wine

AN INTRODUCTION

wine
AN INTRODUCTION

Joanna Simon

Photography   Ian O'Leary

A Dorling Kindersley Book

For Benet, Alice, Emma, Joy, and Heloise,
and in memory of Michael Hoare

LONDON, NEW YORK, MUNICH,
MELBOURNE, DELHI

A PENGUIN COMPANY

Produced for Dorling Kindersley by

Francis Ritter (editorial)
Toni Kay (design)

SENIOR EDITOR
Nicki Lampon

SENIOR ART EDITOR
Anna Benjamin

US EDITORS
Gary Werner and Margaret Parrish

MANAGING EDITOR
Sharon Lucas

SENIOR MANAGING ART EDITOR
Derek Coombes

ART DIRECTOR
Carole Ash

DTP DESIGNER
Sonia Charbonnier

PICTURE RESEARCH
Georgina Lowin, Franziska Marking

PRODUCTION CONTROLLER
Louise Daly

CONTRIBUTORS
Jane Boyce MW (pronunciation guide); Margaret Rand
and Simon Woods (the world's wines)

First American Edition, 2001
First Paperback Edition, 2006

06 07 08 09 10 10 9 8 7 6 5 4 3 2 1

Published in the United States by
DK Publishing, Inc
375 Hudson Street,
New York, New York 10014

A Cataloging-in-Publication record for this title is
available from the Library of Congress.

ISBN-13: 978-0-7566-1886-5
ISBN-10: 0-7566-1886-X

Color reproduction by GRB Editrice, Verona, Italy
Printed and bound in China by SNP Leefung

See our complete catalog at
www.dk.com

contents

introduction

Wine isn't a difficult subject to get to grips with; and yet, when you're faced with hundreds and hundreds of bottles, or dozens of unfamiliar names on a wine list, it can seem extraordinarily opaque. I know, and I sympathize. I only have to open the hood of a car – that's if I can find the mechanism for doing so – to feel daunted. As far as I'm aware, I'm perfectly capable of learning about cars, but I decided long ago that life, however extended, was going to be too short for engines. As a result, I never look at a car manual. Some people feel the same about wine, but the fact that you've opened this book strongly suggests that you're not one of them. Join the club.

One of the appealing aspects of exploring wine is that there are more ways to approach it than in the past, when geographical location ruled the wine world. Nowadays, you can get to know wine through the grape varieties; discover wines you like through the food they go with; take the traditional geographical approach by acquainting yourself with wines by region or country; tackle the subject from the viewpoint of what goes on in the vineyard, winery, or cellar; or approach it from any number of other angles – even via the labels on the back of the bottle, provided you can sift the drivel from the facts and understand the jargon. This book is designed to help with every one of those aspects.

It is also designed to work in different ways and at different levels for different readers. Some people will go straight for the pronunciation guide, instantly increasing the repertoire of wines they can order easily and confidently. Others will be happy with their rough approximations of wine names, but will want to know more about buying wines – in stores, in restaurants, online – or more about matching wine to food and serving wine. Some readers will know which wines they enjoy, but would love to know which others are likely to be to their taste.

Some will feel that they could get more out of wine if they only knew more about the tasting process and how to pinpoint those familar flavors, or if they had a better understanding of where the wine had come from. It's all in these pages. The most appealing aspect of all, of course, is that you can't really get to know wine without the product. You can learn about history by reading; you don't need to have been there at the time. You can appreciate music without being able to play an instrument or knowing your treble clef from your bass. But with wine you've got to absorb its smells, taste it, drink it, savor it, linger over it. So, please, dip into this book, read it, refer to it, look at the pictures – whatever you like, but with a glass at hand.

A WORD ABOUT WINE WORDS

Like all specialized subjects, wine has developed a language of its own. Some of it clarifies the subject as effectively as egg whites clarify red wine (if you didn't know that, see page 130), but some merely serves to cloud and complicate the issue. I've tried to avoid using jargon – whether technical or marketing – and, on the occasions where I have resorted to it, I have explained it, as in varietal (a wine made from a single grape variety, such as merlot). In addition, there are glossary-type lists in the chapters on tasting and buying wine. But there are a few things worth pointing out here.

I have used the terms New World and Old World as a convenient shorthand. Some people don't like them, I know, because they feel they imply two irredeemably divided philosophies; but, from the point of view of this book, "New World" is a lot crisper than listing Australia, New Zealand, South Africa, South America, and North America every time. Likewise, it is more concise to say "Old World" rather than list France, Germany, Italy, Spain, and the other long-established winegrowing countries or regions of Europe.

Grape varieties are written in lowercase, as in chardonnay, muscat, and aglianico. The names of wines (and the places they come from) are written with an initial capital, as in Chablis and Coonawarra. The main exceptions are: grape varieties when they form part of a recognized wine name, for example Aglianico del Vulture or Muscat de Beaumes-de-Venise; and English or anglicized wine names, such as claret, port, burgundy, and champagne.

White, red, or rosé, dry to sweet, light to full-bodied, sparkling, or fortified, the world has wines for you to try in every category.

wine
styles

crisp, dry, light-bodied

Pale, young, light-bodied white wines with delicate flavors, no oak influence, and a finish that is crisply refreshing: a preeminently European style.

wines and grapes

France: Muscadet Sur Lie and Gros Plant; Vins de Pays des Côtes de Gascogne, du Gers, and du Comté Tolosan; Anjou Sec; Bergerac and Bordeaux; Bourgogne Aligoté and inexpensive Chablis

Italy: Soave, Frascati, Orvieto, Bianco di Custoza, Verdicchio; inexpensive pinot grigio; and most Sicilian whites

Germany: Trocken and Halbtrocken of QbA or Kabinett quality and the new Classic and Selection styles

Portugal: traditional dry Vinho Verde

Australia: young Hunter semillon for aging

Many Europeans would argue that California and the southern hemisphere countries do not have the cool-climate regions required to make such wines. Most growers in California and the southern hemisphere would argue that they wouldn't want to make them anyway.

Lightweight, pale, sharpish wines are a European taste, yet even in Europe wine drinkers are showing some signs of moving away from them in favor of bigger, bolder flavors. It would be a great pity if we did abandon them, not just because they are an important part of Europe's heritage but because fresh, light, dry wine has its place.

Wines such as Muscadet, preferably Muscadet Sur Lie, and basic Chablis (not light in alcohol, but fairly neutral) are archetypal for seafood – not elaborately sauced, but fresh and briny or simply cooked.

Many of these kinds of wines, including Italian staples such as Soave, Frascati, and Orvieto Secco, and vins de pays from Gascony, also go well with light and creamy pasta dishes, salads, and antipasti; and they

cope better than most wines with oily fish such as sardines and mackerel. Equally, they can be drunk without food (some of the driest German wines excepted), providing a lighter aperitif than an oaky chardonnay containing 14 percent alcohol.

The New World doesn't set out to make wines such as these, but one region in Australia, the Hunter Valley, while striving for its own unique style, turns out initially sharp, light wines. Traditional Hunter semillon, which is low in alcohol at around 11 percent, starts life thin and sharp and ages into a straw-yellow, intensely toasty, honeyed wine.

aromatic or flowery,
dry to medium-sweet

Whether light-bodied or medium-full, dry or medium-sweet, these whites are marked by their distinctive flowery, spicy, or fruity aromas.

wines and grapes

Germany: riesling and scheurebe grapes, especially Kabinett and Spätlese quality, and especially from the Mosel, Rheingau, and Pfalz regions

France: Alsace gewurztraminer, riesling, tokay-pinot gris, and muscat; dry muscat and lighter viogniers from Languedoc

Italy: Alto Adige pinot grigio and traminer aromatico

Hungary: irsai oliver

Argentina: torrontes

Chile: gewurztraminer

England: medium-dry whites

You might expect wines with a smell that jumps out of the glass to be big and powerful. But wines in this group demonstrate just how little aroma and taste are related to weight and body, especially in white wines. Some of the lightest-bodied whites have the most intense perfumes and tastes. Classic German wines, above all Mosel riesling at Kabinett and Spätlese quality/sweetness levels, may be as little as 7 percent alcohol (occasionally even lower) and yet they have intense flowery, fruity flavors. Like most wines in this group, they also have lively acidity, which is crucial in German wines as a counterpoint to the characteristic fruity sweetness. Without it, they would be vapid (like Liebfraumilch and similar cheap efforts).

Aside from Germany, most of these wines are medium-bodied or medium-full. Alsace is their heartland, but Italy's alpine Alto Adige is also noted for its highly aromatic whites. Other such wines are the dry muscats from France, Argentina's torrontes, irsai oliver from Hungary, and some of the crisper, less rich viogniers from vins de pays areas.

Whether light or full, these whites are unlikely to show any signs of oak. Highly aromatic – all right, smelly – wines aren't aged in (or with) new oak because they need neither its extra flavor nor its softening, broadening effect. With grape varieties such as the pungently and exotically perfumed gewurztraminer, the taste of oak would simply clash.

Aromatic whites are refreshing aperitifs, but often also go well with food – for example, German wines with Chinese dishes, many appetizers, and salads, and Alsace whites with lightly spicy, but not fiercely hot, food.

tangy or steely, medium-bodied

A largely oak-free zone of assertive, sometimes pungent, dry white wines, with a zesty character of green fruit or citrus, and no room for sweetness.

These are incisive, dry wines with a backbone of brisk, food-friendly acidity and sometimes, especially in France, a steely or mineral undertow. Vivid, penetrating fruit is the vital ingredient that stops them from being ascerbic.

Wines in this group are fielded by most countries, but the king grape variety is sauvignon blanc. With its tingling gooseberry fruit, it is at its best in Marlborough (New Zealand) and in the Loire regions of Sancerre and Pouilly-Fumé, but it is coming up in Chile, especially the Casablanca Valley, and in South Africa. There are also softer, less intense sauvignons from around Bordeaux, and lighter, grassier ones from Touraine. Another Loire wine that belongs here, though not a sauvignon, is the strident, long-lived, and rare Savennières. From Burgundy, there is aligoté and a few Chablis wines made in the more austere, unoaked style.

Australia has limited success with sauvignon (as does California in the unoaked style), but, to go with dishes flavored with Asian spices, Australia produces dry, mouthwateringly lime-scented rieslings, especially in the Eden and Clare valleys. Germany has Halbtrocken and Trocken Spätlese rieslings, and new dry styles. Austria has both riesling and grüner veltliner. Spain has Rueda (which often contains sauvignon) and the aromatic but tangy albariño, grown in Rías Baixas in the northwest. Portugal has fernão pires. Greece has assyrtiko and several other notably crisp, flavorsome varieties. Chardonnay doesn't fall naturally into this wine category, but chardonnay addicts can take refuge in the zippy, unoaked chardonnays from Hungary and Italy's Alto Adige.

wines and grapes

New Zealand, South Africa, and Chile: sauvignon blanc

France: Sancerre and Pouilly Fumé; sauvignons from Bordeaux, Bergerac, Côtes de Duras, and Touraine; Savennières; and Bourgogne Aligoté

Australia: riesling

Germany: Halbtrocken and Trocken Spätlese rieslings, and the new Classic and Selection styles

Austria: riesling and grüner veltliner

Spain: albariño and Rueda

Portugal: fernão pires

Greece: assyrtiko and other whites

England: dry whites

full-bodied,
rich-flavored

White wines with power, depth, and oak are almost everywhere. Chardonnay rules, but there is plenty of room for other grapes and flavors.

wines and grapes

New World: chardonnays

France: burgundies, including Chablis; chardonnays from the Pays d'Oc and Pays de l'Ardèche; Hermitage, Châteaneuf-du-Pape, and Condrieu; Graves and Pessac-Léognan

Spain: chardonnays from Navarra and Somontano; white Rioja

Italy: chardonnay from Puglia

California: viognier

Australia: viognier, semillon, marsanne, and verdelho

South Africa: barrel-fermented chenin blanc

This is the category in which you find the great white burgundies – rich yet dry, nutty and honeyed, yet always savory in character – and these are the wines that have been the model for chardonnays everywhere, especially in California and the southern hemisphere. Whether they end up as much riper-tasting but shorter-lived wines, with tropical fruit, butterscotch, and toasty oak flavors (the warm-climate style), or whether, coming from a cooler New World region such as Adelaide Hills or Casablanca Valley, they end up being longer-lived and closer to the burgundian original, they belong in this category. So does Chablis of *premier cru* and *grand cru* quality. Some of it doesn't see a grain of new oak, but good Chablis, with its mineral, nutty, crème fraîche flavors, is a powerful wine.

Other wines that meet the criteria are the big, often herb-scented whites of the Rhône – Châteauneuf-du-Pape and long-lived Hermitage – and a rarer Rhône, the opulent, heady Condrieu, made from the viognier grape. Viognier wines from California and Australia are in the same mold. Australia also has full-bodied marsannes (another Rhône grape) and verdelhos, and an abundance of rich, lemony semillons, especially from the Barossa Valley. Semillon crops up again in Bordeaux's fine white Graves and Pessac-Léognan, wines that can seem lean and taut when young, but which develop deep, creamy, wheatlike flavors with time. Top white Rioja wines from Spain behave in the same way.

rosé

Is rosé neither one thing nor the other, or is it the best of both worlds? Is it pink, vapid, and slightly too sweet, or dry, vibrant, and refreshing?

The answer, of course, is that rosé is all of these things (yes, on the right occasion, it can even be the best of both worlds). Rosé's principal problem today is image, simply because in the past its problem was quality. Long after the wine industry improved the standards of white and red wines, most rosé continued to be decidedly second-rate. Either it was made after lunch by winemakers who would rather have been making red wine (and in their quality time probably were); or it was made in regions that supposedly specialized in rosé, but specialized more in maintaining sloppy, old-fashioned winemaking practices, often involving cloying amounts of residual sugar in the wines. Semisweet Portuguese pink wines and Rosé d'Anjou still often leave much to be desired, and most semisweet Californian blush zinfandels do rosé's reputation no favors either; but, those aside, rosé is not what it was – thank goodness.

Many of today's best – dry and full of fruit – are made from grenache (garnacha in Spain), cabernet sauvignon, merlot, or syrah. Languedoc produces all four (often as Vin de Pays d'Oc); Bordeaux makes some juicy, round cabernets and merlots (sometimes called clairet); and big, dry, peppery Rhône pinks come from Tavel, Lirac, and Gigondas. Everyday Provençal rosés are not much to write home about, but fashionable Bandol, Cassis, and Bellet are more interesting – at a price. Fashion plays its part in the pricing of Sancerre rosé, too. Outside France, very attractive rosados are made in Spain, especially Navarra; Hungary is a source of good value; and Australia produces a few exuberant, full, dark pinks.

wines and grapes

France: Vin de Pays d'Oc; Bordeaux (claret); Tavel, Lirac, and Gigondas; Bandol, Cassis, and Bellet; Sancerre

Spain: especially Navarra

Hungary: cabernet sauvignon

Australia: rosé

rosé

sparkling

Sparkling wines come in all shapes and sizes, but the quality market is dominated by French champagne – the real McCoy – and its imitators.

wines and grapes

France: champagne; Crémant de Limoux and Blanquette de Limoux; Crémant de Bourgogne; Crémant d'Alsace; Saumur and sparkling Vouvray

Australia and New Zealand: especially labels citing chardonnay, pinot noir, blanc de blancs, or a vintage date; also Australian sparkling shiraz

California: especially vintage and blanc de blancs

Spain: cava

Italy: Prosecco

Good champagne – and there is poor, sharp stuff that doesn't deserve the name – is delicate yet incisive, with biscuity, creamy, brioche flavors and a quintessential freshness. These characteristics are rooted in climate: the Champagne region in northern France is one of the wine world's coolest and grapes barely ripen.

Most countries outside France that use the Champagne region's grape varieties and production method are warmer. This brings less depth and finesse to the wines, but riper fruit and lower acidity, which can be very appealing, especially to people who find most French champagne too tart. The wines are cheaper than champagne and are often good value, particularly from Australia.

In favored cool spots of Australia (including Tasmania), New Zealand, California, and even, in a very limited way, the south of England, some producers are succeeding in making wines that come very close to champagne. And it's no coincidence that many of the companies involved are partly owned by champagne producers, such as Moët, Roederer, and Deutz. Their wines usually cost about the same as the cheapest champagnes, but are of much better quality.

The cheaper French sparkling wines, made according to the champagne formula but not necessarily with the same grape varieties, include Crémant de Limoux, Crémant de Bourgogne, Crémant d'Alsace, and Saumur. The best are good value, but quality is variable (Limoux is currently the most reliable).

Spain's answer to champagne is cava, most of it from Penedès. With its appley, earthy flavors, it is much softer, simpler, and cheaper than champagne and has been hugely successful overseas. Germany has Sekt, usually light and sweet. Italy exports its sweet, grapey, low-alcohol moscatos (of which Asti is best known) and dryish Prosecco (its cava equivalent), but its few champagne-method wines are drunk mainly in Italy.

A final variant is sparkling red. Cheap Lambrusco has given red fizz a dreadful name, but try Australia's rich, ripe, spicy, fizzy reds and, if you come across it, the rarely exported, authentic dry Lambrusco.

sparkling

Good champagne is delicate yet **incisive**, with **biscuity**, creamy, **brioche flavors** and a **quintessential freshness**.

fresh, fruity, low-tannin

Simple, juicy, young red wines for drinking today, tomorrow, or next month. Oak is never more than a background whisper, if that, in these wines.

wines and grapes

France: Beaujolais; Sancerre, Menetou-Salon, Gamay de Touraine, Anjou Rouge, Saumur-Champigny, Chinon, and Bourgueil; vins de pays; Alsace and Jura pinot noir

Italy: Bardolino; Valpolicella; dolcetto; barbera; reds from Trentino-Alto Adige

Hungary: kékfrankos

Germany: limberger

Spain and Portugal: young, modern reds

New World:
- the cheapest red blends
- Argentine bonarda and barbera
- South African cinsaut
- Australian and Californian ruby cabernet
- Australian tarrango

While winemakers around the world fashion ever bigger wines, there is still a role for light, refreshing reds that slip down easily without food, reds that are usually better served cool and don't need a year in the cellar.

Beaujolais provides the benchmark. Beaujolais-Villages and its individual *crus* (or villages), such as Fleurie, are the more grown-up versions of the style. The Loire has the pinot noirs of Sancerre and Menetou-Salon, and gamays and cabernet francs from Touraine, Anjou, and Saumur (but excluding the most expensive Chinon, Bourgueil, and Saumur-Champigny). Alsace and the Jura have their pinot noirs. Many vins de pays also fit the bill, although Vin de Pays d'Oc, especially cabernet sauvignon and syrah, can be on the big side, and you should avoid any vins de pays that from their prices are obviously ambitious, and any described as oaked (or *élevé en fûts de chêne*).

Italy has several wines from the north: Bardolino, basic Valpolicella, dolcetto, simple barbera, and many of the reds from Trentino-Alto Adige (merlot, lagrein, Caldaro, and others). Spain and Portugal now make many of their cheap wines in soft, juicy styles, even though light, fresh, unwooded reds are not part of Iberia's heritage. From Hungary there is kékfrankos; Germany has limberger among others.

Light red is not naturally a New World style, but the cheapest reds exported from Argentina, Chile, South Africa, Australia, and California – sometimes with grape names, sometimes unspecified blends – are made to be drunk today.

reds

medium to
full-bodied

Flavorsome reds but not blockbusters, mostly matured in oak but not heavily oaky, this category includes many great French reds and other classics.

Not so long ago, we would have called this middle group "medium-bodied reds," and left it at that. But wines have been getting bigger and fuller: so, medium to full-bodied it is. Because every significant producing country makes wines in this group, it encompasses a large number of wines and a wide spectrum of flavors.

In France, most red Bordeaux (or clarets) and burgundies qualify, although the cheapest Bordeaux in a modest vintage will be light and feeble. The same applies to similar styles from southwest appellations such as Bergerac, Buzet, and Côtes de Saint-Mont. Some of the expensive, ambitious wines from the Mediterranean south, especially Languedoc-Roussillon, are powerful and spicy; but most of the everyday Corbières, Fitou, Minervois, Côtes du Ventoux, Côtes du Lubéron, and so on belong to this category.

Italy has a number of wines in this group, including much ordinary Chianti (that is, not labeled *riserva* and not the more expensive estate-produced Chianti Classico), Barbera d'Asti, and Montepulciano d'Abruzzo. From Spain, most of the wines of Rioja, Valdepeñas, Somontano, and Navarra qualify.

In warmer climates, such as those enjoyed by most areas of California and Australia, cabernet sauvignon and merlot, the two main red grapes of Bordeaux, generally produce riper-tasting, heavier, oakier wines; but New Zealand's cabernets and merlots, being grown in cooler conditions, are more similar in weight to those of a good Bordeaux vintage, as are Chile's least expensive cabernets and merlots, and most from the cooler eastern European vineyards.

As it is relatively difficult to make pinot noir, the red burgundy grape, into a positively big wine – least of all a successful one – most pinot noirs belong to this category, even when they are 13.5 or 14 percent alcohol and have more obvious oak than any classic red burgundy.

wines and grapes

France: Bordeaux, Buzet; burgundy; Fitou, Minervois, Côtes du Lubéron

Italy: Chianti; Barbera d'Asti; Montepulciano d'Abruzzo

Spain: Rioja; Valdepeñas; Navarra; Somontano

NZ, Chile, and E. Europe: cabernets and merlots

New World: pinot noirs

full, powerful,
often spicy

Big, often spicy, and usually oak-matured red
wines with mouth-filling flavors and textures.
Some are tannic when young; others are velvety.

wines and grapes

New World:
- Australian shiraz, grenache, and mourvèdre
- Californian zinfandel, syrah, and merlot
- Chilean cabernet sauvignon
- Argentine malbec
- South African pinotage

France: Rhônes, including Châteauneuf-du-Pape and Cornas; Languedoc-Roussillon, including top Corbières, St.-Chinian, and Collioure; Bandol; Madiran

Italy: primitivo; Barolo and Barbaresco; Brunello di Montalcino; Amarone di Valpolicella

Spain: Ribera del Duero; Toro; Priorato; Jumilla; garnacha and monastrell

Portugal: Alentejo

This category has grown enormously in the past few years, reflecting global changes in taste and winemaking and the emergence of the New World. Before wines such as Californian cabernet sauvignon and Australian shiraz burst onto the scene, the roll call of big, strapping reds extended little further than Châteauneuf-du-Pape, Hermitage, Cornas, Bandol, Barolo, Brunello di Montalcino, and Amarone di Valpolicella.

Today, these wines have been joined by a mass of others – from all over the world – and not so much joined as overtaken, at least in terms of alcohol. Whereas 13.5 percent used to be the ceiling for normal table wines (wines that aren't fortified with brandy), 14 percent is common today, and grape varieties such as grenache, primitivo, and zinfandel regularly clock in even higher.

The high alcohol levels and the typically "sweet," ripe flavors come in a large part simply from leaving grapes to ripen, especially in the Mediterranean and New World climates, for far longer than growers in the past would have dared to leave them. As riper, sugar-rich grapes have lower acidity and softer tannins, this process also leads to fuller-tasting wine.

Some grape varieties have an inherently spicy-sweet character, among them shiraz, grenache, primitivo, zinfandel, malbec (specifically in Argentina), carmenère, and pinotage. And, to complete the picture, the oak barrels in which most of these wines are matured give their own spicy, sweet flavors, together with a smoother, richer texture.

Full-bodied, spicy wines can often take quite strongly flavored food and are good at dealing with modern dishes that mix spices, Mediterranean flavors, and cooking methods such as char grilling and barbecuing. Save the more traditional, tannic European wines for meaty casseroles and game.

The high alcohol content is significant. Although it **tastes** of little, alcohol contributes to the **smooth**, almost **sweet, spicy feel** and **flavor** of the wines.

sweet

From sweet but delicate to luscious and opulent, these are the wines to drink with dessert, instead of dessert, or perhaps as a change with cheese.

wines and grapes

France: Sauternes, Barsac, Monbazillac, and others from Bordeaux and the Dordogne; Loire wines such as Coteaux du Layon (including Bonnezeaux and Quarts de Chaume) and Vouvray Moelleux; Alsace Sélection de Grains Nobles gewurztraminer, pinot gris, and riesling; Jurançon Moelleux; Jura vin de paille; Muscat de Beaumes-de-Venise, Muscat de Rivesaltes, and other muscats

Germany: Trockenbeerenauslese, Beerenauslese, and Eiswein

Austria: Trockenbeerenauslese, Beerenauslese, Ausbruch, Strohwein, and Eiswein

Hungary: Tokaji Aszú and Tokaji Aszú Eszencia

Italy: Recioto di Soave

Australia, New Zealand, and California: botrytized semillons and rieslings

Canada: icewine

Most of the finest sweet wines are made from botrytized grapes – grapes that have been shriveled by a fungus that leaves them high in sugar, glycerol, acid, and fruit flavors. Noble rot, as it is known, gives the wines a complex honeyed palate, and sometimes, as in the case of Sauternes and other semillon-based wines, an unctuous, fat texture. Sauternes is the arch exponent, but there are other important ones: the famous Loires, such as Bonnezeaux and Quarts de Chaume; Alsace Sélection de Grains Nobles wines; the sweet wines of Germany and Austria; Tokaji; and New World botrytis-affected semillons and rieslings.

Most of the other great sweet wines are made from grapes that have been allowed to dehydrate. Like botrytis, dehydration intensifies the sweetness and flavors, but without giving the fat, luscious character. In the case of Jurançon, in southwest France, the grapes are left to dry on the vines. With others, such as Recioto de Soave, Jura vin de paille, and Austria's Strohwein, the bunches of grapes are dried after picking.

Another way of intensifying the flavors of the grapes is, odd as it may sound, to allow them to freeze on the vine in winter. When the frozen grapes are pressed, the ice crystals inside are removed, leaving extremely concentrated, sweet, sharp juice, destined to become Eiswein in Germany and icewine in Canada.

The vins doux naturels of southern France constitute another important group of sweet wines. These are actually fortified wines (grape alcohol is added to them), but those made from the muscat grape are archetypal dessert wines. Muscat de Beaumes-de-Venise, with its grapey, barley-sugar flavors, is the most famous and potentially the best.

sweet

tangy, dry, fortified

Bone dry, tangy wines, strengthened (or fortified) with added alcohol. Sadly unfashionable for now, these are some of the world's great aperitifs.

wines and grapes

Spain: sherry – fino, manzanilla, genuine dry amontillado, oloroso, and palo cortado; pale, dry Montilla

France: Jura vin jaune

Hungary: dry Tokaji Szamorodni

Portugal: dry white port

Australia and South Africa: dry, sherrylike wines

Madeira: sercial and verdelho

Pale, dry fino sherry, which comes from Jerez in southern Spain, is the best known of the dry fortified wines; but, in Spain itself, manzanilla is more popular. Both have a brisk, yeasty tang, but manzanilla, which comes from the coast a short way to the northwest of Jerez, is a little lighter, saltier, and snappier. The darker, nuttier amontillado and oloroso sherries are also naturally dry, but for export markets, such as the UK, the habit has been to sweeten and emasculate them. It is well worth trying the genuine dry articles, including palo cortado, a rarer, dry, nutty style.

One of a dwindling group of dry sherry-related wines, Montilla is still produced to the north of Malaga, but it rarely approaches sherry quality. France has its rare vin jaune from the Jura, and Hungary has its (very loosely related) dry Szamorodni. Australia and South Africa both continue to make sherry-styled wines for their home markets, and some of them are very good. White port can be dry, but often isn't, and it never has the tang of dry sherry.

The other wine in this category is Madeira, in two styles: sercial, the most pungently tangy of all wines; and verdelho, which is a little softer and fruitier, often with a hint of apricot. Cheap dry Madeiras don't carry the names sercial and verdelho (which are the grape varieties) and taste simple in comparison.

fortified

dark, sweet, fortified

The after-dinner brigade – high-alcohol, sweet, dark-hued wines that only show their best after many years in the cellar. Port leads the way.

Port is that rare thing: a sweet red wine; Mavrodaphne from Greece is one of the few others. The finest port is vintage port, made only in the best years and requiring a decade at least before it's ready to drink. Single quinta port – made from the best individual estates in the "no vintage" years – comes a close second. Late-bottled vintage, or LBV, is usually about half the price of single quinta, less rich and complex, and not intended to be cellared; the exception is Traditional LBV, which is made more like vintage port. Ruby ports are younger and simpler than LBVs.

Tawny port is a different style completely. After long maturation in wood, as opposed to bottle, it ends up pale brick (or tawny) in color, mellow and nutty in taste, and should be served lightly chilled. But, beware: cheap tawnies are briefly-aged blends of ruby and white port. The genuine article declares its age on the label, as in 10-year-old or 20-year-old.

Although Australia and South Africa both make portlike wines for domestic consumption, none quite touches port from Portugal. Instead, Australia has its own unique fortified wines: gloriously rich, sweet, viscous, brown liquids, known as "liqueur muscats" and "liqueur tokays," although most producers are trying to get away from the misleading "liqueur" tag.

As with port, there are cheap, ordinary styles of Madeira. The authentic sweet Madeiras are bual and the even sweeter malmsey. However sweet, they always have Madeira's characteristic acid tang. Italy's sweet Marsalas can be complex and raisiny, but only when they are at the quality level of Marsala Superiore Garibaldi Dolce. Spain has syrupy, raisiny, pedro ximénez (or PX) sherries, a few exceptional, sweetened, very old rich (or *muy viejo dulce*) oloroso sherries, and a handful of producers who still make the Victorian favorite, Málaga.

wines and grapes

Portugal: port – vintage, single quinta, LBV and Traditional LBV, tawny

Australia: liqueur muscats and tokays

Madeira: bual and malmsey

Italy: Marsala Superiore Garibaldi Dolce

Spain: pedro ximénez and oloroso sherries; Málaga

tannic versus
nontannic wines

Apart from being the substance in tea that furs up your mouth so unpleasantly, tannin is present in wine, especially in young, red wines that are designed to be aged. In fact, tannin is not only present but essential in a red that is going to be laid down for several years, which means that some of the most expensive red wines – Bordeaux (claret), Barolo, and Hermitage – taste disconcertingly tough, dry, and bitter when very young.

As a rule, warmer climates produce less aggressively tannic wines than cool-climate regions, so New World wines are less tannic than Old World wines. That said, many European reds are now made less tannic than wines of the past, which is one reason why more and more people are drinking red wines. Tannin levels also vary with grape variety. Thicker-skinned varieties, such as cabernet sauvignon, syrah, tannat, and nebbiolo, are more tannic than thinner-skinned varieties, such as pinot noir, because tannin resides in the skins (as well as in the pits and stems). White wines do have tannin, but mostly at imperceptible levels.

old versus
young wines

Buy it today, drink it tomorrow – or, at a stretch, next weekend. We drink much younger wines than previous generations did, partly because we don't have cellars, butlers, and so on, and partly because the majority of today's wines are made for more or less immediate consumption. Wines are softer, less tannic, and much more overtly fruity than in the past, and many have the softening texture and seductive, sweet vanilla and toast flavors of new oak. The result is that mature, old wines can come as a shock to the unaccustomed. Where is the exuberant ripe fruit and toasty oak? The answer (in a good old wine) is that those primary flavors have been replaced by a more complex, interwoven set – potpourri or pomander, dried fruits or autumnal compotes, mellow cedary flavors, coffee and roasted aromas, leather, licorice, undergrowth, truffles, and all the rest. Such wines can take some getting used to, but ultimately you can expect to be well rewarded.

Scores of grape varieties,
growing in widely differing soils
and microclimates, yield an
amazing range of different wines.

wine
grapes

chardonnay

Famous, fashionable, the ultimate crowd pleaser,
but it isn't only consumers who like chardonnay:
it makes growers and winemakers smile, too.

BUTTER A flavor that comes from both the grape and a particular winemaking technique.

PEACH One of many fruit flavors that occur in chardonnay, depending mainly on the climate.

WALNUT Characteristic of white burgundy, especially, but also top Californian chardonnay.

TOAST Toasty aromas come from new oak. Winemakers choose low, medium, or high toast.

Growers like chardonnay because it is very adaptable. It flourishes in a far wider range of climates and soils than most varieties, largely resisting disease and producing generous, financially rewarding crops. Given frost protection, it is happy near the cool fringes of grape-growing, notably in Chablis (the northern outpost of its Burgundian heartland) and in Champagne, where it is the one white grape variety. But chardonnay is equally at home in warm New World regions, such as the Napa Valley, Mendoza, and the Barossa Valley.

Winemakers like chardonnay because it's so pliant. Whereas grapes such as riesling and sauvignon blanc are essentially hands-off varieties, leaving the wine-maker few choices about the style of wine that can be made, chardonnay is like putty. For all the richness and power of the wines, the grapes themselves don't have very assertive aromas or flavors, so the winemaker can tailor the wine to market demands or to his or her own aspirations.

What is it about chardonnay that appeals to wine drinkers? In a word, pleasure. Other wines can be difficult or an acquired taste, but chardonnay is almost always easy to drink: this is especially true of the modern, fruit-driven New World styles. Even a good burgundy uncorked before it reaches its peak is rarely a penitential drink: it's just a waste of a potentially great wine.

In so far as it exists, the average New World chardonnay is full, ripe, fruity, and smooth: naturally high alcohol gives roundness and a sensation of sweetness; naturally low acidity means chardonnay is almost incapable of being tart or aggressive. The fruit flavors range from lemon and apple (in cooler climates) through melon and peach to pineapple and tropical fruit. In burgundies, the ripe fruit is more understated, with more savory, nutty flavors taking its place. Chablis is nutty, but more mineral and steely.

The most obvious add-on with chardonnay is oak. Fermenting and/or aging in new or nearly new barrels gives a toasty-vanilla flavor to the young wine, a more complex flavor as it matures, and a richer texture. It also adds a good deal to the price. Cheaper alternatives, including suspension of staves (planks) or oak chips in tanks of wine, are used to impart oak flavor to everyday chardonnay. Other flavor-influencing techniques include allowing all or some of the wine to undergo a secondary fermentation, called the malolactic, which makes the wine softer and more buttery, and aging it on its lees (spent yeasts) before bottling, to give a nutty-yeasty dimension and richer texture. Chardonnay loves them all.

vines grow
well in a
variety of
soil types

vines bud
early and
thrive in a
range of
climates

wines are
naturally relatively
high in alcohol

blended with
pinot noir in
champagne

WHERE — Burgundy, including Chablis, is the heartland of this grape, regardless of whether or not it originated in the Burgundian village of Chardonnay. Since the 1960s, it has spread to every wine-growing country, from Chile to China, England to Peru.

MAIN STYLES — Full-bodied dry whites, often showing the influence of oak irrespective of quality and price. New World chardonnays are more overtly fruity and oaky; white burgundy is more savory; Chablis is more mineral. Alto Adige and Friuli chardonnays are lighter, crisper, and more floral.

WHEN & WITH — Top white burgundy can be kept 10 or more years, but most chardonnay should be drunk within four years (the cheaper, the sooner). Varied styles allow varied food: the fullest can even cope with steak; most go with fish, but avoid oily fish and vinegar.

ALSO KNOWN AS — MORILLON and FEINBURGUNDER in Austria

GOOSEBERRY
Characteristic fruit flavor,
but in New Zealand can
have more tropical fruit.

GRASS A smell like
a freshly mown lawn
in all sauvignons, but
especially French ones.

CURRANT LEAF Fresh
aroma of blackcurrant or
flowering currant leaves,
especially in Loire wines.

FLINT A smoky, flinty
character is characteristic
of some Sancerre and
Pouilly-Fumé wines.

sauvignon
blanc

If you smell gooseberries, cut grass, flowering
currant leaves, or nettles, it's almost certain that
you have a glass of sauvignon blanc in your hand.

If you detect asparagus, cat's pee, or green beans, the chances are again weighted
in sauvignon's favor, although you may not have such an enticing example.
Sauvignon is one of the most distinctive of white grape varieties. Apart from its
penetrating, fresh, "green" aromas, it is notable for its invigorating high acidity.
If it lacks that acidity, which invariably it does in a warm climate, it lacks appeal.

For a long time, the need for a cool climate kept sauvignon out of much of the
New World, which was good news for the growers of Sancerre and Pouilly-Fumé,
who provided the benchmark style. But, at the end of the 1980s, sauvignon blanc
from Marlborough, New Zealand, sprang onto the scene. It was fruitier than the
benchmarks from the upper Loire, it lacked their sometimes flinty-smoky
character, but it had a particularly mouthwatering clarity and intensity. New
Zealand had created a benchmark, one that sometimes outshone the Loire
originals. Marlborough sauvignon is still in a class of its own, but good examples
are increasingly being produced in South Africa and in Chile's Casablanca region.

The main reasons why the flavors of sauvignon retain their clarity are that
sauvignon rarely takes well to oak (unlike chardonnay), and it doesn't blend well
with other varieties. The main exception is Bordeaux, where the top white wines
of the Graves and Pessac-Léognan regions are fermented and aged in new oak
barrels, and are usually blends of semillon and sauvignon. California Fumé Blanc
is also oak-aged, but it is not a style that has found many fans abroad.

Another reason for sauvignon remaining true to itself is that it is rarely given
the chance to do anything else. Most bottles are drunk within two or three years
of the vintage, simply because it is not a variety that develops interestingly with
age. Most sauvignons start to fall apart after three years: they lose their touchstone
acidity and freshness and have nothing to compensate. A tiny minority, with
especially intense, concentrated flavors, do stay the course for a decade or so,
but staying the course is not the same as improving with age.

shaded grapes produce "green" or "grassy" wines

makes crisp, vibrant wines

grapes exposed to sun by leaf pruning produce riper fruit flavors

provides acidity in blends with semillon in Bordeaux

WHERE — Two focal points: the Loire, especially Sancerre and Pouilly-Fumé; and Marlborough, New Zealand. Also significant in Bordeaux and Bergerac; Rueda in Spain; Styria in Austria; Chile, especially Casablanca; South Africa; and California.

MAIN STYLES — Crisp, dry, and bracing, with riper fruit and more alcohol in New Zealand than the Loire. Seldom oak-matured, except in California and in expensive white Bordeaux (blended with semillon).

WHEN & WITH — Drink young, except the top, oak-matured, white Bordeaux. Drink with fish, vegetable dishes, and lightly spiced meat dishes. Also makes a reviving and delicious aperitif.

NOT THE SAME AS — SAUVIGNONASSE or SAUVIGNON VERT, an inferior variety sometimes passed off as sauvignon blanc in Chile: or SAVAGNIN, an obscure, unrelated variety grown in the Jura.

APPLE Classic German riesling, especially Mosel, has a mouthwatering, fresh apple aroma.

LIME Zesty lime cordial flavors are hallmarks of Australia's Clare and Eden valleys.

HONEY Sweet rieslings, especially German ones, are characteristically ripe, honeyed wines.

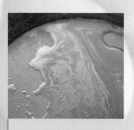

GASOLINE It sounds bizarre, but fine German riesling develops a gas character with age.

riesling

Riesling is as unfashionable as chardonnay is fashionable, but there's no question that it is one of the world's supreme grape varieties.

Riesling is not nearly as accommodating as chardonnay about its vineyard environment, but in the right, cool German climate it produces extraordinarily intense, yet fabulously light and elegant, fruity wines; wines which, because of their acidity, can age over many years and still taste fresh. The wines span the spectrum of sweetness, from modern, bone-dry rieslings to the very sweetest Trockenbeerenauslese, made from grapes concentrated by botrytis cinerea, the benevolent fungus known as noble rot.

Rieslings also span the alcoholic range: more so than any other variety. The classic semisweet German styles (Kabinett, Spätlese, Auslese, and so on) are often 8 percent alcohol or less, while the new dry wines may be 12 percent. Dry Alsace and Austrian rieslings are around 12 percent, while some dry Australian rieslings reach 14 percent, although the norm is lower, especially in the top riesling regions of the Eden Valley (part of the Barossa) and the Clare Valley.

Riesling is not as tractable as chardonnay in the winery either. It doesn't like oak – but there again, it doesn't need to. Its wines have such inherent aroma, structure, and balance, they don't need the added flavor, depth, or richness that new oak barrels give. In fact, new oak destroys riesling's essential integrity.

The hallmark flavors in German riesling range from floral notes, crisp green apples, and slate (especially in the Mosel), to riper fruit (peach and apricot) and spice in the warmer Pfalz, to lemony, mineral characters in the Rheingau. The sweet wines often have aromas of honey, and mature German riesling develops a telltale gasoline smell (which sounds odd but isn't). Alsace rieslings tend to have an appley, steely, mineral character. Australian rieslings are appetizingly lime-scented and become toasty with age (although they are not oak-aged). Australia also produces good botrytis-affected, honeyed, sweet wines, as does New Zealand. California makes sweet, late-harvest rieslings and Canada makes intensely concentrated, sweet icewines.

If riesling is so wonderful, how has it attracted such opprobrium? Although there are some poor wines, the damage has largely been done by wines that have become mistakenly associated with riesling, and by wines posing as riesling. Liebfraumilch and the other very cheap, sugary, watery German wines are mostly made from second-rate varieties entirely unrelated to riesling. Similarly, cheap, semisweet wines from eastern Europe, now labeled laski rizling and olaszrizling, but in the past spelled riesling, have nothing to do with the real thing.

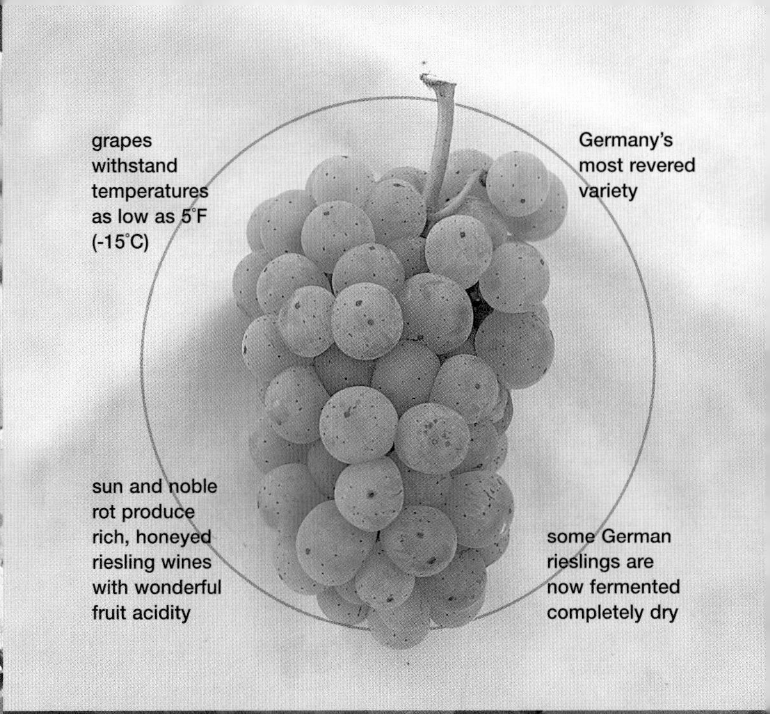

grapes
withstand
temperatures
as low as 5°F
(-15°C)

Germany's
most revered
variety

sun and noble
rot produce
rich, honeyed
riesling wines
with wonderful
fruit acidity

some German
rieslings are
now fermented
completely dry

WHERE

Throughout Germany, but especially Mosel-Saar-Ruwer, Nahe, Rheingau, Rheinhessen, and Pfalz; Alsace; Austria, especially Wachau; and Australia, especially the Clare and Eden valleys.

MAIN STYLES

Every permutation from bone dry to very sweet in Germany, and from very light and low in alcohol to dry and medium-bodied. Elsewhere, mainly dry and medium-bodied, but some very good sweet wines from Australasia and icewines from Canada.

WHEN & WITH

Inexpensive riesling should be drunk young, but others, especially German, can be drunk young or kept many years. An excellent aperitif, good riesling is also a match for many foods that defeat other wines, such as Chinese and lightly spiced dishes.

NOT THE SAME AS

Any kind of RIZLING

MINT An especially
distinctive note in some
South Australian and
Washington State wines.

BLACKCURRANT Found
in most young examples,
but less overt in Bordeaux
than the New World.

PENCIL SHAVINGS The
classic signature of wines
from the Médoc and
Graves in Bordeaux.

CHOCOLATE Not
exclusively, but a feature
of good quality, especially
New World examples.

cabernet sauvignon

Cabernet sauvignon is to red wine grapes what chardonnay is to white: successful, adaptable, widely traveled, and enduringly popular.

Championed by pioneers in the New World since the 1960s, cabernet sauvignon has put down roots in almost every winegrowing country. Despite this globe-trotting, its homeland is undisputedly Bordeaux, its reputation established by the *crus classés* of the Médoc and Graves and the fine, long-lived wines from such châteaux as Lafite, Latour, and Margaux.

As its spread suggests, cabernet sauvignon is an adaptable variety, although it is not quite as forgiving as chardonnay. Because it ripens late, it fails to mature fully in climates that are too cool, producing thin-bodied, "green," herbaceous wines. It is rare in the Loire, even rarer, mercifully, in Germany, and needs nurturing in New Zealand. Equally, in too hot a climate, it can give jammy, simple flavors.

Those areas aside, one of the marks of cabernet sauvignon is that, wherever it is grown, it remains true to itself. A Pauillac (Bordeaux), with its mineral, cedary, cigar-box flavors, is very different from a Coonawarra cabernet sauvignon from South Australia, with its big, incisive cassis, menthol, and clove flavors. But through these regional styles cabernet sauvignon retains its distinctive personality.

This is partly a question of flavor: the blackcurrant, veering to sweeter black fruits in warmer regions; the cedar or pencils of Bordeaux; the mint or eucalyptus that often signal Coonawarra, Langhorne Creek, and Washington State; the green pepper that typifies cooler climates; and the chocolate and clove or licorice of warmer areas. But it is also a question of structure, the feel of the wine in the mouth, and it is the characteristics of the berries that determine this.

Cabernet sauvignon grapes are small, thick-skinned, dark, and bluish. They give deep-colored wines and, because of the high proportion of pits and skins to juice, wines that are naturally tannic and potentially long-lived. With assertive flavors and a tannic framework, the wines are suited to aging in oak barrels, especially French; so the flavors of new oak – vanilla, toast, spice, chocolate, coconut – are frequently part of the profile of the wine.

Another element is the blend. Even where it takes all the glory, cabernet sauvignon is often a blend with softer, juicier varieties, notably merlot and cabernet franc in Bordeaux. In the New World, it stands alone more often, but producers are increasingly trying out Bordeaux blends to add complexity.

small berries yield deep red wine

grapes require late summer sun to ripen

wine is often full-bodied with a powerful aroma of blackcurrant

high tannin levels ensure that costly wines repay cellaring

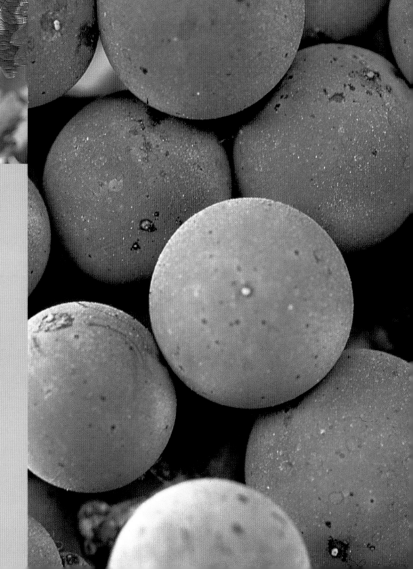

WHERE

Has spread from its Bordeaux heartland to make worthwhile wines in Australia, California, Chile, Argentina, South Africa, New Zealand, France's Vin de Pays d'Oc region, Washington State, Tuscany, and, less reliably, in Bulgaria and Romania.

MAIN STYLES

Dry reds, from medium-bodied to full-bodied, often showing the influence of oak; can be tannic when young. All quality levels, and prices to match, from low, especially in eastern Europe, to the world's highest in Bordeaux and California.

WHEN & WITH

Has cellaring potential – the best Bordeaux keeps 8–20 years – but cheap wines are not for keeping. Most New World cabernets are ready on release, but the more expensive develop over 4–8 years. Generally, a wine for food, especially red meat.

RASPBERRY A flavor in both complex burgundy and inexpensive, fruity New World pinot noir.

WILD STRAWBERRY A haunting hint found in some fine burgundies and pinot noirs.

ROSES OR VIOLETS An elusive floral scent, found especially in top-quality burgundy.

TRUFFLE Mature burgundy develops a rich, gamey, truffley, or even farmyardy bouquet.

pinot noir

Pinot noir has caused more grief to more growers and winemakers than any other grape, but still they persist with this tantalizingly fussy and fickle variety.

Producers in all corners of the world attempt to grow pinot noir because it is the grape of red burgundy – the grape behind Romanée-Conti, Chambertin, Clos de Vougeot, and all the other great Côte d'Or reds – just as chardonnay is the variety behind the great white burgundies. But, while chardonnay will settle almost anywhere, pinot noir is frustratingly persnickety about its climate, its soils, the way it is handled during the growing season, and the way it is handled once the grapes are picked and the wine is being made in the cellar. As the Burgundians say, there is far more to their wine than mere grape variety.

Pinot noir can be coaxed into giving reasonably deep color and significant tannin, but generally it produces light to medium-colored red wines with relatively low tannin and acidity. It takes well to French oak, judiciously used, but not to the more robust, spicy flavor of American oak. In too cool a climate – perhaps an off year in Burgundy or Alsace – it ends up thin and pallid. In too warm a climate – which includes many of the places it has been tried in the New World – it becomes jammy. But, when everything goes right, it has the most seductive of perfumes and silkiest of textures. Raspberries, strawberries, and cherries mingle with roses, violets, incense, and hints of oriental spice. In burgundy, with time, some of the sweet fruitiness gives way to richer, more savory, game and truffle flavors – a *goût de terroir*, or local taste, that has almost entirely eluded the New World.

Some of the finest red burgundies from the Côte de Nuits need several years to reach their peak and then, gratifyingly, stay there for a long time; but most pinot noirs are ready to drink more or less as soon as they are bottled and don't last nearly as long as cabernet sauvignon of equivalent quality.

Among the New World regions making headway with pinot noir are Oregon, cooler areas of California (such as Carneros, Russian River Valley, and Santa Maria), and New Zealand (including Martinborough, Marlborough, and Central Otago regions). Australia has had some success in the cooler regions of Victoria (for example, Yarra) and in Tasmania, but much is used, as it is in Champagne, to produce sparkling wines. South Africa and Chile are both having a try.

Aside from France, the European countries that take pinot noir most seriously are Germany (where it appears as spätburgunder) and Austria (under the name of spätburgunder or blauburgunder). Pinot noir has also spread across eastern Europe, but the Burgundians need not lose any sleep over that.

grapes are thin-skinned and susceptible to rot and mildew

wines are mostly low in tannin

vines bud early, making frost a hazard

used for red wines, but also (without their skins) for champagne

WHERE
Burgundy, Burgundy, and Burgundy; but the Burgundians should keep an eye on what is starting to be achieved in California, Oregon, New Zealand, and Australia.

MAIN STYLES
Medium-bodied, often not very deep-colored red with alluring perfume, sweet fruit, and silky texture. Doesn't make cheap wines and its cheapest are rarely worth bothering with. Can be very expensive – and worth it.

WHEN & WITH
Most pinot noir should be drunk young; only the finest burgundies have long cellaring potential. Can be drunk on its own, but is food-friendly – it goes with game and most meat, and is the best red wine to drink with fish.

ALSO KNOWN AS
SPÄTBURGUNDER (Germany and Austria), BLAUBURGUNDER (Austria and Switzerland), PINOT NERO (Italy), BURGUND MARE (Romania).

BERRIES Blackberry
dominates in Australia,
blackcurrant, raspberry,
and herbs in the Rhône.

BLACK PEPPER Most
distinctive in the northern
Rhône and Australia's
cooler Victoria vineyards.

SPICE Warmer climates
produce shiraz with spicy
flavors, often enhanced
by aging in oak barrels.

CHOCOLATE Rich,
chocolaty flavors are
characteristic of warmer
vineyards in Australia.

syrah/shiraz

For years, whether it was called syrah or shiraz made no difference: it was little regarded either way. But in the last decade the tide has turned.

Deep-colored, full-bodied, spicy-toned wines are now all the rage and syrah/shiraz is the red king. Producers throughout the New World and Mediterranean Europe are planting new vineyards and nurturing old ones that were little thought of when cabernet sauvignon reigned triumphant. Syrah's home is the northern Rhône Valley, where it makes muscular, dark, tannic, long-lived wines epitomized by Hermitage and Cornas and the more perfumed Côte Rôtie. But it is in Australia, especially the Barossa Valley, that the greatest plantings of old shiraz are found. Hundreds of acres of gnarled, unruly-looking, bushlike vines, some of them over 130 years old, produce tiny yields of very concentrated grapes that make quite a different style of red from that of the Rhône.

In the northern Rhône, the berry fruit (tasting of blackcurrants, blackberries, and raspberries) is dense, inky, and more herbal, the acidity is higher, the spice is a vigorous whiff of freshly ground black pepper, and there is often a suggestion of smoke, tar, or burnt rubber (much nicer than it sounds). As the wines age and mellow, they develop more complex gamey, sometimes leathery, flavors.

In old-vines shiraz from the Barossa Valley, the berry fruit is riper and fuller, there is a rich, mouth-filling, chocolaty character, sometimes a suggestion of mint, and the spice element, which is intensified by aging in oak, is sweeter and more exotic. The wines are intense, but altogether more succulent, and the best last for many years, as proved by wines such as the famous Penfolds Grange. Another warm Australian region where shiraz has long been at home is the Hunter Valley. Shiraz grown further south, in the cooler vineyards in Victoria, gives distinctly peppery wines that have more in common with northern Rhône syrahs.

Syrah/shiraz doesn't only make expensive, top-of-the-line wines. In Australia, where it has regained its postition as the most planted red grape, it is responsible for masses of everyday, smooth, spicy, blackberry-flavored reds. It is also blended very successfully with cabernet sauvignon at all quality levels (an idea that growers in Provence have copied), and is made into a delicious, full-bodied, ripe, spicy, sparkling red.

All across the south of France, but especially in Languedoc, syrah has been planted in recent years as a so-called "improving variety" to raise standards. It appears in traditional reds such as Corbières and in vins de pays with syrah, or even shiraz, declared on the label. It is also being increasingly planted and cosseted in South Africa, California, Chile, and Argentina.

wines have a
characteristic
spicy, smoky,
peppery,
fragrance

can produce
tannic wines
that age well

reputed to have
been introduced
to the Rhône from
Shiraz in Persia

deep
color,
heavy
perfume

WHERE
Rhône, especially the northern stretch; all over Australia, but especially the Barossa Valley; southern France, especially Languedoc; and almost anywhere else where it is warm enough.

MAIN STYLES
Full-bodied, spicy reds: big, muscular, and tannic in the northern Rhône, fatter and riper in Australia. Also makes simpler, fruity, cheaper wines; blends well with cabernet sauvignon in Australia; and is an "improving variety" in almost any Languedoc red.

WHEN & WITH
The best from the Rhône need long cellaring, but Crozes-Hermitage and St.-Joseph can be drunk after a few years. Top Australian shiraz can be drunk when released, but ages well. Cheaper wines shouldn't be kept. Use big wines for big flavors – game, casseroles, sausages, cheese.

NOT THE SAME AS
The PETITE SIRAH of California and Mexico.

albariño

Spain has few distinguished white grapes, which makes the aromatic albariño of Galicia in the northwest all the more important – and, in recent years, modish and expensive.

Albariño produces wines with good acidity, fairly high alcohol, and rich, but dry, peachy fruit. In many ways, it's like a more tangy and steely version of viognier but with the advantage of higher acidity, which makes it a better match for food, including seafood. Most albariño isn't matured in oak, but it can be – with success – and most is drunk young, although it can age well. It is most important in Rías Baixas, where albariño may feature on the label more prominently than the name of the region or producer. It's also grown, and appreciated, across the border in the Vinho Verde region in the far northwest of Portugal.

ALSO KNOWN AS:
• ALVARINHO in Portugal

ALSO KNOWN AS:
• PINEAU in the Loire
• STEEN in South Africa

chenin blanc

This is a grape with an extraordinarily wide repertoire – wines in every style from bone dry to gloriously sweet, sparkling wines, and some of the longest-lived of all white wines.

Yet chenin blanc remains one of the least popular of the main French varieties, for the simple reason that, given unripe, overcropped, or badly handled grapes, it can deliver some of the world's nastiest, tartest wines, such is its natural high acidity. Its homeland, Anjou-Touraine in the Loire Valley, still delivers many a drab, cheap bottle, but it also produces superlative chenins: wines with crisply floral, apricot and apple, marzipan, straw, and honey flavors; and wines that range from sec, demi-sec, and moelleux (dry, medium-dry, and sweet) styles, from appellations such as Savennières (dry) and Vouvray (dry, medium-dry, and sweet), to lusciously sweet, botrytis-affected wines from the Coteaux du Layon. In the New World, especially in South Africa and California, chenin is used for churning out large volumes of cheap, basic wine, but a few Cape producers are now cosseting low-yielding, old vines to make impressive, oak-fermented dry whites.

white grapes

colombard

It can't be said that colombard is one of the most characterful varieties, but that's what made it useful in the Cognac and Armagnac regions.

Light-bodied, modestly flavored wine is the ideal kind for distilling. It was only when the Armagnac market slumped in the 1980s that producers came up with the idea of trying to make drinkable table wine instead. Applying modern wine-making methods, they started to produce light, crisp, leafy, fruity wines – and Vin de Pays des Côtes de Gascogne became one of the great success stories. Colombard is also grown – widely – in California's hot Central Valley and in South Africa, in both cases to provide large volumes of simple, fruity wine. In Australia, colombard is primarily blended.

gewurztraminer

Not only does the distinctive pink coloring of a ripe gewurztraminer crop make it one of the easiest varieties to identify, the wine produced is also the most instantly recognizable, especially from Alsace.

Yellow-gold, full-bodied, low in acid, and slightly oily in texture, gewurztraminer has an unmistakeable trademark in its smell: an exotic blend of lychees, rose petal, turkish delight, and sometimes ginger. If sweet, either late harvest (Vendange Tardive) or botrytized (Sélection de Grains Nobles), it adds honey to its other flavors. Although grown in Germany, Austria, Italy's Alto Adige, Switzerland, and eastern Europe, nowhere is it quite so rich and pungent and nowhere taken quite so seriously as in Alsace. Most of the New World is too warm for the variety, but New Zealand, Oregon, and Washington State, and a handful of Chilean examples demonstrate that it can be worth pursuing in a cooler climate.

grüner veltliner

It is grown in Hungary and the Czech Republic, but, above all, grüner veltliner is Austria's specialty and most extensively planted grape.

As is so often the case, familiarity bred contempt, with much of Austria's output being drunk in wine taverns as inexpensive Heurige (young wine). It still is, but, in the last decade or so, grüner veltliner has been revalued, with the wines from the Wachau, Kremstal, and Kamptal regions emerging as the finest and most long-lived. In structure, the wine is similar to riesling, but its flavors are different – a hallmark white pepper character combined with white peach and a herbal/mineral or sometimes smoky seam.

ALSO
KNOWN AS:

• ERMITAGE BLANC in Switzerland

marsanne

As the principal grape of white Hermitage and other northern Rhône whites such as St.-Joseph, marsanne has enjoyed the vogue for Rhône grapes and is now part of most white appellations in Languedoc, including varietal vins de pays.

With its mouth-filling weight, relatively low acidity, and affinity with oak, marsanne has also benefited from the domino effect of chardonnay's popularity. Its aromas often combine jasmine, hazelnuts, and herbs; but its character is far more about body and richness. While marsanne is relatively new in California, adopted there by the Rhône Rangers (as the growers of Rhône grapes are known), the state of Victoria in Australia has long nurtured the grape to produce typically rich, oak-matured whites with citrus and tropical fruit flavors. Marsanne is also a specialty of the Valais in Switzerland.

muscat

The one grape variety that, fermented into wine, can still smell unmistakeably of fresh grapes is muscat.

ALSO KNOWN AS:
• FRONTIGAN
• MOSCATO
• MUSKATELLER
• MOSCATEL
• MUSCADEL (but not Muscadelle)
• ZIBIBBO and many others

Light, sweet, fizzy muscats – Clairette de Die Tradition; Asti and other Italian moscatos – often taste simply of sweet, juicy grapes; but dry muscats can have an aroma of roses as well, and sweet muscats such as Muscat de Beaumes-de-Venise and other vins doux naturels of France often have enticing scents of orange and spice. There are several muscat grapes: the finest is muscat blanc à petits grains, which has far too many common synonyms to list here. There are also golden, pink, red, and darker-berried versions: in Australia, where it's the variety behind the immensely concentrated, rich, raisiny "liqueur muscats" of Rutherglen, it's called brown muscat. In Europe, petits grains is found all around the Mediterranean, from Greece via Italy to the south of France, but it often cohabits with muscat of alexandria, the next best strain, and, in Alsace, with muscat ottonel, which comes further down the pecking order again.

pinot blanc

Originally from Burgundy and still found in a few vineyards there, pinot blanc's French base is now Alsace, where it produces soft, rounded wines with a gentle perfume of apples, talcum powder, and, just occasionally, hints of spice.

In the Pfalz, Baden, and eastern Germany, pinot blanc is grown as weissburgunder and used for drier, fatter wines than the classic German styles and grape varieties, often aged in oak and intended to be served with food. In Italy and much of eastern Europe, it makes fairly simple, fresh whites, but Austria produces notable dry and botrytized sweet pinot blancs. Although there are some good Californian pinot blancs, it isn't – yet – a variety that has captured New World imagination.

ALSO KNOWN AS:
• WEISSBURGUNDER in Germany and Austria
• PINOT BIANCO in Italy

pinot gris/grigio

As with pinot blanc, pinot gris originated in Burgundy, and it can still be spotted there – but, whereas pinot blanc hides in among Burgundy's chardonnay, pinot gris is scattered among the pinot noir, red-wine vineyards.

This isn't quite as odd as it sounds: pinot gris is a mutation of pinot noir and a more characterful variety than pinot blanc (at least in France). In Alsace, pinot gris produces rich, perfumed whites, with a nutty, smoky, spicy, sometimes honeyed character; these can be dry, sweet, or botrytized and ultrasweet. Such wines are not the pinot gris that wine drinkers familiar with pinot grigio will know, however. Italian pinot grigio – that from Collio excepted – is mostly crisp, fairly light, and neutral. Pinot gris is also widely grown in eastern Europe, Austria, and Germany; and, from a small base, is gaining ground in California, Australia, and New Zealand, having already won acclaim in Oregon.

ALSO KNOWN AS:
- RULÄNDER and GRAUBURGUNDER in Germany
- PINOT BEUROT in Burgundy
- MALVOISIE in the Loire and Switzerland

semillon

Overshadowed by sauvignon in Bordeaux and chardonnay in Australia, semillon rarely enjoys the limelight, but it is pivotal and plentiful in both places.

Dry semillon tends to be broad and fat with a lanolin character and low acid – ideal for splicing with the tang and aroma of sauvignon in Bordeaux, whether in a mass-market blend or a long-lived, barrel-fermented white Graves. When it comes to sweet Bordeaux – Sauternes et al – there's no question that semillon is supreme. Given morning mist and afternoon sun, it succumbs to noble rot, resulting in opulent, golden, honeyed wine. Australia makes a few botrytized semillons – convincing, if slightly heavier than Sauternes – but semillon's main role down under is to be dry. The Barossa style is smooth and oaky with a rich lemon flavor. Traditional Hunter Valley semillon is unoaked and idiosyncratic: light, sharp, bone dry, altogether fairly charmless when young, but toasty, honeyed, and lemony with age – and it can be great age. In cooler Western Australia, New Zealand, and Washington State, it tends to be more intensely fruity and grassy.

viognier

Now ultrafashionable, viognier is all too difficult to get right. It's treacherous in the vineyard, can be almost as tricky in the winery, and doesn't improve with age.

Not surprising, then, that up until the 1980s it was hardly found outside its home territory, the tiny, steep, terraced area centered on Condrieu in the northern Rhône, and not surprising that it should be expensive. There are some cheaper viogniers now, especially from Languedoc, where much was planted in the 1990s, and they are begining to come from Australia and Argentina; but, while they have the characteristic peach and apricot perfume, they lack the original's sumptuousness. Condrieu and the best viogniers of California and Australia are high in alcohol, voluptuously scented with freesias, musk, peaches, apricots, and ginger, and have an unctuous, creamy texture.

gouais blanc

This isn't a name you will have seen on any wine label, nor will you have tasted any wine made from gouais blanc, and it's almost certain that you never will.

What you have almost certainly tasted, however, is wines, probably many, made from the offspring of this obscure and lowly grape variety. DNA testing in California in the late 1990s sent tremors through the wine establishment when it showed that the pale-skinned, acid gouais, which was common in northeast France in the Middle Ages, had crossed with one of the noble pinot family (pinot noir is the most likely) to produce 16 new grape varieties, including gamay (as in Beaujolais), melon (as in Muscadet), and no lesser star than chardonnay, the variety of white burgundy, many champagnes, and so many esteemed New World wines.

aligoté
Very much the second white grape of Burgundy in both stature and acreage, producing simpler, sharper, shorter-lived wine than chardonnay. It's at its best in the village of Bouzeron, and is the traditional wine for making Kir. Also grown widely in eastern Europe.

assyrtiko
One of several indigenous Greek grapes capable of producing high-quality wines with piquant acidity. Pithy, citrus, herb, spice, and apricot flavors. Originally from Santorini, but increasingly grown on other islands and the mainland.

catarratto
Italy's second most cultivated white grape, although confined to Sicily. Traditionally used for Marsala, but increasingly being used for table wines, sometimes blended with chardonnay, which complements its fresh grapefruity flavor.

chasselas
A fairly neutral table grape that nonetheless produces some lively, worthwhile wine in Switzerland, where it is by far the most important variety (known as **fendant** in the Valais). Produces less memorable results in Alsace, Savoie, and, as **gutedel**, in Germany.

clairette
A low-acid, southern French grape yielding full, but often flaccid, wine that needs blending with other, crisper varieties (or using to make vermouth). Confusingly, the principal grape in sparkling Clairette de Die isn't clairette but muscat – hence the fruitiness of that wine.

cortese
The grape behind Gavi, Italy's modish white wine from Piedmont. Racy and fruity at best, and a good match for the fish of the Ligurian coast, but at other times nothing more than overpriced and overfashionable.

fernão pires
Portugal's most widely planted white grape, making medium-bodied whites with a slightly pungent spiciness. Important in the Ribatejo region and, as **maria gomes**, in white Bairrada.

furmint
The characterful, high-quality mainstay of Hungary's great, sweet (botrytized) Tokaji wines. It also makes powerful dry wines in Hungary, and is grown in Slovakia, Slovenia, and Austria.

gros plant
An even tarter, more neutral version of the melon grape of Muscadet, from the same Nantais region of the Loire. It is also distilled for brandy, and in that case usually called **folle blanche.**

irsai oliver
A Hungarian table grape (a relatively new crossing) that is increasingly being turned into crisp, light to medium-bodied wines with a grapey, muscat scent. Also grown (spelled **irsay**) in Slovakia.

kerner
The most successful and recent of Germany's many crossings, especially popular in the Pfalz and Rheinhessen. Early-ripening (the aim of most such crossings), crisp, flowery, and more like riesling than most.

macabeo
An important Spanish grape, mildly scented with herbs and flowers, grown all over the north, including in Rioja (known there as **viura**) and in Catalonia, where it's one of the key components of cava. Also grown in Languedoc-Roussillon.

malvasia
The grape behind sweet malmsey Madeira and a name applied to a confusing array of grapes and wines over the years – dry, sweet, white, red, brown, still, and sparkling. Especially important, in many incarnations, throughout Italy. Malvoisie in France and Switzerland is usually pinot gris.

Top to bottom:
aligoté
chasselas
macabeo
müller-thurgau

other whites

manseng, gros & petit
Sibling grapes with intense, tangy fruit (tangerine, nectarine, quince), producing dry and sweet Jurançon in southwest France and contributing to Gascony's Pacherenc du Vic-Bihl. Gros manseng is used more for the zingy, dry wines, the smaller-berried petit for the fine, sweet wines. Now being planted in California and Languedoc.

melon de bourgogne
Originally from Burgundy, as the name implies, but now the grape of Muscadet and nowhere else. Neutral, acid grape that can cope with the Atlantic-influenced weather, but is otherwise unloved.

müller-thurgau
A highly productive German riesling crossing, but almost entirely deficient in riesling character and quality, and usually the chief ingredient in Liebfraumilch and other cheap bottles from Germany and Eastern Europe. Produces better results in Italy, Switzerland, and New Zealand. Also important in England.

muscadelle
The third and least fashionable white grape of Bordeaux and Bergerac, mainly used in the sweet wines. Also the grape used, under the name tokay, in Australia's dramatically sweet, rich, brown "liqueur tokays" (fortified dessert wines).

palomino
The grape behind most sherry, but not a name that was ever used on labels until recently. It has also found a niche for itself recently as a table wine grape in the Canary Islands, and occasionally appears as **listán** in the south of France.

pedro ximénez
Often just called **PX**, this is responsible for the syrupy, brown wines used for sweetening some sherries; the rich, raisiny-sweet, fortified wines of Málaga; and the similarly sticky, pure PX of Jerez. It also makes the sherrylike dry and sweet wines of Montilla.

picpoul
An old Languedoc variety that usefully retains its refreshing acidity in the warm climate. At its best in the full, dry, lemony whites of Coteaux du Languedoc Picpoul de Pinet.

prosecco
The grape used to make wines of the same name in the Treviso hills, north of Venice. Both still and sparkling wines exist, but the soft, off-dry, almond-scented, fizzy wines predominate.

roussanne
Finer and more aromatic and herb-scented than marsanne, its partner in blends from the northern Rhône, but trickier to grow and therefore less common. Also present in white Châteauneuf-du-Pape, in Savoie (known as **bergeron**), and increasingly in Languedoc. It was catching on in California, too, until some worryingly large plantings turned out to be viognier.

roussette
A high-quality grape producing crisp, perfumed, sappy whites in the Alpine hills of the Savoie region. Also known there as **altesse.** Possibly the same variety as furmint.

scheurebe
One of the most successful of Germany's many crossings, delivering dry as well as sweet wines with a characteristic pink-grapefruit flavor and often a touch of spice, especially in the Pfalz. Known as **samling 88**, it produces some very good sweet wines in Austria.

seyval blanc
Relegated to the bottom of the class by the wine establishment because it's a hybrid, but can give crisp, appetizingly fruity wines in the cool climates of England, Canada, and New York State.

silvaner
Spelled **sylvaner** in Alsace and Austria and widely grown throughout central Europe and Germany. An early-ripening variety with high acid, it's often used as something of a workhorse, but can achieve a fine, mineral quality, particularly in the Franken region of Germany.

tocai friuliano
A variety that makes a significant body of fresh, fragrant, floral whites in Friuli, northeast Italy. It has no connection with Alsace's tokay-pinot gris, but some authorities claim a link with the furmint of Tokaji (Hungary). Others say it is the commonplace sauvignonasse of Chile, the variety that some Chilean producers misleadingly market as sauvignon blanc.

torrontes
A grape from Galicia in northeast Spain, but now more of an Argentine specialty. Aromatic and decidedly muscatlike, the wines are often full-bodied and high in alcohol, yet refreshingly crisp.

trebbiano/ugni blanc
So thin and uninspiring is the wine made from this grape in Italy and France (as trebbiano and ugni blanc, respectively), it's rarely mentioned on labels. Why mention it here? It's the most planted white grape in both countries: most of it is blended.

verdejo
One of Spain's few high-quality, ageworthy white grapes. Aromatically verdant, sometimes nutty specialty of the Rueda region, where it is often blended with sauvignon blanc.

verdelho
Best known as the medium-dry, typically tangy style of Madeira, but increasingly seen as a full-bodied Australian wine with a taste of lime marmalade. Probably the same as Galicia's delicious, but rare, **godello**.

verdicchio
Famous for Verdicchio dei Castelli di Jesi, a crisp, lightly perfumed, lemon and almond-flavored dry white wine that comes from the Italian Marches in an unforgettable amphora-shaped bottle.

vermentino
Aromatic grape making lively whites in Sardinia, Liguria, Corsica, and Languedoc-Roussillon; probably the same as the **rolle** grape of Provence.

vernaccia
A name applied to several grape varieties in Italy, but the wine everyone knows is the nutty Vernaccia di San Gimignano. This is Tuscany's most interesting white – and arguably Tuscany's only interesting white.

welschriesling
Whether it's called welschriesling, **olasz rizling**, **laski rizling**, or **riesling italico**, this grape of central and eastern Europe and northern Italy is unrelated to the real, and higher-quality, German riesling. It can produce crisp, light, reasonably aromatic wines, but is at its best in the sweet (botrytized) wines of Austria.

barbera

Although it is Italy's second most planted red grape, barbera isn't responsible for any of the great and famous red wines, so it doesn't have the standing of sangiovese or nebbiolo.

The defining characteristic of barbera is high acid (for a red wine) combined with low tannin, which gives it a tart cherry-and-damson fruit flavor, especially on its home ground in Piedmont, northwest Italy. The variety has always played second fiddle to nebbiolo there; but growers, especially in the zones of Barbera d'Alba and Barbera d'Asti, are now taking it more seriously, softening its edges and giving it greater depth by aging it in oak. Barbera is widely grown in California's Central Valley for everyday reds and is producing some increasingly worthwhile results from large plantings in Argentina.

ALSO KNOWN AS:
- BOUCHET in St.-Emilion
- BRETON in the Loire
- MENCÍA in Galicia, northwest Spain (but confusingly, mencía is also used for another light red variety in Spain)

cabernet franc

The third red grape of Bordeaux, cabernet franc is a lighter, less tannic version of cabernet sauvignon, with berry flavors that can have some of the green-pepper, currant-leaf freshness of cool-climate cabernet sauvignon.

Because it ripens earlier and, in cooler conditions, more fully than its distinguished cousin, cabernet franc is most important on the right bank of the Gironde, especially in St.-Emilion, where it's the principal grape in, among others, the illustrious Château Cheval-Blanc. Its other main claim to fame is as the variety behind the best reds of the middle Loire, including Bourgueil, St.-Nicolas-de-Bourgueil, Chinon, and Saumur-Champigny. It is also significant in northeast Italy, especially Friuli, where it produces medium-bodied, soft, leafy-flavored wines. In the New World it is mainly used as a minor blending partner, as in Bordeaux, but some growers are starting to give it more attention.

red
grapes

gamay

The grape famous for one wine: Beaujolais. No other region makes gamay with the same fresh intensity and the lively, sappy, strawberry fruit achieved in the granitic hills of Beaujolais.

Just to the north of Beaujolais, in the Mâconnais, gamay is the grape behind most (rather dull) red Mâcon and some basic Bourgogne Rouge. It also appears in Bourgogne Passe-Tout-Grains, a blend with pinot noir that finds its echo in Switzerland's Dôle. In and around the Loire Valley, it produces such wines as Gamay de Touraine, Coteaux du Giennois, Côtes du Forez, and Côte Roannaise. Wines labeled gamay in eastern Europe and California are usually, respectively, blaufränkisch and pinot noir.

grenache

Until a few years ago, the world's most widely planted red grape, grenache, was not a name seen much on labels. If people had heard of it, it was usually as the most important of the 13 grape varieties that are permitted, but rarely all used, in Châteauneuf-du-Pape.

Grenache found favor in the late 1990s, when full-bodied red wines with spicy, ripe fruit became fashionable. Not that all grenache – or garnacha in Spain, where it is even more important than in the south of France – has this character, or the signature raspberry and white pepper flavors. Young grenache vines, and vines allowed to overproduce, give high-alcohol but pallid wines. Both Australia and California grow it on a large scale for cheap, high-volume wines; but, in Australia especially, old grenache vines are now being diverted to the production of big, fruity, characterful reds. Grenache is also a good variety for rosé, or rosado.

ALSO
KNOWN AS:

• CANNONAU in Sardinia

Below: ripening
cabernet franc

malbec

Like syrah/shiraz and grenache, malbec is a grape variety on a roll. At least, it is in its adopted country of Argentina.

In Argentina, and on a much smaller scale also in Chile, malbec produces full, richly fruity, spicy reds with flavors of mulberries and blackberries. In its native Cahors in southwest France, it is better known for harder, leaner wines with dry tannins, higher acid, a mineral, pencil-shavings character, and restrained blackberry fruit. Small amounts of malbec are still used in Bordeaux and other reds from the French southwest, and a few Californian winemakers incorporate it in their Meritage wines (Bordeaux blends). Just recently, a handful of producers in Hawkes Bay, New Zealand, have started to use malbec with more conviction in their – mostly merlot – blends, and with success.

ALSO KNOWN AS:
• AUXERROIS and COT in Cahors

merlot

Hi-C for grown-ups; cabernet sauvignon without the pain: as technical descriptions they may lack gravitas, but, as thumbnail sketches, they are right on.

Merlot is broadly similar to cabernet sauvignon, but softer, lusher, less austere. Like cabernet, it takes well to oak, but has less tannin and acidity and a more plummy, less incisive, blackcurrant flavor. More widely planted in Bordeaux than cabernet, merlot predominates in all the basic wines (simple Bordeaux, Premières Côtes, Côtes de Bourg et al), as well as in St.-Emilion and Pomerol, but was traditionally regarded as cabernet's understudy – a useful, earlier-ripening blending partner. Famous tiny-production Pomerols such as Château Pétrus and Le Pin raised its profile in the 1990s, and there was a rash of planting throughout the New World – everywhere from Washington State to Hawkes Bay, Casablanca to Coonawarra, and, above all, California. There, it produces wines at every level from simple and jammy to exceptionally rich and correspondingly expensive.

Below left: a merlot vine
Below right: merlot grapes

mourvèdre

Called monastrell in Spain, the robust, dark-berried mourvèdre has always been one of the key Spanish varieties; but it was little talked about under its French name in France or anywhere else until recently.

Mourvèdre was known, if at all, as the principal grape of the long-lived, but rather obscure, Provençal red wine Bandol, and as a bit-part player in a few other southern French reds. Its fortunes changed when it was recommended as one of several "improving varieties" throughout Languedoc-Roussillon, recognized for its firm-structured wines with their concentrated, gamey, leathery, black-fruit flavors. As mataro, it languished on the sidelines in California and Australia for many years; but, since Rhône grapes and other southern French varieties have become the vogue, mataro has been rehabilitated as sought-after mourvèdre.

ALSO
KNOWN AS:

- MONASTRELL in Spain
- MATARO in California
  and Australia

nebbiolo

One of the most stay-at-home of all grapes, nebbiolo has its heartland in a relatively small, hilly, and misty corner of northwest Italy, centered on Piedmont.

Here, it is celebrated, above all, in Barolo and Barbaresco – both majestic reds, high in tannin and acid, that need years to unveil their complex flavors of tar and truffles, roses and violets, prunes and dark chocolate. Nebbiolo has been transported to both North and South America and to Australia, all without much success; but the determination with which the fashion for Italian varieties is being followed in California and Australia may produce some more interesting nebbiolos in the coming years.

ALSO
KNOWN AS:

- SPANNA in Piedmont
- CHIAVENNASCA in the
  Valtellina (Lombardy)

pinotage

South Africa's own red variety, a 1920s' crossing between pinot noir and the lowly southern French cinsaut, pinotage is a grape unlike either of its parents.

Because it was treated pretty disdainfully by most producers until recently, pinotage hasn't developed one signature style. The wines vary from light and juicy, with a distinctive bubblegum-cum-banana flavor, to bigger, more serious, tannic and oaky reds with plummy, slightly marshmallowlike fruit. With its idiosyncratic taste, it's not a variety likely to catch on in other countries, but it does provide South Africa with its answer to Australian shiraz, Californian zinfandel, and Argentine malbec.

sangiovese

Italy's most planted variety, sangiovese provides the framework for all of Tuscany's great reds – Chianti, Brunello di Montalcino, Vino Nobile di Montepulciano, and Carmignano – as well as the less familiar Morellino di Scansano and Parrina.

Inherently, sangiovese is late-ripening, fairly acid and tannic, with plum and cherry fruit, an herbal, tobacco-leaf accent, and a slightly gamey-leathery flavor; but, because there are so many different clones, wines vary from the light and simple (much Sangiovese di Romagna) to Tuscany's exalted, chewy reds. Other regions where the grape makes its mark include Umbria, where it's at its best in Torgiano, and the Marches, especially in Rosso Piceno. In the New World, it generally produces softer, more supple wines than in Tuscany. California, in particular, is producing some good, if expensive, sangiovese; Argentina is starting to get more characterful results; and there is eager interest in Australia.

ALSO KNOWN AS:
- SANGIOVETO, BRUNELLO, MORELLINO, and PRUGNOLO GENTILE in Tuscany
- NIELLUCCIO in Corsica

Below left:
pinotage grapes
Below right:
sangiovese grapes

tempranillo

Quantitatively, tempranillo is not Spain's most important grape variety; qualitatively, it is.

Although usually blended, tempranillo forms the backbone of both Rioja and Ribera del Duero and appears throughout north and central Spain, including Navarra, Penedès, Costers del Segre, Somontano, Valdepeñas, and La Mancha. The thick-skinned grape gives good color, aging potential, and spicy, tobacco, and strawberry flavors, but it is hard nonetheless to disassociate the taste of most tempranillo-based wines from that of the oak, especially American, in which most are aged. Vanilla, spice, toast, even coconut – flavors traditionally linked with Rioja – are more than anything signs of oak maturation, as is a relatively pale color. Under the names aragonez and tinta roriz, tempranillo is significant in Portugal – in the Douro region – for both port and fine table wines. It makes soft, easy-drinking reds in Argentina, and is likely to make more rewarding ones in future from Australia and California.

ALSO KNOWN AS:

- TINTO FINO, CENIBEL, ULL DE LLEBRE, TINTO DEL PAÍS and TINTA DE TORO in Spain
- ARAGONEZ and TINTA RORIZ in Portugal

zinfandel/ primitivo

It took DNA fingerprinting in the 1990s to confirm what experts had begun to suspect: California's zinfandel grape and the primitivo of Apulia in southern Italy are one and the same.

This proved good news for primitivo, which was important locally, but until then, hardly known beyond Apulia. Because vines adapt to environmental conditions, zinfandel and primitivo have developed personalities of their own. Both are headily aromatic and alcoholic (often 15 percent or more alcohol), with notably sweet, spicy fruit, but zinfandel's fruit is sweeter, with a ripe, raspberry, sometimes porty, bramble-jelly quality. Primitivo tends to be a bit earthier, with more plum and cherry notes. Their uses vary, too. Although both are made into big, dry reds – their natural style – zinfandel is also used for bland, semisweet pink wine, known as blush wine or white zinfandel.

Top to bottom:
blaufränkisch
carmenère
petit verdot
pinot meunier

agiorgitiko
An important Greek variety, also known as **st. george**, that on its own is responsible for the velvety, fruity red Nemea, but is often blended with other varieties, including cabernet sauvignon.

aglianico
A distinguished Italian grape of Greek origin with a penchant for the volcanic soils of southern Italy. Its two finest wines are Aglianico del Vulture from Basilicata and Taurasi from Campania – dense, long-lived reds with rich fruit and a gunflint-and-spice character.

baga
A small, thick-skinned Portuguese grape that produces dark, tannic, astringent reds with a pronounced berry flavor in the Bairrada region, and, incongruous as it may sound, provides some of the raw material for Mateus Rosé. Also planted in the Dão and Ribatejo areas.

blaufränkisch
Grown in central and eastern Europe – as **limberger** in Germany and **kéfrankos** in Hungary – the fruity, peppery blaufränkisch makes particularly rewarding, oak-matured reds in Burgenland, Austria. It also blends well there with both cabernet sauvignon and pinot noir. Known as **lemberger** in Washington State.

bonarda
Originally from northern Italy, and still a strong presence in Oltrepò Pavese, but now much more significant in Argentina, where it's the most widely planted red grape, used mainly to produce juicy, relatively light reds, including blends.

brunello
A clone or subvariety of sangiovese that famously produces the tannic, long-lived reds of Brunello di Montalcino, toward the south of Tuscany, as well as a softer, younger version called Rosso di Montalcino.

carignan
Rarely seen on labels, but France's most extensively cultivated red grape, with a firm grip on the south. Very old vines in the Languedoc hills can produce flavorsome wine, but carignan's basic characteristic is astringency. In other countries it usually disappears into blends, but it is rightly celebrated in Sardinia's rich, supple Carignano del Sulcis and occasionally (as **carignane**) in California.

carmenère
Thought to have all but died out since Bordeaux's growers abandoned it more than a century ago, carmenère has recently made a dramatic comeback – not in Bordeaux but in Chile, where, in the 1990s, much of the "merlot" was discovered to be carmenère. Produces darker, richer, riper reds than merlot, with more spice and coffee flavors.

castelão/periquita
One of the most popular varieties in southern Portugal where, under a muddling array of aliases (including castelão francês, its official name until recently), it produces wines with ripe, sweet fruit and good structure. They can be drunk young, but develop with age and are worth cellaring.

cinsaut
Workhorse variety of Languedoc, Provence, the southern Rhône, and Corsica, largely used in blends to give softness and a sweet perfume to firmer reds, but stands alone in rosés. Also significant in volume, rather than quality, in South Africa, Morocco, and Lebanon.

corvina
One of Italy's many fine reds, although seldom encountered either alone or on labels. Corvina is the principal grape of Valpolicella, especially the powerful Amarone, and of the reds and rosés (aka chiaretto) of Bardolino.

other
reds

dolcetto A key variety in Piedmont, northeast Italy, not least because it has low acidity, which contrasts with the high-acid barbera, and means it can be drunk much sooner than the high-tannin nebbiolo. The best – lively, full wines with cherry and almond flavors – come from the Dolcetto d'Alba and di Dogliani zones.

dornfelder Deep color, sweet fruit, and good acidity make this Germany's most successful red crossing: particularly successful in the Pfalz and Rheinhessen.

kadarka At one time, this was Hungary's most important red, producing the original, full-bodied Bull's Blood wines; but its star has waned in favor of more resistant varieties such as kéfrankos.

lambrusco Not just the semi-sweet, fizzy red and whites wines sold in large screw-cap bottles, but the name of the grape (with many subvarieties) grown in Emilia Romagna. When it is made in the traditional, nonindustrial way, the wine is sharp and refreshing.

mavrodaphne A Greek grape best known for a sweet, fortified, port-like red wine, the Mavrodaphne of Patras.

mavrud A respected Bulgarian variety that produces full-blooded, quite tannic wines that take well to oak and aging, particularly in Assenovgrad.

montepulciano Grown extensively in central Italy, the montepulciano grape produces full-bodied, sturdy but supple reds, including Montepulciano d'Abruzzo and Rosso Cònero. Oddly, the variety has nothing to do with the Vino Nobile di Montepulciano of Tuscany.

negroamaro The widespread "black-bitter" grape of the far south of Italy. It is used there to provide the backbone of reds such as Salice Salentino, Brindisi, Copertino, and Squinzano – all of them deep, powerful wines with flavors of damsons, dark chocolate, and roasted chestnuts.

nero d'avola Also known as **calabrese**, this is Sicily's most prominent red grape in volume and quality. It produces heady, aromatic wines.

petite sirah The source of strong, tannic reds in Mexico and South America, but most closely associated with California, where it's often blended with less muscular zinfandel. Despite DNA testing, its identity is still foggy – partly because there seem to be more than one variety involved.

petit verdot Traditional Bordeaux variety that ripens nail-bitingly late, but is increasingly valued by top Médoc châteaux for the depth of color, perfume, and spice a small percentage can give to cabernet blends. Used similarly in California, and starting to appear in impressive varietal form in Spain and Australia's Riverland.

pinot meunier Or just **meunier**, but either way the unsung grape variety of champagne – largest in acreage but lowest in standing, and thus little grown by producers making champagne-style sparkling wines elsewhere. Its contribution to champagne is a simple, fresh fruitiness.

ruby cabernet A Californian crossing of carignan and cabernet sauvignon that produces basic, often jammy reds. South Africa and Australia obtain similar results.

st. laurent An Austrian specialty that, with tender, loving care, delivers wines uncannily like pinot noir – even burgundian pinot noir, although it ages more quickly. Cheaper versions can be rather bland.

saperavi Robust, high-acid Russian grape that makes correspondingly robust, long-lived wines in Georgia, Ukraine, Moldova, and most states in the CIS. Blends conveniently well with cabernet sauvignon.

tannat A brawny, tannic variety cornered in southwest France, above all in Madiran, but also in reds from Irouléguy, Tursan, and Côtes de Saint-Mont. Tannat's other heartland is Uruguay, where it produces softer reds with raspberry/blackberry aromas.

tarrango Australia's answer to Beaujolais: a 1960s' crossing of sultana and the Portuguese touriga nacional, designed to give low-tannin, juicy, light-bodied reds. It does – but cannot be said to have caught on there in a big way.

teroldego A distinctive, high-quality grape confined to Trentino in northern Italy. Teroldego Rotaliano is a rich, berry-scented red with a balancing bitter-almond twist.

touriga nacional Already Portugal's top grape for port – dark, aromatic, rich in fruit, and tannic – but also on the increase as a grape for making fine, ageworthy red table wines, both in the Douro (the port region) and Dão. Emerging in table wine form in Australia, too.

zweigelt Austria's most extensively planted red grape, a crossing of blaufränkisch (for its snappy fruit) and st. laurent (for its fullness). Still popular, but little is now being planted in the country.

Below: touriga nacional

Learning to identify and appreciate
the fine flavors of bottles from top
producers is the natural next step
from enjoyment of everyday wines.

tasting wine

getting the most
from your wine

Can anyone really need to be told how to taste wine? Surely, you pick up the glass, take a sip, swallow, and, all being well, enjoy the taste?

Well, yes and no. Simply sipping a glass of wine, or even swigging it, doesn't mean you are tasting it to any great effect – which is fine if all you require is liquid refreshment, or if what you're drinking is a liter bottle of the cheapest vin de table (no amount of painstaking tasting is ever going to turn a humdrum wine into an exciting taste sensation). But if you drink wine because you particularly like it and find that it adds an extra dimension to food – a strong likelihood if you're reading this book – then you'll appreciate that wine isn't like other drinks. It's altogether more complex in its flavor and behavior, with the potential in the best wines to reflect precise provenance and to change and improve with age.

Faced with this potentially fascinating liquid, it makes sense to ensure that you get the most out of every mouthful, glass, and bottle. That means tasting, not just drinking, but it doesn't mean going in for all the facial contortions, sucking noises, and extensive note taking of the professional wine taster, whose livelihood

LOOK Viewed against white paper or some other light background, the color of your wine can give clues to grape varieties, place of origin, and age.

TWIRL Swirling the wine aerates it and releases its aromas; and the way it runs back down the glass may tell you something about its alcohol or age.

SNIFF Inhale deeply and don't be afraid to put your nose right down into the glass. While your sense of smell is at its most receptive, try to identify the aromas.

depends on accurate assessment of the quality, aging potential, and commercial possibilities of wines. It means thinking drinking, a happy medium between pouring it down without a second thought and the pro's clinical approach. And anyone can do it. It just takes experience, the more the better (and what could be nicer?), and the effort involved in memorizing and recalling smells and tastes. You'll find that making brief notes, especially if you're tasting and drinking more than one wine, will speed up the learning process dramatically (*see page 72*).

WINE-TASTING PRACTICALITIES

For a social wine tasting, you need a smell-free room, with reasonably good but not fluorescent light, plus some simple equipment, above all, clean, smell-free glasses: at least one generously sized, plain, tulip-shaped, stemmed wineglass for each person (for more on glasses, *see page 158*). When using one glass for a series of wines, rinse it out when you progress from white to red, or make any other major change, by swirling a little of the new wine around the glass and pouring it out. If the new wine is expensive, you can use a cheaper one to rinse the glass, but watch that it doesn't overwhelm the fine wine – otherwise, use a little water.

You will also need some kind of pale background, such as white paper, a white cloth, or a sheet, against which to view the wines; a bucket, bowl, or pitchers, or proximity to the kitchen sink, for those who want to spit; water and either bread or water crackers for clearing tiring palates; pencils and paper for the diligent to write notes; a means to chill white and sparkling wines (but don't overchill them because you'll numb their aromas); and aluminum foil to wrap around the bottles if you are planning a blind tasting.

Don't forget that wine tasting is apt to be a slightly messy business. Even the best pourers and spitters sometimes miss, so don't wear anything that a spot of red wine would spoil. In the event of a full-scale spillage, white wine lifts red wine to some extent, and salt soaks it up, provided you pile it on and don't rub it in.

distractions

Appreciating wine aromas and flavors is made more difficult when other factors are affecting your nose and palate.

- Cooking smells (however delicious), scent, aftershave, tobacco smoke, and any other strong odors.

- Toothpaste, chewing gum, chocolate, chile, curry, and anything else that leaves a strong or lingering taste.

- The great outdoors: although you may lose distracting scent and cigarette smells into the air, you also lose the all-important wine aromas in the same way. And you won't smell anything standing near a barbecue.

SIP Take a generous sip, concentrating on how the wine feels in the mouth and on the tongue. Analyze the wine and search for flavors – and textures.

MANEUVER Move the wine around your mouth to reach all the taste buds of your tongue. Draw in air to carry the aromas to the back of the throat.

SPIT OUT If wine tasting, rather than social drinking, is your primary aim, you need to keep a clear head. Spit out after tasting to keep your faculties at their best.

look at the wine

Looking at the wine may tell you a lot or very little, depending on the wine, but it's always worth the brief effort. Even if you achieve nothing else, at least you'll know whether there are any pieces of cork floating around in your glass (entirely harmless, but distracting if you get any of them in your mouth).

1 LOOK DOWN Pour a small amount of wine into the glass – not more than a third full, and the same amount in each glass if you intend to compare wines. Look down on the wine from above to check how clear and bright it is and whether it contains any tiny bubbles, and to assess its depth of color.

Determine the depth of color by checking how easily you can see the stem of the glass through the sample of wine.

CHECK THE CLARITY

A wine in good condition should be appetizingly clear, not hazy or cloudy-looking. Fortunately, cloudy, contaminated bottles rarely reach the retail market nowadays, and a single smell and taste should quickly confirm that something is wrong. A muddy appearance is more likely to be due to sediment (deposited coloring matter, tannin, and tartrates) that has been disturbed in moving the bottle, and this is far more common in red wines.

With the trend away from heavy filtering, in some cases to no filtration, we are seeing more wines with sediment these days, and they aren't necessarily old wines. A good two-year-old Australian cabernet sauvignon/shiraz blend may start to throw a sediment. It can have a rather mucky taste and texture, so, if you think there is any possibility of sediment in the bottle, pour gently and don't pour to anywhere near the end of the bottle (leave an inch at the very least). Sometimes labels point out that the wine is unfiltered or may have thrown a sediment.

In white wines, you are more likely to see colorless crystals at the bottom of the glass, or tiny bubbles, usually just below the surface of the wine. The crystals are harmless tartrates which show, like sediment, that the wine has not been overtreated. The bubbles, equally harmless and found in young wines, are carbon dioxide. They give a slight – and refreshing – prickle in the mouth. Any wine, red or white, that is starting to referment (turning sour) will also have bubbles, but in the company of an unmissable whiff of vinegar.

COLOR INDICATIONS

The color of a wine gives tantalizing hints at its age, origin, grape varieties, fermentation, maturation methods, and, by extension, quality. White wines generally reveal less about themselves than red wines, but they nonetheless vary from almost colorless, sometimes with the merest hint of green (a young Mosel Kabinett, for example), to deep gold and even darker. Age is one of the key factors. White wines go darker with age, eventually turning brown, at which point, with the exception of fortified wines such as sherry and Madeira, they are usually well over the hill.

Origin is another factor. The cooler the climate the grapes are grown in, the paler the wine, the higher the acid, and the slower the color will darken – hence water-white Mosel riesling. Conversely, the warmer the climate, the yellower the wine, the lower the

2 TILT THE GLASS To assess the color of the wine – its hue, not just its depth – and to see how much it lightens toward the rim of the glass, hold the glass by either its stem or its base, so that your hands are neither obscuring the wine nor warming it up unnecessarily. With a white background before you, tilt the glass at an angle of about 45 degrees and view the wine through the glass.

3 QUICKLY TWIRL Before you go on to smelling the wine, give the glass a quick twirl and look at the way the wine clings to the glass and then runs down it. (Giving the glass a twirl isn't as easy the first time as it sounds, so it's not something to try out with red wine if you're sitting next to someone. A few minutes with a glass of water over the sink might be time well spent. Try twirling it counterclockwise if you're right-handed, and vice versa.)

acid, and the quicker the wine will age, as in the case of yellow Hunter Valley chardonnay. But there are exceptions. Botrytis-affected grapes produce deeper colors; so, a German Riesling Trockenbeerenauslese will be yellower than a Kabinett of the same region and vintage, and Sauternes in a good vintage will be yellower than the equivalent dry white Bordeaux.

Fermentation and maturation in oak barrels can also deepen the color of whites, but, to complicate the picture, oak-fermented whites are often aged in the barrel with their lees (dead yeasts) and the lees will impede the yellowing.

Color is more indicative in red wines. Where white wines darken with age, red wines become paler, shedding their color as sediment. Like white wines, they also become progressively browner. This means that the deep purplish red of youth gradually gives way to ruby, to garnet, to brick, and finally to a faded, past-its-best tawny. And the more mature the wine, the greater the gradation of color from the center, the darkest part, to the rim, the palest (look at this through the tilted glass). In an old wine, the rim can be almost colorless. In addition, red wines aged for a long time in wooden barrels

lose more color than wines aged predominantly in bottles. Until recently, the superior grades of traditional oak-aged Spanish wines, such as reserva and gran reserva Riojas, were often quite pale, but the fashion now is for Riojas that are deeper, if not actually deep, in color. Tawny port is the archetypal example of a wood-lightened, literally tawny-colored, wine. The other styles of port, aged largely in bottle, are much darker.

With red wines, as with whites, the warmer the climate, the deeper the color, which explains the very dark, inky hues of so many New World reds.

After a twirl, a full-bodied, viscous wine runs slowly down the side of the glass in "legs" or "tears."

The cooler the climate, the paler the wines usually are (as in Alsace and Germany). But color also varies according to grape variety and production and aging processes. The pigments are in the skins (most wine grapes have colorless flesh and juice), with thicker-skinned varieties, such as cabernet sauvignon, syrah, mourvèdre, barbera, and the Portuguese baga, producing darker wines, and thinner-skinned varieties, such as pinot noir, giving paler wines. Winemakers can manipulate the depth of color of red wines by lengthening the period over which the skins remain in the vat with the newly fermented wine, or by adding a little press wine – dark, tannic

wine made from pressing out the skins (*see* In the Winery, *page 130*). And deep-colored red wines are most definitely in vogue.

VISCOSITY

As for that preliminary swirl of the wine, it doesn't tell you a great deal, but wine that runs down slowly in distinctly viscous "legs" or "tears" is likely to be quite high in alcohol and/or sweet. Wine in which the edge seems to crumble away rather than flow in streams is likely to be quite old or very light-bodied and dry. Or it may just be that detergent or cloth residues are breaking the surface tension, in which case you might like to look at the section on glasses (*see page 158*).

smell the wine

You can learn more about a wine from its nose – that is, by smelling it – than by looking at it or sipping it, but simply putting your nose to the glass won't give you much to go on.

Some reassuringly familiar smell may jump out at you – gooseberries or blackcurrants, for example – and you may suddenly feel that you understand the whole business of wine tasting. But it's equally possible that you cannot instantly pinpoint any particular

aromas – least of all the kind of barrage of exotic fruit, flowers, and vegetables that some tasters always seem to be able to detect. Instead, you find that, even after a second aerating twirl, the wine just seems to smell of, well, wine, and not even of grapes.

① **SNIFF THE AROMAS** You need to put your nose right down into the glass and sniff deeply. Smell it again if you like, but not repeatedly, particularly if you have several wines to taste, because your nose and palate can tire quickly.

IDENTIFY THE AROMAS

Very few wines actually smell of fresh grapes, and those that do are mostly made with and labeled muscat. Identifying what you are actually smelling is a matter of practice – no hardship there, then – but some wines are unquestionably easier than others. For example, it's hard to miss the ebullient lychee, cold cream, and turkish-delight aromas of the gewurztraminer grape. Similarly, modern, fruity, often oaky, young wines made predominantly from one grape variety, such as cabernet sauvignon or sauvignon blanc, are usually relatively accessible. Cooler climates generally produce more restrained aromas, while age (in a wine of sufficient quality to improve with keeping) gradually yields more intricate, complex smells, and these need more unraveling.

Try using the broad groupings of my initial prompt list (*see page 66*) to help you identify the flavors in your glass. The list is not official or definitive, so add and delete your own categories as you wish. In addition, the checklist of aromas and flavors (*see pages 70–1*) names the wines most commonly associated with each aroma or flavor. If, for example, you smell pepper, mint, or lime, you can look up which wines or grape varieties might be implicated.

Whatever you do when puzzling over a wine, have faith in what your own senses tell you. Don't fall into the trap of citing all sorts of aromas and flavors because you think they're supposed to be present. If a white Mâcon reminds you of a sheepskin blanket with a hint of cream cheese, it'll be far more useful to you if you remember that, rather than try to persuade yourself that it smells of apple, walnuts, buttered toast, and a hint of honey. Equally, don't be afraid of sounding pretentious. Wines really can smell of green pepper, rose, raspberry, pear, banana, grass clippings, and a host of other fruits, vegetables, and common

substances – although not all at once – because grapes share with those things many of the same chemical compounds. Methoxypyrazines, for example, give the green-pepper aroma often found in cabernet sauvignon, and the gooseberry and canned-asparagus aromas in some sauvignon blancs. But it would be unhelpful, not to say pretentious, to say: "Mmm, I'm getting distinct methoxy-pyrazine on the nose from this claret."

SOURCES OF AROMAS

Identifying individual aromas is satisfying and useful, but it's only one aspect of wine tasting. The idea is not to produce a wine description like a grocery list, but to see how the aromas and flavors interrelate and to build up a picture of a wine's style, character (including age), and quality. That way, you'll know not only what you like, but why, and, crucially, what else you might like.

When getting to know a wine style, it's worth remembering that the smells come from three main origins or stages. The first, the so-called primary aromas, often brightly fruity, floral, or vegetal, come from the grapes themselves. The secondary aromas are those from the wine-making processes. Smells of butter or cream, for example, are found particularly in white wines that have undergone a malolactic fermentation (*see* In the Winery, *page 128*). Smells of vanilla, wood shavings, and toast are associated with the use of new oak in the course of fermentation and/or aging. Many wines are never intended to get beyond these first two stages. They're made to be drunk when young and won't improve with keeping.

OLDER WINES

The third group, the tertiary aromas, often the hardest to pin down at first, are the complex, mellow aromas that develop as a high-quality wine matures in its bottle. Gradually, the vivid, fresh-from-the-press, fruit aromas are replaced by interwoven layers of deeper smells. The wine won't smell as briskly fresh and bright as a young wine, but it should still smell clean, not stale and tired.

In white wines, the most obvious bottle-age smells include honey (in dry as well as sweet wines), toast (even in unoaked wines such as champagne and Hunter Valley semillon), grilled nuts, and gasoline (in riesling, especially German). In red wines, the fruit usually becomes gentler but somehow sweeter and more autumnal, sometimes with suggestions of dried fruit or potpourri; often savory, gamey, leathery smells emerge, too. At this stage, professional tasters often start talking about a wine's "bouquet."

These aging smells can be quite pungent, perhaps disconcertingly so, in which case you have discovered a wine or style of wine you don't like. Some wine drinkers find the gasoline (or kerosene) smell of fine old riesling unexpected and unattractive. Others are shocked by their first whiff of the farmyard in a mature red burgundy. Some old red wines, especially red Bordeaux, can have a slightly mushroomy odor. None of these should dominate, but as elements in a multifaceted bouquet they can add enticing, savory notes. And unpleasant smells are not limited to old wines; the aromas of sauvignon blanc and müller-thurgau have been likened to cat's pee.

- **Fresh fruit** (is the wine overtly fruity and are there any fruits that stand out – lychee or raspberry, for example?)
- **Dried fruit** (raisins or prunes, perhaps?)
- **Floral** (roses?)
- **Vegetal** (green pepper, grass?)
- **Mineral** (flint, wet stones?)
- **Animal** (leather, game?)
- **Buttery** (butter or crème fraîche?)
- **Spicy** (black or white pepper?)
- **Nutty** (walnuts, almonds?)
- **Oaky** (vanilla, toast?)
- **Honey** (but dry or sweet?)

If you do happen to come across a smell that makes you sit up, but which you don't think signifies an actively bad wine (*see* Wine Faults, *page 73*), consider it as a kindred spirit to one of those awesomely stinky but delicious cheeses from rural France.

SMELL INTENSITY

Once you've got a few ideas about what the wine smells of, and whether it seems young, old, or somewhere in between, think about the intensity of the smells. Are they piercing, exuberant, refined, modest, or almost nonexistent? If the nose is very muted, there are three main possibilities: it may be a wine made from one of the least aromatic grape varieties, such as the melon de bourgogne of Muscadet; it may be a cheap, ordinary wine made from heavily cropped vines that have delivered dilute-flavored grapes; or it may be a good-quality wine that isn't ready for drinking and is going through a so-called dumb phase. Sometimes you can reawaken such a wine by putting your hand over the top of the glass and giving it a shake (as with twirling and spitting, you might first want to practice this with water). Often the wine simply needs more time in the bottle, perhaps a few months, perhaps a few years, to reemerge from its shell. If you have purchased several bottles of such a wine, be brave, and be patient.

taste the wine

Strange as it may seem, your taste buds tell you less about wine than your sense of smell can. But taking a sip will add to and qualify the impressions you have already received.

You can't taste a wine properly if you can't smell it: you can test this by holding your nose, putting a clothespin on it, or waiting for your next bad cold. But that doesn't mean your mouth is redundant as a sensory agent. Your taste buds play a vital part in "feeling" the weight and texture of the wine and assessing key, nonvolatile flavors.

To set your taste buds to work, you need to take a good sip and then maneuver the wine around your mouth. At this stage, you can either swallow, spit, or go in for an optional extra practiced by professional tasters (but, be warned, it's not something to try out at a dinner party). Open your mouth slightly and draw in some air. (If you think this sounds alarming, just wait until you get to spitting.) The purpose is to aerate the wine and send

(1) **TAKE A SIP** Once your eyes and nose have told you everything they can about your wine, take a generous sip, but not so large a mouthful that you can do nothing but swallow. Think carefully about the taste as you sip – the first tasting is usually the most vivid.

2

MANEUVER THE WINE

Move the wine around your mouth, particularly over your tongue, which is home to the vast majority of taste buds. Some tasters also suck air through the wine, carrying its aromas to the back of the throat.

the volatile compounds up the back of your mouth to your olfactory bulb, from where messages are sent to the brain. When you have tasted and "felt" the wine, and either swallowed or spat, consider how much and which aspects of the taste linger. The length and the finish or aftertaste are key indications of quality in all wine. The longer and more pleasant, the finer the wine. Try counting the seconds.

NONVOLATILE FLAVORS

Your first impressions of the taste will probably reinforce much of what you found from smelling the wine, because the same aromas have traveled up the back of your mouth to the olfactory area. But you will probably find that the relative intensity of the various aromas has changed because you're now experiencing them in conjunction with other flavors and textures. One of your main goals at this stage is to work out whether all the various components in the wine are in balance.

Taste buds are sensitive to five basic nonvolatile flavors: sweetness, acidity, bitterness, saltiness (although there is not much of the latter in any wine), and umami (a savory taste). Many people are most sensitive to sweetness at the tip of their tongue, to acidity at the sides, and to bitterness (as found in the tannin in some red wines) at either side at the back; but this pattern is by no means universal, so don't rely on it unless you're sure that you conform.

ACIDITY

Start by considering how sharp or acid the wine is, how sweet it is, and whether the two are in balance. Sweet wines, in particular, need acidity: if they do not have enough, they can be horribly cloying. In dry wines, there may be a small amount of residual sugar (grape sugar that hasn't been converted into alcohol). In addition, ripe fruit flavors, alcohol, and glycerol (a fermentation byproduct) can all give a suggestion of sweetness. Remember, too, that warm climates generally give riper fruit flavors, and higher alcohol and glycerol, than cool climates, so that dry New World wines can seem "sweeter" than Old World wines made from the same grape varieties. A higher alcohol and glycerol content will also give fuller-bodied wines with a smoother, sometimes even slightly oily, texture.

Acidity, which is correspondingly higher in cooler climates, gives wines an essential freshness and crispness, especially white wines; but the wines will simply taste tart if the acidity isn't balanced by fruit and alcohol. In the warm Australian climate, acid is added to most white wines, and they taste the better for it. But winemakers don't always get the balance right and sometimes the acid, far from giving liveliness and zip to the wine, ends up sitting clumsily apart from it.

LONGEVITY

Acidity is also the principal contributor to the longevity of white wines, softening gradually as the wine ages. A young white wine destined for the cellar will need to have relatively high levels of acid at the outset. Oak-fermented wines (such as chardonnays, and including Côte d'Or burgundies), with their extra dimension of flavor and richness of texture, will not seem as obviously acid as unoaked wines. German and Austrian rieslings, Savennières, traditional Hunter Valley semillon, and Greek white wines made from indigenous grape varieties can sometimes seem startlingly acid when young. It is not easy to assess whether the acid balance is right in a white wine that is intended to be aged in the bottle; the key is having sufficient fruit for it not to have faded by the time the acidity has softened to perfection. Getting it right is largely a matter of experience – sometimes tooth enamel-stripping, but largely enjoyable.

TANNIN

Acid is important for red wines, too, but far more important, especially in reds intended to be laid down in the cellar, is tannin, the mouth-coating substance also present in brewed tea.

Tannin can be detected by the taste buds sensitive to bitterness. As the wine matures, the tannins soften and mellow, but in some very young, high-quality red wines they can be unpleasantly high-profile. When you taste the wine, try to gauge whether the tannins seem overbearingly hard and harsh, or whether, under the tannin, you can discern a depth of ripe fruit flavors – enough to outlast the tannin.

Nowadays, wines worldwide are being made from riper grapes with riper tannins, which makes them fruitier and more approachable at a younger age. But there is also a trend toward ever bigger, increasingly concentrated red wines, and this can lead to winemakers, anxious to extract every last drop of flavor from their red grapes, extracting too much tannin as well. And until someone succeeds in controlling the weather, there will always be poor vintages in cool climates producing barely ripe grapes with hard, unripe-tasting tannins.

The opposite of a tannic red wine is one that is silky and smooth (glycerol gives smoothness). This may sound seductive, but a wine can be too soft, with not enough tannin and/or acidity, in which case it will seem bland and spineless. The taste will probably pall before the end of the first glass and the wine will have no aging potential.

OAK

Another potential source of imbalance is the taste of oak. You will pick up oak aromas when you smell a wine, but you become more aware of oak when you taste. When carefully used, the right kind of oak – new or nearly new barrels, French, and the finest American – gives complexity of flavor and a richer texture to both red and white wines. But oak has its own seductive vanilla and toast flavors and is increasingly used in various cheaper forms (oak chips, staves suspended in stainless steel tanks) to give a straightforward oak flavor to cheaper wines. There's nothing wrong with that, provided you end up with a glass of wine, not a glass of liquid oak with a hint of wine. Oak is also sometimes used overenthusiastically, in the form of expensive barrels, by ambitious but insufficiently skilled or experienced winemakers. If the concentration of fruit and acidity or tannin is lacking, the oak will dominate the taste when the wine is young and will still be dominating when fruit and other flavors have faded.

BODY

Having thought about all the flavors and textures of the wine and the way they work together, you should have an impression of the wine's weight, of whether it is light-, medium-, or full-bodied. Alcohol is one of the principal

The influence of oak must be carefully controlled to prevent it from overwhelming other flavors and aromas of the wine.

contributors to the weight of a wine, although it's not the only one. It has a slightly sweet taste and, at high levels, a slightly "hot" aftertaste. Like everything else, the alcohol should be in balance with the other flavors. An overalcoholic wine will taste heavy and "hot," and will be lacking in refreshing qualities.

BALANCE

Balance is essentially a matter of quality – the greater the harmony between sugar, acid, tannin, and alcohol, the greater the wine – but it has to be considered in conjunction with the style of the wine. A Sancerre should have notably high acidity; a Condrieu or other viognier wine should not, because viognier only develops its distinctive varietal character when the grapes are very ripe and the acidity levels are comparatively low. Red burgundy should not be as tannic as red Bordeaux of the same quality and age. Similarly, a Californian pinot noir from Santa Barbara County shouldn't be as tannic as a cabernet sauvignon of the same vintage and caliber produced at Howell Mountain, to the north of Santa Barbara in Napa County.

AFTERTASTE

Finally, when you've despatched the wine either down your throat or into the nearest spittoon, think about the taste you're left with. Is it clean, pleasing, and balanced, and does it last? If it fades within a few seconds, you are tasting a simple, everyday wine. But if it lingers for as much as 30 seconds or more, you probably have something rather special in your glass. Congratulations.

describe the wine

Professional tasters have their own vocabulary to describe many aspects of wine. Try using the terms to express your own wine-tasting experiences.

aggressive notably tannic or acid; not invariably a criticism if the wine is not ready for drinking

aromatic plenty of fruity and/or floral aromas (smells) in a young wine

astringent mouth-puckering tannin

austere rather hard and unyielding, perhaps because the wine is young

baked fruit flavors that seem baked and lacking freshness, from overripe grapes or too-hot fermentation temperatures

chewy tannic, but not aggressively so

closed not showing much aroma and flavor, usually not ready for drinking

concentrated packed with flavor and substance

crisp fresh, positive acidity

dried-out old wine in which fruit flavors have faded; past its best

dumb same as closed, usually just a phase in the wine's life

extract the combination of tannin, coloring matter, sugar, and glycerol (that is, the non-water substance of wine)

extracted implies too much tannin and color in a red wine; that is, unbalanced

fat full-bodied but often implying inadequate acidity

finesse high-quality, refined, with everything in balance

firm positive tannin and/or acid

flabby lacking acid, the opposite of crisp

flat lacking acid and freshness

fleshy full and generously flavored

forward more mature or ready than you would expect

green young, acid, raw; may just be too young to drink

hard acid or tannic or both

heavy full-bodied, high alcohol, usually implying unbalanced (except in fortified wines when categorized as "heavy wines")

hollow lacking flavor; has a start and a finish but no middle

hot overalcoholic and therefore unbalanced

jammy jam rather than bright fruit flavors, lacking freshness

lean short on fruit

long high praise for flavors that last

meaty full-bodied, flavorsome, and sometimes literally savory, meat flavors

mouth-filling wine with richness of flavor and texture that seems to fill the whole mouth

neutral wine that offers little in the way of aroma or flavor

oily the slightly oily (smooth, heavy) texture of grape varieties such as gewurztraminer and viognier, and of botrytized semillon wines, such as Sauternes

rich depth and breadth of fruit, other flavors, and texture

round no hard edges, ready to drink

short flavors that don't last, therefore not of high quality

silky fine, smooth texture

soft not too tannic or acid

spritz tiny carbon-dioxide bubbles giving a refreshing prickle on the tongue

steely a firm, intense, positive quality in dry wines with good acidity, such as Chablis

structure the balance and intensity of the basic components (acid, tannin, alcohol, coloring matter) that support the fruit; a wine with good structure will age well

supple round, smooth, not too tannic or acid, ready for drinking

tangy lively and crisp from start to finish

thin lacking flavor and body

tough too tannic

velvety smooth texture, similar to silky but perhaps richer

volatile all wines have volatile acidity, but a volatile wine is on its way to vinegar

woody usually implies an unpleasant, old, or dirty wood character rather than positive oak flavors

zesty fresh, crisp, lively (in whites)

aromas
& flavors

Noting certain flavors in a blind tasting can give you a shrewd idea of the provenance of a wine, the grape variety or varieties involved, and the age of it.

almond many dry Italian whites, such as Soave and Prosecco, but also Valpolicella

apple many whites, including German riesling; some cool-climate chardonnay; and wine made from mauzac, especially Gaillac

apricot viognier wines, including Condrieu; botrytized sweet wines, especially from the Loire (such as Bonnezeaux)

asparagus sauvignon blanc, especially from the New World

banana young, inexpensive whites; South African pinotage; Beaujolais Nouveau

biscuit champagne, especially vintage and any good mature champagne; a few top sparkling wines from elsewhere

blackberry Cahors; Madiran; Argentine malbec; zinfandel; mourvèdre

blackcurrant cabernet sauvignon, including young claret; to a lesser extent, cabernet franc and merlot

bread (freshly baked) champagne

brioche champagne

bubblegum Beaujolais Nouveau; pinotage

butter white wines that have undergone a malolactic fermentation, above all chardonnay, including burgundy

cat's pee müller-thurgau; French sauvignon blanc

cedarwood/cigar box red Bordeaux; some other high-quality cabernet-based reds (such as Washington State, Western Australia, and New Zealand)

cherry many Italian reds; red burgundy

chestnut (roast) southern Italian reds

chocolate many medium- and full-bodied, often oak-aged reds, Old and New World, but especially Australian shiraz and southern Italy's negroamaro

clove cabernet sauvignon

coffee beans various oak-matured reds, usually of quite high quality, including burgundy and Chilean carmenère

cream (creamy flavor and texture) good champagne; some chardonnay, including burgundy

currant leaf sauvignon blanc; cool-climate young cabernet sauvignon (such as New Zealand); Loire cabernet franc

earth/gravel/stone red Graves above all; some more rustic reds

eucalyptus New World cabernet sauvignon

flint Pouilly-Fumé; Sancerre; and Chablis

floral (a general flowery aroma) German riesling and kerner

game red wines, especially mature northern Rhône, burgundy, shiraz, and Ribera del Duero

gasoline mature German and Austrian riesling

gooseberry sauvignon blanc

grape muscat; sometimes Argentine torrontes and Hungarian irsai oliver

grapefruit scheurebe; Sicilian catarratto

grass sauvignon blanc

herbaceous sauvignon blanc

honey sweet white wines, especially botrytized ones; mature dry whites, including burgundy; Alsace pinot gris

lanolin Sauternes and other botrytized semillons; dry Barossa semillon

leather robust red wines, especially syrah-based and Bandol

lemon a great many young whites

licorice young, tannic, red wines

lime Australian riesling and verdelho

lychee gewurztraminer

melon New World chardonnay

mineral Pouilly-Fumé; riesling; Chablis

mint New World cabernet sauvignon, especially South Australian and Washington State; South Australian shiraz

nivea/pond's cold cream gewurztraminer

nut (walnut, hazelnut, cashew) white burgundy; mature champagne; other chardonnays, especially oak-matured

oak many, many wines, red and white, but traditionally Rioja

olive cabernet-based wines

orange many sweet and/or fortified wines

peach many whites, especially viognier and chardonnay

pear young, light-bodied, fairly neutral whites; Beaujolais Nouveau

pepper (green capsicum) cabernet franc and cool-climate cabernet sauvignon

pepper (ground black) grenache; many Languedoc reds; Côtes du Rhône; shiraz

pepper (ground white) Austrian grüner veltliner

plum many red wines

quince Loire whites, dry and sweet, made from chenin blanc

raisin sweet fortified wines (such as Rutherglen liqueur muscat and PX sherry)

raspberry red burgundy and other pinot noirs; red Rhônes; Beaujolais

rose Alsace muscat; burgundy; Barolo

salt manzanilla sherry

smoke full-bodied, oak-matured syrah; Alsace pinot gris; Pouilly-Fumé

spice many full-bodied, oak-aged reds, especially shiraz, Rhône, zinfandel, and primitivo; gewurztraminer

stone (wet stones) Chablis

strawberry Beaujolais; red Rioja; red burgundy

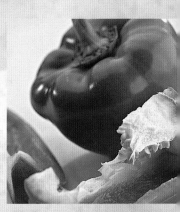

tar Barolo; northern Rhônes

toast any wine that has been aged in new oak barrels; mature champagne; mature Hunter Valley semillon

tobacco/tobacco leaf many reds, including Chianti and other sangioveses, and red Bordeaux

turkish delight gewurztraminer

vanilla any white or red wine aged in new oak (especially American oak)

yeast (bready) champagne

after the tasting

I know it hurts to spit out good wine, and it goes against what you were taught as a child, but spitting is best practice if you're tasting a lot of wines.

The avid swallowers at extensive tastings are the ones with the rosy glows and benevolent smiles. They're the same people who wake up the next morning unable to remember what they tasted, but with a vague recollection of having ordered rather a lot of something from the obliging wine merchant who was holding the tasting. Spitting doesn't mean you don't swallow anything – a little always goes down and is gratefully tasted by the taste buds at the back of the throat – but you keep a clearer head and sharper mind. If you feel shy about it – and most people do at first – practice with water at home. When tasting, keep ties, scarves, necklaces, and long hair out of the way, and don't wear pale colors.

MAKING NOTES

There is nothing complicated about making notes and no reason for it to be seen as pretentious. It's a case of common sense, especially if you're tasting several wines, and it makes learning easier and quicker. Unless you are blind tasting (with the labels hidden), make sure that you have the wine's vital statistics before you start – there's nothing worse than reading a mouthwatering tasting note and then finding you haven't recorded the name of the wine. Labels vary in the information they give: some show the essentials instantly, others are determinedly obtuse. The section Reading the Label (*see pages 142–7*) will help, but, as a start, look for an appellation or region of origin, vintage, grape or grape varieties, style (such as sec or blanc de noirs), the name of a producer and/or property, and a vineyard name or name of a particular bottling, cuvée, or blend.

To make life simple, I write the vintage first, as in 1999 Château Quelquechose, Coteaux du Languedoc, but there's no rule about it. Include where and when you tasted, where and when you bought the wine, and the price, if relevant. The notes aren't for publication, so there's no need for ornate prose. Just jot down or key in things as you go along and as we've looked at them. Include initial impressions of the color – both its hue and depth; aromas and their intensity – from the grapes, the winemaking, and the aging process; sweetness, acidity, and tannin; balance; weight; length of flavor and finish; and then your overall impression of style, quality, age, and aging potential, if any. You won't have a comment on all these, but make sure your remarks go further than a simple yes or no.

Discussions with other tasters will broaden your appreciation of wine – but don't lose sight of what your own senses told you during the tastings.

GIVING SCORES

Scoring wines has become a peculiarly sensitive subject thanks to the influential American wine writer Robert Parker, whose scores out of 100 for every wine written up in his bimonthly magazine, *The Wine Advocate,* can make or break the reputation of a wine, an estate, or a vintage. One of the criticisms of his system is that many people buy according to the scores alone. They neglect to read the all-important tasting notes, which would tell them whether they might expect to like the wines in question.

So, should you or shouldn't you? By all means, if you find it helps you to choose between wines at a tasting or wine fair, for example. But don't use digits as an alternative to notes, and choose a system that is useful to you – perhaps marks out of five, 10, or 20. I use either a 20-point rating, or, if it's just a very quick indication I need, a three-star rating: three for very good or better; two for good; one for quite good; none for anything less. And often I just write notes, with no scores.

wine faults

Thanks to the enormous improvements in winemaking, faulty wines are fewer than they used to be, especially cloudy, moldy-smelling wines spoiled by bacteria.

CORKED WINE

Today, the most common fault is corked wine: its incidence has risen as worldwide demand for corks has increased. Despite recent efforts by the Portuguese-based cork industry, cork taint or corky wine remains a real bugbear. In concentrations of just a few parts per trillion, the principal culprit, trichloroanisole, or TCA, gives wine a dank, moldy, musty smell. To make matters worse, the smell increases with exposure to air, so a bottle that appears to be only slightly corked on opening will soon taste far more unpleasant. You should always reject corked wine in a restaurant, or return it to the store from which it was bought, if possible.

VOLATILITY AND OXIDATION

A wine that smells of vinegar almost certainly has undrinkably high levels of volatile acidity (VA): acetic acid produced by acetic bacteria. White wines that smell pungently of pear-drops, bananas, or nail polish remover have a similar problem: they're unlikely to do you any harm, but you probably wouldn't want to

drink them anyway. The same applies to any white wine that smells of sherry, indicating that it is oxidized (or maderized) – past its best, in other words. Oxidized red wines tend to have an unappetizing stewed, flat smell, or sometimes a sharp, acetic acid-affected one.

SULFUR FAULTS

The other main group of wine faults is sulfur-related. Sulfur dioxide is the main preservative and disinfectant used in winemaking. Applied judiciously it has a lot going for it, but used heavy-handedly it flattens wine aromas, sometimes giving a coarse, meaty overtone, and it can catch unpleasantly in the nose and back of the throat. Overuse is less of a problem than in the past, but it still occurs, especially in German wines and sweet French wines. Some asthmatics need to be cautious with wines that have high sulfur dioxide.

The rubbery, rotten-egg smell of hydrogen sulfide is much stronger, but can be reduced by dropping a copper coin into the wine, either into the glass or a pitcher into which you've decanted the whole bottle. But if the sulfide has already formed even smellier compounds called mercaptans (reminiscent of acrid boiled cabbage, sewage, or burned rubber), your coin won't do anything. On the other hand, a mild smell of sulfide may just be something called bottle stink (*see right*), which fortunately disappears soon after the wine is opened.

common worries

- **Crystals** resembling sugar or glass: harmless tartrates.

- **Pieces of cork** floating in your wineglass: inexpert serving but emphatically not a corked wine.

- **Tiny bubbles** in still white wine, but no vinegary smell: carbon dioxide, which gives the wine a refreshing spritz.

- **A murky, bitty** final glass from a bottle of red wine: harmless but sometimes muddy or bitter-tasting sediment; inexpert serving again.

- **Bottle stink:** not very enticing name for so-called reductive odors that are apparent when the bottle is opened but which quickly disappear after the wine has come into contact with air.

Knowing that you enjoy certain wine styles can be a springboard to discovering wonderful new wines from all over the world.

exploring wines

french whites

Let the benchmark white wines of France be your starting point for an exciting exploration of whites from the rest of Europe and the New World.

if you like
alsace gewurztraminer

There is no grape variety quite like the powerfully and exotically perfumed gewurztraminer, and no region where it is quite as at home as in Alsace; but it is worth looking out for occasional bottles from New Zealand, Chile, Alto Adige (northern Italy), and Oregon and Washington State.

Wines simply labeled traminer from central and eastern Europe are rarely in the same league as these gewurztraminers. A better alternative is Alsace pinot gris, often labeled tokay-pinot gris. Other alternatives include highly aromatic grapes such as muscat, most of which ends up as sweet wine but in Alsace and in a few other places, including the Vins de Pays d'Oc vineyards of Languedoc-Roussillon, is made into a dry wine. The fashionable viognier grape is another; it used to be confined almost exclusively to expensive Condrieu, but spread rapidly in the 1990s, especially to California (it tends to be expensive there, too), Australia, and Languedoc. The muscatlike torrontes of Argentina is also worth a try.

try:

- New World and Alto Adige gewurztraminers
- Alsace tokay-pinot gris
- Alsace and Vins de Pays d'Oc dry muscats
- Condrieu, Californian, Australian, and Languedoc viogniers
- Argentine torrontes

whites

if you like
bordeaux & entre-deux-mers

Dry white Bordeaux comes in two main types: cheap, medium-bodied, usually unoaked, and, if quality is up to par, fresh and grassy; and, from the Graves and Pessac-Léognan areas, expensive, oak-aged wines designed for aging.

For the cheaper wines, substitute whites from the Dordogne and further southwest (Bergerac Sec, Côtes de Saint-Mont, Vin de Pays des Côtes de Gascogne), dry whites from the Loire (such as Anjou Blanc Sec), Alsace sylvaner, and inexpensive Chilean and South African sauvignons. Alternatives to the expensive wines are less obvious because few regions make semillon and sauvignon blends and then age them in oak (there are a few producers around Bergerac). California's oaked sauvignon style, Fumé Blanc, is not very similar; nor are Australia's almost chardonnaylike oaked semillons. But mature Hunter Valley semillon (from Australia), though unoaked, would probably please a Graves fan.

try:

- whites from the Dordogne and southwest France
- dry whites from the Loire
- Alsace sylvaner
- inexpensive Chilean and South African sauvignon blancs
- mature Hunter Valley semillon

if you like
burgundy

If your taste is for the gently nutty, buttery chardonnays labeled white burgundy, Bourgogne, or Mâcon Blanc, the better Mâcon (with a village name such as Mâcon-Davayé), Pouilly-Fuissé, Viré-Clessé, and St.-Véran should all be a step up in quality.

Rully, Montagny, and Mercurey (all from the Côte Chalonnaise) should be a step up again. Wines labeled chardonnay are almost always more overtly fruity and often oaky, but Vin de Pays de l'Ardèche and Limoux tend to be less so. Vin de Pays d'Oc, Puglia (Italy), and South African chardonnays can be a halfway house between burgundy and the full-frontal New World style.

There is no shortage of expensive chardonnays trying to capture the savory, nutty, yet honeyed character of the great Côte d'Or classics – Meursault, Puligny-Montrachet, Chassagne-Montrachet et al. Some of the most convincing come from California, especially from Carneros and the South Central Coast (Edna, Santa Maria, and Ynez valleys). But there are others from Oregon and New York State, regions such as Yarra Valley and Margaret River in Australia, New Zealand, South Africa, and even Austria. Price is a guide, at least to ambition and intention.

try:

- Pouilly-Fuissé, St.-Véran, and Côte Chalonnaise appellations
- Vin de Pays de l'Ardèche, Limoux, Vin de Pays d'Oc chardonnays
- chardonnays from Puglia
- South African chardonnays
- California, Oregon, and New York State chardonnays
- Yarra Valley, Margaret River, and New Zealand chardonnays
- Austrian chardonnays

if you like
chablis

Chablis is part of Burgundy, its northern outpost, but its minerally, steely wines are unlike burgundy or any other wines.

Chablis fans, therefore, must either head off into fatter, fruitier, or oakier chardonnays, or try other firm, dry whites. Australian and other chardonnays labeled unoaked, and chardonnays from Marlborough, New Zealand, are worth considering. Other wines to try are Bourgogne Aligoté (burgundy's other white grape); Alsace's minerally rieslings; Pouilly-Fumé, Sancerre, and Savennières (three from the Loire); Verdicchio dei Castelli di Jesi; Austrian grüner veltliner (especially from Wachau, Kamptal, and Kremstal), and Spanish albariño.

try:

- unoaked Australian and New Zealand chardonnays
- Bourgogne Aligoté, Alsace rieslings, Pouilly-Fumé, Sancerre, and Savennières
- Verdicchio dei Castelli di Jesi
- grüner veltliners and albariños

if you like
champagne

The sparkling wines that come closest to champagne in quality and style, capturing some of its creamy, biscuity complexity, are the best from California, Australia (including Tasmania), and New Zealand, most of them made by, or jointly with, well-known companies from Champagne itself.

Most of the top New World sparkling wines are priced just below champagne and specify that they are made from chardonnay and pinot noir, or chardonnay alone. Many carry a vintage date. There are also many simpler, softer, less dry sparkling wines from these same countries, and even more from France (including Saumur, Blanquette de Limoux, and Crémant de Bourgogne) and Spain, which has huge success with its sparkling wines, called cava.

try:

- Californian, Australian, and New Zealand sparkling wines made of chardonnay and pinot noir
- Saumur, Blanquette de Limoux, and Crémant de Bourgogne
- Spanish cava

if you like
muscadet

With its crisp, dry, relatively unobtrusive flavors, Muscadet is the antithesis of the archetypal New World style. No other wine, from either the New or Old Worlds, is made from the same grape variety, so obvious alternatives are sparse.

Gros Plant, Muscadet's sharp and ascetic neighbor, is one – albeit an acquired taste. Sauvignon de Touraine is similar in weight and crispness, but with sauvignon's more grassy flavor. North Italian whites, such as Soave and pinot grigio, are similarly dry and relatively low-key in flavor, but tend to be a little softer. Other wines to consider are Vin de Pays des Côtes de Gascogne, authentic dry Vinho Verde, Chablis, Bourgogne Aligoté, and German dry wines.

try:

- Gros Plant, Sauvignon de Touraine, Chablis, Bourgogne Aligoté, and Vin de Pays des Côtes de Gascogne
- north Italian whites (such as Soave and pinot grigio), dry Vinho Verde, and German dry wines

if you like
muscat de beaumes-de-venise

The French alternatives to this extra-sweet, grapey young wine from the Rhône are the similarly made vins doux naturels from further south in the Midi, including Muscat de Rivesaltes, Muscat de St.-Jean-de-Minervois, and Muscat de Frontignan.

But you don't have to stay in France: Spain has its moscatels, above all the inexpensive Moscatel de Valencia; Greece has its Samos; Italy its rarefied Moscato Passito di Pantelleria, made from sun-dried grapes; California has its aptly-named orange muscat under the Essensia label; and South Africa is again producing tiny quantities of the historic Constantia. There are also long-aged muscats with deeper, more complex flavors – the so-called liqueur muscats of Australia (mostly from Rutherglen) and Portugal's Moscatel de Setúbal. No grape makes sweet wines with the same grape-essence quality of muscat, but the unctuously sweet brown pedro ximénez (or PX) wines of Spain are worth investigating if you have a particularly sweet tooth. Sweet rieslings, such as botrytized versions from Australia, are a lighter, crisper option.

try:

- Midi vins doux naturels
- Spanish moscatels and PX wines, and Portugal's Moscatel de Setúbal
- Samos from Greece
- Moscato Passito di Pantelleria from Italy
- Californian orange muscat
- South African Constantia
- Australian liqueur muscats
- Australian botrytized rieslings

if you like
sancerre & pouilly-fumé

These two crisp, grassy, flinty Loires were the only widely known wines made from sauvignon blanc before New Zealand's Marlborough region rose to prominence in the 1980s.

Now there are alternatives from most New World countries. All tend to be fruitier-tasting than the Loire originals, but the New Zealand, Chilean, and South African styles are tangier than those from California and Australia. Alternatives from France include Menetou-Salon, Quincy, Reuilly, and the chenin-based Savennières from the Loire, and wines specifying sauvignon on the label from Touraine, Haut-Poitou, Bordeaux, and Bergerac. Outside France, try sauvignons from Hungary and northern Italy, Rueda from Spain, and Austrian grüner veltliner, sauvignon, and riesling.

try:

- sauvignons from New Zealand, Chile, South Africa, California, and Australia
- Loire sauvignons and other French wines labeled sauvignon
- Hungarian and northern Italian sauvignons, and Rueda from Spain
- Austrian grüner veltliner

if you like
sauternes

Sauternes (including Barsac) should be opulent, sweet, and honeyed, but never cloying. Wines modeled on Sauternes in nearby Ste.-Croix-du-Mont, Cadillac, and Loupiac, and also from a little farther away in the Dordogne regions centered on Monbazillac, can be of good value.

There are also some convincing Sauternes-style wines being made in the New World, especially Australia, usually labeled botrytis or botrytis-affected semillon. New World botrytized rieslings are less opulent, but worth trying.

Of the European countries other than France, Austria's sweet wines are most similar in weight and style, although made from different grape varieties. Germany's sweet wines are much lighter-bodied, but extraordinarily intense in flavor. Hungary's Tokaji Aszú and Eszencia are also different – sweet and uniquely tangy.

try:

- Ste.-Croix-du-Mont, Cadillac, Loupiac, and Monbazillac
- New World botrytized semillons and rieslings
- sweet wines from Austria and Germany; Hungary's Tokaji Aszú and Eszencia

other whites

Up to now, white wines from Italy, Germany, and the New World may have been your first port of call.

if you like
australian chardonnay

Australian chardonnay, in general terms, is full-bodied with ripe, tropical, fruit flavors, seasoned with vanilla-tasting oak.

The style is repeated in Chile, Argentina, California, South Africa, and New Zealand. The wines don't all taste the same – just as Australian chardonnays don't all taste the same – but there is a family resemblance, one that is shared by examples from Puglia and Salento in southern Italy, Navarra in Spain, Vin de Pays d'Oc (and other vins de pays from the south of France), and occasionally Bulgaria and Romania.

Other grapes, when oak-aged like chardonnay, can give wines of similar weight and structure, but with their own flavors. They include semillon, especially from the Barossa Valley, but also from Chile and New Zealand, and marsanne and verdelho in Australia. It's also true of barrel-fermented South African chenin blanc.

try:

- other New World chardonnays
- Puglia, Salento, and Navarra, and French vins de pays
- Barossa Valley, Chilean, and New Zealand semillons
- Australian marsannes and verdelhos
- South African oaked chenin blanc

if you like
frascati & other italian whites

The archetypal Italian dry white is lively and refreshing, crisp, light to medium-bodied, and relatively neutral in flavor.

Obvious substitutes for Frascati, Orvieto Secco, and Soave are other Italian whites (excluding the top end and chardonnays) – Lugana, Bianco di Custoza, pinot grigio, Verdicchio dei Castelli Jesi, and blends from Sicily, to name a few.

French answers come from the southwest, especially Vin de Pays des Côtes de Gascogne, the Loire (although the Loires – Muscadet, Vins de Pays du Jardin de la France, Cheverny – are more acid and therefore sharper), and from Alsace, but only its least expensive whites. New-wave German wines are an alternative from the other side of the Vosges. Muted flavors are rare in the New World, but cheap Chilean, Argentine, and South African blends are often modestly flavored.

try:

- other Italian whites, barring chardonnays
- whites from southwest France, the Loire, and Alsace
- new-wave German whites
- cheap blends from Chile, Argentina, and South Africa

if you like
mosel & other german rieslings

There is no wine with the sweet-fruit intensity, vibrant acidity, yet light body and low, low alcohol of a classic German riesling.

Almost all other countries' rieslings are drier – often completely dry – and fuller bodied. Alsace and Austrian rieslings are also less floral and more mineral than the German, while Australian rieslings, especially from the Clare and Eden valleys, have a distinctive lime flavor. Light-bodied, freshly fruity, but nonetheless dry whites worth considering include English wines, Vin de Pays des Côtes de Gascogne, and Puglia and Vin de Pays d'Oc wines made from the muscat grape. If it is the sweetness in German riesling that you like, try demi-sec, or even moelleux, Loire wine such as Vouvray, or a medium-dry English wine.

try:

- rieslings from other countries
- Vin de Pays des Côtes de Gascogne and English wines
- muscat from Puglia and Pays d'Oc
- demi-sec or moelleux Loires

if you like
new zealand sauvignon blanc

A taste for New Zealand sauvignon is a taste for assertively fruity, tangy white wines free of the flavors and softening influence of oak.

No other country's sauvignons achieve quite the same intensity of flavor, but the more expensive Chilean sauvignons, especially those from the Casablanca Valley, and those from regions in South Africa such as Elgin, come close. Sancerre and Pouilly-Fumé are the French answer to New Zealand sauvignon, but with more grassy, green, and mineral flavors. Other sauvignons that can have modest shades of New Zealand include the best of southwest France – Bordeaux, Bergerac, Côtes du Duras, and Côtes de Saint-Mont – and Vin de Pays d'Oc, as well as Hungarian sauvignons. Other wines and grape varieties to try are Australian rieslings from the Clare and Eden valleys, Alsace riesling, Austrian riesling and grüner veltliner, and Jurançon. And you might want to renew your aquaintance with Chablis.

try:

- more expensive sauvignons from Chile and South Africa
- Chablis, Sancerre, and Pouilly-Fumé
- superior Bordeaux and south-west France sauvignons
- Hungarian sauvignons
- rieslings from Australia, Alsace, Austria, and Jurançon

oaky & oak-free

Contact with oak can fundamentally affect the flavors of any white wine, regardless of its country of origin.

if you like
oaky whites

If you like the flavors given by new oak – vanilla, buttered toast, coffee, grilled nuts, coconut – think in terms of full-bodied wines, especially from the New World, and wines made from chardonnay.

Unless the label specifies unoaked, most chardonnay will have been exposed to oak at some point during the production process. Oaked wines are sometimes named as such, as in oaked viura (a Spanish white); and French wines, not necessarily chardonnay, may be labeled *élevé en fûts de chêne* (or *fûts neufs*). The European white in which oak was traditionally quite a pungent ingredient is Rioja. After a flirtation with lighter, unoaked wines, the pendulum has swung back to oak, but in a cleaner, more modern style. In Australia, another white grape that takes well to oak is semillon, especially in the Barossa Valley.

try:

• New World chardonnays and other full-bodied whites

• French whites labeled *élevé en fûts de chêne* (matured in oak barrels) or *fûts neufs* (new barrels)

• oaked viura and white Riojas

• Australian oaked semillons

if you like
oak-free whites

If you prefer your whites oak-free, there is a heartening trend away from heavy oak, seen in the rise of unoaked chardonnays.

There are also plenty of white grapes that rarely see oak, including sauvignon blanc, riesling, gewurztraminer, pinot grigio, albariño, torrontes, and other fairly aromatic varieties. French regions where oak is largely absent from the white wines include the Loire (all the way from Muscadet to Sancerre), Alsace, Mâcon (except the more expensive wines), most Bordeaux and Bergerac, Jurançon, and most non-chardonnay vins de pays. Chablis is also traditionally unoaked, although it has to be said that a hint of oak can be detected in several these days. Other countries where few white wines are oaked are Germany, Italy, and Hungary.

try:

• aromatic varietals, including sauvignon blanc and riesling

• Loire, Alsace, Mâcon, Bordeaux and Bergerac, Jurançon, non-chardonnay vins de pays, Chablis

• German, Italian, and Hungarian whites

french reds

France has such a wealth of reds that it can be tempting to stick with them, but Europe and the New World offer many spectacular alternatives.

if you like
beaujolais

There aren't many reds with the same crisp, sappy, strawberry flavors as Beaujolais, but there are young, medium and light-bodied reds with similar youthful, fruity appeal.

Any wine based on the gamay grape, such as Gamay de Touraine, Côte Roannaise, Mâcon Rouge, and Switzerland's Dôle, is a good start. Light Alsace pinot noir, red Sancerre (also made from pinot noir), and Loire reds such as Chinon (not the expensive ones) are other possibilities, as are German reds, Hungarian reds made from kékfrankos, and northern Italian reds such as Bardolino, simple Valpolicella, dolcetto, and grignolino.

This is not a red wine style found much in the New World, but bonarda gives some juicy, light reds in Argentina, cinsaut does the same in South Africa, and tarrango has been developed as Australia's answer to Beaujolais. Some Australian grenache wines are also made in a simple, drink-it-young style.

try:

- gamay wines; pinot noirs from Alsace and Sancerre, and Chinon
- German and Hungarian reds
- Bardolino, Valpolicella, dolcetto, and grignolino
- tarrango and lighter grenache wines from Australia
- Argentine bonarda

reds

if you like
bordeaux

The alternatives to basic Bordeaux fall into two main camps: red wines from near that area, which are often very similar, and wines from farther afield, which are often fuller and riper.

Bergerac, Buzet, Côtes de Duras, and Côtes de Saint-Mont are all within reach of Bordeaux and belong to the former group. Vins de Pays d'Oc cabernet sauvignons and merlots, cheaper examples from Chile and South Africa, and red wines from Bulgaria and Romania fall into the latter group. North Italian merlots may fall into either camp, or, if they are very light and grassy, neither.

try:

- Bergerac, Buzet, Côtes de Duras, and Côtes de Saint-Mont

- Vin de Pays d'Oc cabernets and merlots; cheaper Chilean and South African examples

- north Italian merlots

if you like
burgundy

Red burgundy is the wine that has most frustrated wine-makers trying to make their own versions of the French classics elsewhere; so, you won't find many dead-ringers for the great Chambertins, Volnays, and Vosne-Romanées.

Most New World pinot noirs are more obviously fruity and oaky than burgundy. Little by little, however, producers are beginning to capture some of the elusive, sweet yet savory, delicate yet rich flavors and seductive, silky textures of the original wines. Some of the best come from the US – from the cooler regions of California, especially Carneros, Russian River Valley, and Santa Barbara County, and from Oregon to the north. But every country tries: South Africa has had success in the Walker Bay area; Australia in the Yarra Valley and Adelaide Hills; and New Zealand on both islands. Chile is producing some good-value, simple, fruity pinot noirs and has hopes pinned on the cool Casablanca region.

France also delivers some simple pinots from vins de pays regions, and a few more serious examples from Alsace. In the rest of Europe, Austria, Germany, and Switzerland all produce some inspiring wines (usually called spätburgunder in the two former countries and blauburgunder in Switzerland).

try:

- California and Oregon pinot noirs

- South African (Walker Bay) pinots

- Yarra Valley, Adelaide Hills, and New Zealand pinot noirs

- Chilean pinot noirs from Casablanca

- Alsace and vins de pays pinots

- Austrian, German, and Swiss spätburgunder (or blauburgunder)

if you like
châteauneuf-du-pape

A taste for red Châteauneuf-du-Pape is a taste for big, richly flavored, spicy wines, a style much in vogue worldwide, although there are not many true replicas of Châteauneuf-du-Pape.

The main ones come from nearby – Gigondas, Vacqueyras, and Lirac – together with good, but less intense and complex, examples from the best Côtes du Rhône-Villages (including Cairanne, Sablet, and Valréas). Other French alternatives are Mediterranean reds such as Collioures (Roussillon) and Bandol (Provence), and obviously ambitious Languedoc-Roussillon wines – those at half the price or more of Châteauneuf from appellations such as Fitou, Corbières, St.-Chinian, and Faugères – and vins de pays specifying grape varieties such as syrah (shiraz), mourvèdre, and grenache. These are grape varieties to look for in New World countries, too, especially Australia; although the New World wines are usually riper and fruitier tasting.

You may also like California zinfandels; Carignano del Sulcis from Sardinia; wines from southern Italy (including Cirò, Copertino, Salice Salentino, and the primitivos and negroamaros); garnachas and monastrells from Spain, as well as the rare and expensive Priorato; and the best reds from the Alentejo region of Portugal, including its subappellation Borba.

try:

- Gigondas, Vacqueyras, Lirac, and good Côtes du Rhône-Villages
- Collioures, Bandol, and ambitious Languedoc-Roussillon wines
- vins de pays labeled syrah (shiraz), mourvèdre, and grenache, and their New World equivalents
- Californian zinfandels
- wines from southern Italy and Carignano del Sulcis from Sardinia
- Spanish garnachas and monastrells, and Priorato
- reds from Alentejo in Portugal

if you like
côtes du rhône

This is the basic Rhône Valley red, and with 10,000 producers making 300 million bottles a year, some is very basic indeed.

If you don't want to stray far, try some of the less well-known Rhônes, where growers work harder for recognition – Côtes du Ventoux, Côtes du Vivarais, Cotes du Lubéron, Coteaux du Tricastin, or Vin de Pays des Coteaux de l'Ardèche. If you are searching for a red with more character, move up to a Côtes du Rhône-Villages or a wine from the south, such as a good Coteaux du Languedoc or Minervois. For something different, try a malbec from Argentina, a tannat from Uruguay, or a carmenère from Chile.

try:

- wines from less well-known Rhône appellations and Côtes du Rhône-Villages
- wines from Languedoc
- Argentine malbecs, Uruguayan tannats, Chilean carmenères

if you like
médoc & graves

There is hardly a country worldwide that doesn't now produce quality red wines based on cabernet sauvignon, or cabernet sauvignon mixed with merlot (the so-called Bordeaux blend).

Most of these are fuller-bodied and have more intense cassis and oak flavors than the wines of the Médoc and Graves regions. Correspondingly few have the hallmark pencil shavings/cedar/cigar-box accent. That doesn't mean you can't confuse them. Professional tasters do it all the time, especially higher up the quality scale. One of the regions now emerging as a producer of outstanding cabernet/merlot blends, although only in small quantities and favorable vintages, is Hawkes Bay in New Zealand. Regions with longer-established reputations for top cabernets include Napa Valley (and its several subregions), Coonawarra, Western Australia, and Maipo in Chile. Others to try are Argentina, South Africa, and Greece.

try:

- cabernet-merlot blends from Hawkes Bay, New Zealand
- cabernets from Napa Valley, Coonawarra, Western Australia, and Maipo in Chile
- Argentine, South African, and Greek cabernets

if you like
st.-emilion & pomerol

The merlot-dominated wines of St.-Emilion and Pomerol are the rounder, softer, fleshier face of red Bordeaux.

As with the cabernet sauvignons, most New World merlots have riper fruit flavors and more oak, but Hawkes Bay in New Zealand, with its comparable climate, again comes quite close. Chile also produces some very good merlot-based reds, as does the Napa Valley in a fuller, more tannic style. Other sources include Washington State (often distinctly minty), Vins de Pays d'Oc, Romania, and, after struggling uncharacteristically with this variety, Australia.

try:

- Hawkes Bay merlots
- Napa Valley and Chilean merlot-based reds
- Washington State, Vins de Pays d'Oc, Romanian, and Australian merlots

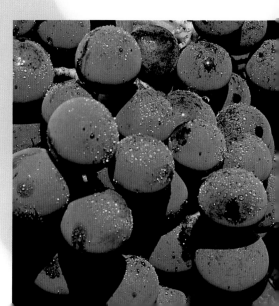

other reds

If you favor Italian, Spanish, or New World reds, follow your grape, but also try other local ones.

if you like
australian shiraz

A few years ago, if you said you liked shiraz, it could only mean one thing: Australia. But, seeing the success of that warming, full, spicy red, other countries have started copying the style.

You can now find shiraz wines from South Africa, New Zealand, and even, much to the French authorities' disgust, from Languedoc regions such as Minervois. Wines labeled syrah (from California, New Zealand, Vin de Pays d'Oc) tend to be more French in style – slightly more structured, less exuberantly full and fruity.

Other spicy, warm reds include Châteauneuf-du-Pape; wines from Puglia in southern Italy, especially primitivo, Copertino, and Salice Salentino; Carignano del Sulcis from Sardinia; Australian grenache and (same grape) Spanish garnacha; Californian zinfandel; South African pinotage; and malbec from Argentina.

try:

- shiraz/syrah from South Africa, New Zealand, California, and Languedoc
- Châteauneuf-du-Pape
- wines from Puglia, and Carignano del Sulcis from Sardinia
- Australian/Spanish grenache
- Californian zinfandel, South African pinotage, and Argentine malbec

if you like
barolo

Barolo is an acquired taste. It's not as tannic as it once was, but it's still a difficult wine to understand, and needs time to develop.

It's also so quintessentially Italian that there is nothing like it outside its Piedmont homeland, and that includes the handful of New World nebbiolo wines. Authentic alternatives are Barbaresco, Gattinara, Ghemme, and Carema, and a few softer, less expensive Piedmont wines in which nebbiolo forms part of the name. Other Italian reds to try are barberas from Piedmont, the big Tuscan red Brunello di Montalcino, and Aglianico del Vulture from Basilicata. Outside Italy, apart from New World nebbiolos and blends, try northern Rhône wines: Crozes-Hermitage and St.-Joseph, moving up through Cornas to Côte-Rotie and Hermitage.

try:

- Piedmont nebbiolos and barberas
- Brunello di Montalcino and Aglianico del Vulture
- Hermitage and other northern Rhône wines
- New World nebbiolos and blends

if you like
chianti

Confusingly, Chianti comes in all qualities and all prices, depending to some extent on the subzone in which it is produced (Classico is the best and most important). But, even at its cheapest and thinnest, it still has a distinctive, slightly astringent, typically Italian finish.

It is the Italian finish that has proved hard to reproduce in other countries. Wines made from the sangiovese grape in California, Chile, Argentina, and Australia are invariably a little (and sometimes a lot) softer and suppler. That's not to say they aren't as good – some of the Californians are particularly inspiring – but they're not Chianti. Italian substitutes for mid-priced Chianti Classico include Morellino di Scansano, Parrina, and Rosso di Montalcino (junior Brunello di Montalcino), all three from Tuscany; and Rosso Cònero and Rosso Piceno Superiore, from the Marches. A more rarefied Tuscan alternative to top-notch Chianti Classico is Carmignano.

try:

- New World sangioveses
- Carmignano, Morellino di Scansano, Parrina, and Rosso di Montalcino
- Rosso Cònero and Rosso Piceno Superiore

if you like
chilean cabernet sauvignon

You can buy cabernet sauvignon from almost any country, but Chile has established itself as a benchmark for reliable quality and appealing flavor at a reasonable price.

If you like Chilean cabernet sauvignon – medium to full-bodied, supple, oak-matured with an alluring cassis flavor – the chances are you will enjoy cabernets from California, Australia, and Washington State, but they generally cost more for the same quality. Argentina is less consistent, but at best offers the same quality/price ratio as Chile. There are also some worthwhile Vins de Pays d'Oc cabernet sauvignons and a few good cabernets and merlots from Romania. South African cabernet is still finding its style, but is usually drier and firmer. New Zealand, except at the top end, tends to be greener and less ripe.

Merlot is the obvious alternative grape variety, but also consider Chilean carmenère and Argentine malbec, and the Spanish grape tempranillo, which is increasingly appearing on labels, not just in Spain but in the New World.

try:

- cabernets and merlots from California, Australia, Washington State, and Argentina
- Vins de Pays d'Oc
- Romanian, South African, and New Zealand cabernets and merlots
- Chilean carmenère, Argentine malbec, merlots from both countries
- Spanish and New World tempranillos

if you like
rioja

If you like the oaky – to some people, the coconutty – taste traditionally associated with Rioja, you will probably like a lot of the reds offered by other regions of Spain.

There is a distinctly spicy Spanish-oak character, which oaky New World wines don't share (and their producers probably don't aspire to). Valdepeñas reds are particularly soft and traditional in style; those from Navarra are far more modern, but still admirably Spanish; both are cheaper than Rioja. Ribera del Duero is similar to Rioja, but bigger-bodied, more fashionable, and, inevitably, more expensive. If you want to branch out into the New World, follow the tempranillo grape. If it's oak in almost any form that you like, be guided by the section on oaky reds (*see opposite page*).

try:

- Valdepeñas and Navarra reds
- Ribera del Duero
- New World tempranillos
- oaky reds

if you like
valpolicella, recioto, & amarone della valpolicella

Like many other Italian red wines, Valpolicella has no close disciples because few wines (perhaps none in the case of Valpolicella) are made from the same grape varieties.

Many Italian reds also have a refreshing sharpness or astringency on the finish that seems reluctant to appear elsewhere. This leaves the alternatives to Valpolicella largely in Italy. Try almost any red from the north except for the heavyweights from Piedmont (Barolo et al): for example, Bardolino, Barbera d'Alba or d'Asti, dolcetto, grignolino, Lago di Caldaro, and lagrein; and revisit Chianti and Montepulciano d'Abruzzo further south. Outside Italy, look for wines made from sangiovese and bonarda, particularly in California, Argentina, and Australia.

When it comes to Recioto, the concentrated, sweet Valpolicella made from specially dried grapes, Sagrantino Passito from Umbria is made in a similar way. Non-Italian substitutes include port and the red vins doux naturels of Banyuls, Maury, and Rivesaltes, but these are not remotely mirror images of Recioto.

Amarone della Valpolicella, also made from dried grapes but a dry, complex, powerful wine, stands alone, with barely a handful of New World imitators. In its absence, try a Sagrantino di Montefalco, a mature northern Rhône such as Hermitage, a Priorato from Spain, or a top Portuguese red.

try:

- Bardolino, Barbera d'Alba or d'Asti, dolcetto, grignolino, Lago di Caldaro, and lagrein
- Chianti and Montepulciano d'Abruzzo
- Californian, Argentine, and Australian sangioveses and bonardas
- Sagrantino Passito and Sagrantino di Montefalco
- French vins doux naturels, and mature northern Rhônes
- Priorato from Spain and top Portuguese reds

oaky & oak-free

Oaky reds are currently popular, but you can escape from vanilla and spice flavors if you want to.

if you like
oaky reds

Devotees of oaky wines are spoiled with choices. A generation ago, the only really oaky red was Rioja. Other wines were oaky only when they were considered too young to drink.

But that was before the vanilla, toast, and spice flavors of new oak became an end in themselves, rather than a passing by-product of maturation. Nowadays, most New World reds are oak-influenced, and the bigger-bodied the wine, the more oak it is likely to have. Shiraz, cabernet sauvignon, malbec, merlot, pinotage, and even pinot noir all usually reveal oak intervention. Most traditional European reds remain less oak-influenced, but Spanish wines labeled crianza, reserva, or gran reserva have always relied on oak. And the new and rejuvenated European regions, such as Languedoc and Puglia, which are making wines to compete with the New World, lean more heavily on oak.

try:

- New World shiraz, cabernet sauvignon, malbec, pinotage, and merlot
- Spanish wines labeled crianza, reserva, and gran reserva
- reds from Languedoc and Puglia

if you like
oak-free reds

The cheapest red wines and any others made to be drunk within a year are unlikely to carry oak.

By contrast, at the other end of the price scale, expensive, classic wines, especially French (for example, burgundy), are aged in oak barrels to make them rounder and more complex, but are not intended to taste of oak. In between these two extremes, the number of wines free of oak has shrunk. Those hanging on include Beaujolais and most of the alternatives to Beaujolais (*see page 84*), together with modern, juicy, modestly priced wines designed to be drunk young and made from grape varieties such as grenache (or garnacha), tempranillo, pinot noir (in the Loire), bonarda, and sometimes merlot.

try:

- top burgundy
- Beaujolais and similar wines
- young grenache, tempranillo, and bonarda wines
- Loire pinot noirs
- some merlots

Good food deserves good wine, but it doesn't have to be expensive – the trick is to match or contrast the food's key characteristics.

food & wine

principles

Our parents would be surprised by some of the wines we serve alongside certain foods, but that is because both food and wine have changed.

Any discussion about matching wine and food has to start with the disclaimers. First, there are no rights and wrongs, no absolutes. If you like a particular match, no matter how eccentric, feel free to indulge – and with any other consenting adults. But you need to be aware that there are combinations which will please more of the people more of the time, and combinations for which it would be hard to win a single vote. You may not get a second chance if you give your guests Muscadet with chocolate mousse (or any dry wine with sweet food), and serving tannic red wines with oily or smoked fish won't win you any friends either.

Disclaimer number two: you are not looking for the world's one and only perfect match. Most dishes can be partnered with several different and often contrasting types of wine. One wine may seem better on one day; another on another occasion. It depends on the place, the company, the season, and quite possibly the budget. The simple, young white that seemed so refreshing with all kinds of dishes while on vacation by the sea probably won't be such a convincing all-around choice back home in chilly midwinter.

OLD RULES FOR OLD WINE STYLES

Disclaimers out of the way, how do you find the crowd-pleasers, or at least avoid the no-votes? In the past, it was simple. If you lived in a wine-producing region or country, you drank the local wines with the local food. Vacationers did the same – indeed, the "when in Rome..." principle is still an eminently sensible and mostly pleasurable one to follow. If you lived far from winegrowing regions, you followed established rules: white wine with fish and white meat; red wine with red meat and game; and to hell with the vegetarians. You also drank light wines before heavier, stronger wines, and dry wines before sweet, while acknowledging the well-known exceptions: sherry or Madeira (strong/heavy) with soup, and Sauternes (sweet) with foie gras.

The color code was limited and limiting, but it wasn't groundless or irrelevant: it rested on a handful of sound observations. The most striking was that fish made most red wines, but not whites, taste metallic or bitter, often horribly so. At the same time, white wines were higher in acid, neatly complementing the acid, in the form of lemon or vinegar, that was an essential ingredient or garnish for many fish dishes.

Meaty fish, like **tuna** and **salmon**, can be partnered with **red wines**, as long as they are relatively low in tannin. **Pinot noir** is especially successful.

You may prefer **red** wine with **roast turkey**, and enjoy a full-bodied **chardonnay** with **steak**.

An oaky chardonnay can sometimes accompany steak just as enjoyably as a red wine.

Meanwhile, tannic red wines tasted decidedly softer and less tannic when partnered with a substantial slab of red meat. No less important, fish and white meat were mostly lighter foods than red meat, just as white wines were mostly lighter-bodied than reds.

But that was then. Wine has changed enormously in the past 20, and even 10, years. Reds, particularly from Europe, are rarely so aggressively tannic – and it's the tannin that becomes unpleasant with fish. White wines are not the generally light-bodied brethren that they were. Think of all those full-bodied, 14 percent alcohol, oaky chardonnays. Wine, both red and white, is now much more overtly fruity, which often gives it instant, easy-drinking appeal, but, perversely, makes it less accommodating with food.

It's all part of the globalization of both wine and food. In the past, far more of the world's wine was produced for merely local consumption (with local food, of course). Nowadays, wine styles, grape varieties, processes, and winemakers all globe-trot. To give just one example, two decades ago the viognier grape could scarcely be found outside a small area of the northern Rhône, centered on Condrieu. Now it's established in Languedoc, California, South Australia, and Argentina.

NEW FOODS, NEW WAYS WITH WINE

Food has traveled and interchanged even more. It's not just that we think nothing of cooking Tuscan, getting take-out Thai, or creating an authentic Moroccan couscous; we also think nothing of mixing, matching, and borrowing techniques and flavors, especially spices, from any number of cuisines: hence Pacific Rim, MediterAsian, and other so-called fusion cuisines.

The old rules are unquestionably out of date, but the color code can still be a useful springboard – one from which to discover, for example, that chicken and pork go with as many reds as they do whites. Fish, particularly meaty fish, like tuna or salmon, and any fish cooked in a red-wine sauce, can be partnered with red wines, so long as they are relatively low in tannin. Pinot noir is especially successful, but New World sangiovese and merlot, and Beaujolais and Loire reds are all worth trying (*see also page 18*). You may also find that you prefer red wine with roast turkey, and that you can enjoy a full-bodied chardonnay with steak. But wherever wine is a significant ingredient in a dish – for example, coq au vin – its color will usually dictate that of the accompanying wine, whatever the color of the protein.

FOODS, COOKING METHODS, AND SAUCES

The first consideration when choosing a wine accompaniment is usually the weight of the dish – the ingredients involved, and how they were put together, cooked, and sauced. Poaching, steaming, and stir frying, for example, produce lighter results than braising, roasting, or conventional frying. Marinading meat, game, and poultry gives them richer, more intense flavors. And then there are the sauces. Among other things, sauces for savory dishes can be bouillon-light, dairy-rich, egg-rich, heavily reduced, meaty and concentrated, acid-sharp, hot and spicy, mildly spicy, herby, salty, caramelized, or sweet. And they can be a combination of these things: hollandaise sauce is both rich and lemony. You ignore sauces at your peril.

In most cases, your goal will be to balance the weight of the wine and food evenly, so that one doesn't overwhelm the other. To give a few examples, a rich, warming casserole flavored with red wine, bacon, garlic, and mushrooms deserves a full-bodied red wine, whether the basis of the dish is chicken, beans, or beef. A light, fresh-tasting stir-fry or a salad will be flattered by a crisp, light-bodied wine, and flattened by something big and strapping. If it's a salad involving strips of rare roast beef, think fresh red: Beaujolais, for example. Chicken in a rich, cream sauce will need a fuller, fatter white wine, such as a Sonoma chardonnay or an Alsace pinot gris; chicken poached with lemon grass will be happier with an Italian pinot grigio or a Chilean sauvignon blanc.

Inevitably, there is the odd exception. Light, crisp, wines with a fruity sweetness can sometimes work as a foil for rich foods. On their home turf, particularly in the Rheingau, it's traditional to serve German Spätlese and Auslese rieslings with roast goose and duck. The wines not only cut through the fatty meats, but have the acidity and fruity sweetness to handle their sweet, fruity garnishes and sauces, which would make many red wines taste dry and lean.

Below left: pinot grigio and chicken poached with lemon grass.
Below: red Rhône accompanies a beef and bean casserole.

Asparagus is echoed by sauvignon blanc, which may itself have a hint of asparagus in its flavors.

Other examples of opposites attracting are light, frothy Asti (or other moscato spumante) with heavyweight holiday desserts; vintage champagne, including rosé, as a contrast to the dense, close texture of cold roast partridge and other game birds; and the fruity freshness of a good Beaujolais, such as Fleurie or Chiroubles, set against the richness and weight of a cassoulet.

INTENSE FLAVORS

Another consideration is the intensity of flavor, which isn't necessarily linked to weight. Light foods can be intense in flavor and need correspondingly intense-flavored, but not heavy, wines. The distinctive flavor of asparagus finds its match – even its echo – in the assertive sauvignon blanc grape.

Similarly, the spices and herbs of East Asia can give even the lightest dishes very intense flavors. Grape varieties with good natural acidity, well-defined fruit, and no need of oak influence or buttery malolactic fermentation are often best – grapes such as riesling, sauvignon blanc, dry versions of muscat, cortese, and, when they are crisp enough, unoaked semillon and viognier. Gewurztraminer is so powerfully and exotically flavored that it tends to overwhelm most dishes, but it does occasionally come into its own with Chinese and Indian dishes (*see pages 108 and 109*).

Sauces based on heavily reduced meat glazes are another source of intense, concentrated flavors, even when accompanying relatively light meats, such as guinea fowl and young pheasant. Choose a fairly full-bodied wine, but not something that is simply ripe, jammy, and high in alcohol (such as a mass-market Australian shiraz or grenache). You need to match the intensity of flavor with something like a more expensive Australian shiraz, a good red burgundy, or a Rhône such as a Gigondas or Crozes-Hermitage.

ACIDITY

You also need to be alert to acidity levels and sweetness. As well as the rich, fatty foods that sometimes benefit from the contrast of a crisp, cutting wine, acidity on the plate – whether it comes from a generous squeeze of lemon, apple sauce, vinaigrette, the wine in a beurre blanc sauce, or something less obvious – needs to be matched by acidity in the glass. If it isn't, the wine will taste flat and flabby. The higher acidity levels are found in white wines: in wines from cooler regions (the principal white wine regions of France and, in the New World, areas such as Casablanca, Eden Valley, Yarra Valley, Marlborough, and Oregon); in grape varieties such as sauvignon blanc, riesling, and chenin blanc, rather than chardonnay, semillon, and marsanne; and in champagne and its closest imitators. Red wines are more difficult, not only because there are few high-acid red wines, but because acid in food doesn't go with tannin. Beaujolais, barbera, Chianti, dornfelder, and any light-bodied red wines are likely to be reasonable bets.

SWEETNESS

There are no rights, no wrongs, and no absolutes, but there's one rule that always holds good: drink sweet wines with sweet food, and make sure the wine is at least as sweet as the food. If it's any less so, it will taste tart and mean. A sweet element (usually a fruit or vegetable) in a savory dish is less straightforward. You don't want a sweet wine with your rabbit or lamb just because it's being served with a sweet onion marmalade or jelly, but the concentrated sweetness of the relish will make most red wines seem thinner, drier, and more tannic or bitter. Traditional European and other tannic reds suffer most, so head for the riper, fruitier flavors, fuller body, and softer tannins of New World reds; head for Europe's warmer parts, such as Puglia in the far south of Italy and Alentejo in Portugal; and think in terms of grape varieties such as grenache and primitivo, with their natural sweet-berry tastes. If white wine seems suitable, choose full, ripe, New World-type flavors, with some acidity – New Zealand sauvignon blanc or chardonnay and Australian riesling are possibilities.

OAK AND FRUIT

Assertive flavors aren't restricted to food. Heavily oaked wines – with their flavors of toast, vanilla, coconut, and smoky bacon – tend to be unfriendly to food. If you like those kinds of wines, you need food with fairly robust flavors, such as casseroles, barbecued meat, red peppers, and cooked dishes with cheese either in or on them. Similarly, the big, ripe, full-on-fruit styles of wine can seem out of kilter with anything but powerful flavors and heavy seasoning.

A chocolate tart is complemented by the richness and sweetness of Banyuls, a vin doux naturel from southern France.

Drink **sweet wines** with sweet food, and **make sure** that the wine is **at least** as sweet as the **food**.

matching flavors & ingredients

There are matches here for the most popular and the most problematic food groups and ingredients – but they are suggestions, nothing more than that.

wines that go well

Australian riesling and German Kabinett riesling: Chinese and lightly spiced food, sun-dried tomatoes, red peppers, salads, roast vegetables, fish (including smoked fish), cold roast meat.

Sauvignon blanc: Thai food, asparagus, goat's cheese, salads, vegetables (but not mushrooms), fried fish, shellfish, sorrel sauce and other sharp sauces.

Chablis: almost all fish except the most oily, from oysters to richly sauced, brandade to kedgeree; high-fat cheeses such as Chaource.

Alsace pinot blanc and pinot gris (not late-harvest sweet): fish, quiches, chowder, risotto, pasta with creamy sauces, chicken.

Chilean cabernet sauvignon or merlot: a good choice when everyone is eating different things: meat, poultry, bean dishes, and, if the wine isn't oaky/tannic, tuna.

Pinot noir: red mullet, monkfish, salmon, tuna, mushrooms, pork, duck, quail, and, especially with red burgundy, partridge.

Italian reds: the characteristic bitter-cherry astringency complements many savory foods (but avoid fish with the tannic wines).

Shiraz/syrah: roast turkey, goose, duck, sausages, barbecued meat and vegetables, meaty casseroles, game (especially with Rhône syrah).

You're perfectly free to dislike my choices, and I hope you'll also find mouthwatering combinations of your own. Some items have asterisks: look on them as warning lights – flavors, and sometimes textures, that can distort the taste of wine. You don't have to avoid them at all costs; but, if you're aware of them, you should be able to avoid spoiling any treasured bottles (and equally treasured friendships). In the event of a clash, bread and water are useful palate-clearers. Another tip: cooking with cream and butter can usefully soften strange or powerful flavors – for example, the metallic or bitter taste that spinach can produce in some wine, or the penetrating flavor of fennel. Similarly, judicious additions of cheese, although often a difficult food to match on its own (*see page 104*), can also have a useful mellowing effect.

SALADS The main thing to remember with salads is the dressing. Sharp dressings need wines with good acidity – sauvignon blanc, for example, or a fresh young Vin de Pays des Côtes de Gascogne. Dressings made with strongly flavored oils such as pumpkin seed, and spiked with ingredients such as soy and ginger, will also need assertive wines, such as sauvignon blanc again, or unoaked Australian chardonnay, marsanne, or verdelho.

EGGS* Depending on the other ingredients, soufflés, quiches, and egg emulsion sauces such as mayonnaise (provided they are not too sharp or lemony) can be matched by round, medium to full-bodied white wines such as chardonnay, including white burgundy (especially Mâcon), and Alsace pinot blanc. The difficulty with eggs is the mouth-coating texture of runny yolk: try chardonnay or pinot blanc, but not your best bottles.

PASTA All you need to remember is that it's the sauce or the stuffing that you're matching. Spaghetti with vongole (clams) calls for a crisp, dry, lightish white, while tagliatelle with cream and mushrooms can take a fuller white. An intense tomato sauce will need tomato-friendly wines.

Oysters are close to **perfection** with **champagne** (ideally blanc de blancs) or premier cru **Chablis**.

A meaty lasagne would suit a red wine such as a Montepulciano d'Abruzzo or a Rosso di Montalcino. Or you could even try a shiraz.

FISH Simply cooked fish can be matched by simple, crisp, light whites, with the wine taking the part of a squeeze of lemon. But, equally, a luxury fish, such as turbot, deserves a grander bottle – a fine white burgundy or other chardonnay. Match fish in creamy sauces and fish pie to pinot blanc, pinot gris, chardonnay, or Vouvray demi-sec. Low-tannin red wines, especially pinot noir, often go well with more meaty fish, especially salmon and tuna. But it's also worth trying Loire reds, such as Saumur-Champigny and Sancerre (the latter made from pinot noir), Beaujolais, New World sangiovese, and, if it's not too oaky, merlot.

Oily fish* Few wines go with sardines and mackerel, but fairly neutral, crisp, dry whites tend to survive intact. Try Muscadet Sur Lie, Picpoul de Pinet, and young north Italian whites, such as Soave and Bianco di Custoza.

Shellfish Oysters are close to perfection with champagne (ideally blanc de blancs) or Chablis of premier cru quality. Other than those, aim for a crisp, dry, unoaked white (Muscadet Sur Lie, Verdicchio, Sancerre, or albariño from Rías Baixas in Spain), but preferably not something as powerfully flavored as a New Zealand sauvignon blanc. The same applies to the classic plateau de fruits de mer (plain mixed shellfish) and simply cooked mussels. Once you start adding cream to your shellfish sauces, you can go for richer wines, such as chardonnays. If you're splurging out on lobster, splurge out on the wines – any fine white burgundy (from Chablis to Meursault), champagne, or Condrieu. Condrieu and other viognier wines also go well with the sweetness of crab.

Smoked fish* Kippers deserve an Islay malt whisky, but smoked salmon is an excuse, should you need one, either for champagne, perhaps vintage blanc de blancs, or for a fine Chablis. As a variety, riesling also works well. Smoked mackerel is difficult, but will accommodate a good Mosel Kabinett or an Australian riesling if you give it a light coating of cracked black peppercorns and plenty of lemon.

POULTRY Chicken is admirably broadminded. Medium-bodied whites and reds go with the basic flavor of chicken, but avoid tannic and/or pungently flavored wines, unless you're matching them to a specific flavor – sauvignon blanc with lemon grass, for example. Because of its mild flavor, you will be taking sauces and flavorings into account most of the time with chicken. The same applies to guinea fowl, although, when plainly roasted, its slightly deeper, more gamey flavor goes notably well with pinot noir-based wines.

Turkey is also broadminded, but generally better with red wine. Served with the robust flavors of traditional Christmas and Thanksgiving trimmings, it needs full, fairly fruity/spicy wines, such as Australian shiraz (including sparkling shiraz), Châteauneuf-du-Pape, and New World cabernets and merlots. If you are a Bordeaux fan, choose a St.-Emilion or Pomerol, rather than a Médoc.

With duck, pinot noirs, including burgundy, are especially well matched. Australian shiraz and wines from Puglia in southern Italy are also good. If you prefer white wine, a medium-sweet German riesling, especially from the Pfalz, makes a successful contrast, particularly when the duck is served with a sweet fruit sauce.

The same applies to goose, but goose also provides a perfect opportunity to savor a top-quality, mature red from the Old World or a red of similar caliber from the New. You should avoid tannic reds, and for that reason, as with turkey and duck, St.-Emilion and Pomerol are more successful than the leaner Médoc wines.

GAME With a few exceptions, such as champagne with cold roast feathered game (see page 98), and rich whites such as chardonnay and Alsace pinot gris with pheasant in cream sauces, game calls for red wine. With game such as grouse, and with the fairly strong flavors of hare, pigeon, and most game casseroles, you need powerful wines. The syrah-based wines of the northern Rhône, such as Côte Rôtie, Crozes-Hermitage, and St.-Joseph, are particularly successful, as are Californian Rhône-style blends, but most countries have something to offer. Australia has shiraz (avoid the cheap, jammy ones) and shiraz/mourvèdre blends. Italy has Barolo, Barbaresco, and barbera; Spain has Ribera del Duero and Priorato; France has Bandol, as well as Rhône wines (*see also page 20*). With milder game, such as partridge, especially when it is plainly roast, think fine red burgundy.

MEAT Pork is very accommodating, going well with a wide variety of reds (preferably not too tannic) and medium to full-bodied whites. The choice is yours, but check the other ingredients and the cooking method – and beware of that sharp, sweet apple sauce with roast pork.

Lamb loves cabernet sauvignon (and classic cabernet blends), anything from the finest mature Bordeaux with a simple roast to a big Californian cabernet with a more intensely flavored dish. Lamb also goes particularly well with Rioja and Ribera del Duero. And cold lamb goes surprisingly well with white wines.

Beef is happy with many reds, so choose according to the dish and your budget. And if you generally prefer white wine to red, try a full-bodied

chardonnay, not too cheap, from, say, New Zealand, with a grilled steak.

With the delicate flavor of veal, think in terms of medium-bodied whites, or gentle, medium-bodied reds, and be guided by the other flavors and the cooking method used.

VEGETABLES

Many vegetables, either because of their acidity (*see* Tomato, *below*), their sweetness (carrots, onions, parsnips, peppers), or their flavors (asparagus and fennel), go better with the acidity of white wines than with the tannin of reds. But mushrooms, eggplants, and rich, baked-vegetable dishes are usually better with red wines, including full-bodied reds, as are many bean dishes.

Artichokes* Globe artichokes make wine taste either strangely sweet or metallic/bitter, depending on the wine and the taster. Dress them with lemon, lemony homemade mayonnaise, or

vinaigrette, then choose a high-acid white wine. Greek whites made from indigenous varieties (in preference to chardonnay) are notably successful.
Tomato* Don't underestimate the acidity of tomato. If it's the principal flavor, think in terms of sauvignon blanc. If it's a strong presence in a dish that otherwise seems to call for red wine, try a barbera or other young Italian red, or perhaps something with a Mediterranean flavor from Languedoc-Roussillon.

SEASONINGS

Salty foods Although salty foods can help to mask tannin, tannic wines are rarely the best partners for them. Crisp white wines with marked acidity or fresh, fruity reds are often better, or, in the case of salty cheese, sweet wines (for example, Sauternes and Roquefort).
Soy sauce* The saltiness of soy calls for white wine with good acidity, but the dish may seem better suited to red.

Chile and other hot spices* Chile doesn't distort wine flavors so much as numb and burn the palate, so don't waste anything special, subtle, or old. Crisp, young, moderately aromatic whites are best. Tannic reds are the worst, so my first choice of red would be a Beaujolais-Villages, which has the acidity but not the tannin.

Curry* There's no question that, put to the test, most people find that white wines work better than reds with curry, and that crisp, moderately aromatic, unoaked whites are more successful than full-bodied, oaky, buttery whites.

Pepper Freshly ground peppercorns can mask the complexities of a fine, old wine, but can pep up a simple, light, young wine, making it seem bigger. Use your grinder accordingly.

Mustard* Dijon is fine, but beware very hot, vinegary, or sweet mustards.

Horseradish* A killer. Use plenty of cream in your horseradish sauce, or abandon the horseradish.

Vinegar and lemon* Be wary of the vinegar in the vinaigrette, the capers, the Japanese pickles, the mint sauce, the chutneys and other relishes, and the béarnaise and tartar sauces. Be equally alert to the lemon in the hollandaise, the preserved lemons in the Moroccan dishes (sauvignon blanc goes well with these), and the lemon in the tarte au citron (a botrytized riesling, with its higher acidity, is likely to work better than a botrytized semillon).

CHEESE* Sadly, cheese is not the friend of dry red wine we would all like it to be. The flavors and, no less important, the textures can be difficult. When tannin and cheese clash, the wine suffers. In fact, dry whites are often better, and sweet wines the friendliest of all – think of the classic combinations of Sauternes with Roquefort and port with Stilton.

If you want to drink red wine, choose hard cheeses: examples are Manchego; French ewe's-milk cheeses such as Etorki, and the many simply called Brebis (sheep); English ewe's cheeses (such as Berkswell); Parmesan; Cantal (of *entre deux* maturity rather than *doux* or *vieux*); English cheddar; and Double Gloucester. Bear in mind that reds with some maturity and complexity work better with most cheeses than young, fruit-driven wines; but, equally, don't make anything very venerable and special undergo an assault course of cheese.

Soft cheeses, such as Camembert, Brie, and Pont l'Evêque are usually the most difficult, especially if they are mature and mouth-coatingly runny in texture. A Côte d'Or white burgundy may go with Brie, and a mature red burgundy, St.-Emilion, or Chianti Classico Riserva with Camembert. For blue cheese, follow the sweet wine/port example set by Roquefort and Stilton.

With goat's cheese, sauvignon blanc, especially Sancerre and Pouilly-Fumé, is hard to beat, but also try red wines from the same part of the world – Loire cabernet francs, such as Saumur-Champigny, Bourgueil, and Chinon.

DESSERTS A simple rule: the wine needs to be as sweet or sweeter than the dessert. In practice, labels rarely spell out how sweet the wines are, so it's a matter of knowing your sweet wines: the section on sweet wine (*see page 22*) will help. Bear in mind that German wines need to be at least of Trockenbeerenauslese or Beerenauslese quality to cope with desserts (Spätlese and even Auslese are almost never sweet enough), and that inexpensive moelleux Loire wines are seldom sufficiently rich and sweet. Those that should be able to cope with most desserts, except chocolate and ice cream (*see below*), include the more expensive Loires from the Coteaux du Layon, Sauternes, sweet wines from Austria, botrytized Australian sweet wines, Eiswein and Canadian icewines, and the very sweet vins doux naturels – Muscat de Saint-Jean-de-Minervois and Moscatel de Valencia, for example.

Chocolate* Death by chocolate: one of the quickest ways to kill off a perfectly good wine. Chocolate isn't just very sweet, it's mouth-coating, and it takes a very sweet, very powerful wine to stand up to this double whammy. Wines made from muscat are the most successful, above all the fortified, aged Australian muscats from Rutherglen. Other largely capable wines include the muscat vins doux naturels from the south of France, such as Muscat de Beaumes-de-Venise and Muscat de Frontignan; the two red (grenache-based) vins doux naturels, Maury and Banyuls; orange muscats from California and Australia; Tokaji Aszú (of 5 or 6 puttonyos sweetness level) from Hungary; Málaga from Spain; and 10-year-old tawny port.

Ice cream* Fortified Australian liqueur muscats and pedro ximenez sherry are the only wines invariably powerful enough to cope with the numbing effects of ice cream, but inexpensive Moscatel de Valencia and vins doux naturels muscats from the south of France, such as Rivesaltes and Frontignan, won't come to much harm.

FRUIT AND FRUIT-BASED DESSERTS Remember that the wine needs to be sweeter than the fruit or dessert, and then head for a sweet wine that has refreshing acidity – a German wine (Beerenauslese or Trockenbeerenauslese riesling); an Austrian sweet wine; a New World botrytized riesling; a Loire, such as Coteaux du Layon or Bonnezeaux; or a sweet Jurançon (which may or may not be described as moelleux or vendange tardive on the label).

With cheese, dry **whites** are often better, and **sweet wines** the **friendliest** of all – think of **Sauternes** with Roquefort.

COOKING WITH WINE

Wine can transform a perfectly ordinary dish into something special, but don't think that the finer the wine, the finer the resulting dish. You need to use an appealing, drinkable wine, but it's a waste to use a premier cru burgundy or cru classé Bordeaux. Full-bodied, flavorsome wines will give correspondingly more flavor than light-bodied, neutral wines. Both acidity and sugar will be concentrated by the cooking process, so use high-acid and sweet white wines with a light hand. If you use white wine in a recipe that says red, start with half the quantity of wine and be prepared to finish with stock and water. Tannin doesn't intrude in the same way as acid and sugar, but oak in a very oaky wine can. In dishes where the wine isn't cooked – syllabub, for example – the "don't-use-it-if-you-wouldn't-drink-it" rule is even more to be respected.

some classic food &
wine combinations

Everyone has their favorite combinations of food and wine, but over the years some have emerged as acknowledged classics.

FOIE GRAS **with Alsace pinot gris vendange tardive** Exceptionally sweet wine with savory liver may sound a surprising combination, but it is the unctuousness of the foie gras that needs matching. Alsace has the advantage over Sauternes in that it has a touch of enlivening spice.

Other wines to try with foie gras:
- Sauternes or Monbazillac
- Alsace gewurztraminer vendange tardive
- Jurançon moelleux
- Tokaji Aszú (5 puttonyos)

GOAT'S CHEESE **with Sancerre or Pouilly-Fumé** Goat's cheese has a tang and saltiness that is complemented by the piercing, grassy sharpness of unoaked sauvignon blanc. Try the cheese on its own, or grilled and served on a bed of lightly dressed salad leaves.

Other wines to try with goat's cheese:
- Menetou-Salon and Quincy
- New Zealand sauvignon blancs
- South African sauvignon blancs
- Chinon, Bourgueil, and Saumur-Champigny

PARTRIDGE **with red burgundy** This should be the best burgundy you can afford – a Vosne Romanée, perhaps – and it should have some maturity, so that it has some of the haunting, gamey, truffley, decisively burgundian aromas that so complement a partridge's gentle gaminess.

Other wines to try with partridge:
- New World pinot noirs, especially Oregon
- mature Pomerol
- mature Crozes-Hermitage
- Ribera del Duero reserva

Classic food/wine partnerships are in **perfect balance**, each partner enhancing the **flavors** of the other.

Oysters: blanc de blancs champagne or premier cru Chablis

Plateau de fruits de mer: Muscadet Sur Lie

Charcuterie: cru Beaujolais, such as Fleurie, or Beaujolais-Villages

Stilton: vintage port

Roquefort: Sauternes or Barsac

ROAST LAMB **with Haut-Médoc, Pauillac, or St.-Julien** It's not simply that cabernet sauvignon goes with lamb. It's the cedary, cigar-box flavors and the medium-bodied elegance of the cabernet-based blends of the Haut-Médoc, and particularly of Pauillac and St.-Julien, that have an affinity with roast lamb. Ideally, it should be a leg or rack of the new season's lamb, simply roasted with just a little rosemary and garlic.

Other wines to try with roast lamb:
- New Zealand cabernet-merlot blends
- top Chilean cabernets and merlots
- Rioja reserva or gran reserva
- Coonawarra cabernet sauvignon

PEAR TART **with Coteaux du Layon, Bonnezeaux, or Quarts de Chaume** The long-lived, botrytized chenin blancs of the Loire have an extraordinary, honeyed, sweet-fruit intensity. They have an affinity with pear, but partner most fruit tarts well, including apple and apricot.

Other wines to try with pear tart:
- Sauternes and Barsac
- Vouvray and Montlouis moelleux
- Californian and Australian botrytized rieslings
- German and Austrian Beerenauslese rieslings

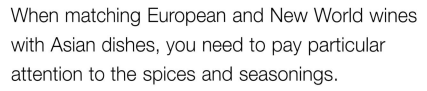

international
accents

When matching European and New World wines with Asian dishes, you need to pay particular attention to the spices and seasonings.

CHINESE

It's the gentle sweetness and delicacy of many Chinese dishes that makes them a challenge for wine. Most wines are too powerful, too dry, or too acid. The best choice is the riesling grape – medium-dry Kabinett and Spätlese Halbtrocken from Germany, and dry, or almost dry, fruity rieslings from Australia, New Zealand, and the US. Demi-sec and even brut champagnes are also generally successful. The exotic gewurztraminer is far too powerful for most Chinese dishes but is a good match for sticky spare ribs and for the two sweet, spicy Chinese sauces, hoisin and sweet bean. Red wines are more difficult (although not for the rich Hong Kong businessmen who drink the most expensive Pomerols), but lightly chilled New World pinot noirs and German spätburgunders do well.

THAI

The top choice for Thai food, with its piercing flavors of chile, lime leaves, lemon grass, coriander, and fish sauce, is the sauvignon blanc grape – classic Sancerre and Pouilly-Fumé, as well as New World sauvignons. New World riesling and unoaked, lemony semillon are also worth trying. No red emerges unscathed from a confrontation with chile, but good Beaujolais-Villages and inexpensive New World reds served lightly chilled don't come to much harm.

JAPANESE

Japanese food looks light, healthy, and innocent enough, but don't be fooled. The essential accompaniments – the pickles, the dipping sauces, and, above all, the pungent, horseradish-related wasabi – pack a powerful punch. While no wine is built to withstand a mouthful of wasabi, there are some that cope better than others. German rieslings, both Kabinett and Halbtrocken styles, go well with sushi and sashimi, as do brut champagne, especially blanc de blancs, and the champagne-quality, dry, New World sparkling wines (from New Zealand, for example). Sauvignon is also adept at standing up for itself, as are fino sherry and manzanilla. The advantage of these two pale, dry sherries (which have some resemblance to sake) is that they also go well with the ubiquitous miso soup. Other dry whites worth considering are Chablis, Pouilly-Fuissé, Jurançon, Verdicchio dei Castelli di Jesi, and pinot bianco. Beef dishes such as teryaki are best accompanied by low-tannin red wines, including Loires, Beaujolais (preferably cru), and pinot noirs (including Côte de Beaune burgundy). And, if money is no object, try a Pomerol.

INDIAN

It's not just the hot spices, but the sheer complexity of flavor in many Indian dishes that makes it hard to find the right wine. Most people find that white wines are the most successful, and preferably unoaked whites, although an oak-matured New World chardonnay can go with a creamy, coconutty dish. In general, think in terms of varieties such as semillon, verdelho, marsanne, muscat, and riesling – and when things get really tricky, remember that gewurztraminer sometimes comes in useful with hard-to-match, highly spiced dishes. White wine is the popular choice, but some people swear by red Bordeaux, and others by fortified wine, especially the verdelho and bual styles of Madeira. I have known Bordeaux to work (a fine, mature Médoc from a hot, ripe vintage), but I still think of it as more fluke than a reasoned match. To the committed drinker of red wines, I would prefer to recommend Beaujolais-Villages; Rioja Crianza or a younger, modern Spanish red; Copertino, Salice Salentino, or primitivo from Puglia, southern Italy; or a mid-priced Australian shiraz.

Chinese food is not as **easy** on **wine** as you might expect. Its **delicacy** and gentle **sweetness** are the challenge.

Good wine needs good grapes and a good winemaker. No wonder vineyards and wineries work closer together than ever before.

growing &
making wine

in the
vineyard

Odd as it may sound, many winemakers have only relatively recently come to recognize how important the vines themselves are to wine quality.

What did they think was important before? In the 1970s and 1980s, as the New World emerged, and the Old World metamorphosed in its wake, those who made wine, whether or not they also grew the grapes, believed that the most influential elements were the equipment in the wineries and their own skills as winemakers. "Give us grapes and brand-new facilities and we'll give you good wine," or so the thinking went in this brave, new, high-tech wine world.

There was a lot in it: wine did become far better and more reliable. But it became apparent – and it sounds so obvious with hindsight – that no amount of clever or inspired winemaking could produce a good wine out of mediocre grapes, or a great wine out of merely good grapes: a case of silk purses and sows' ears. Suddenly, winemakers who had only ever moved between fermentation tanks, maturation cellars, and the occasional quality-control lab were getting into their boots and pacing the vineyards. The new mantra became "wine is made in the vineyard." Californians started talking about "farming for flavors." Viticulturalists (vine horticulturalists) became as important as winemakers.

NEW WORLD VINEYARDS

It was a different way of thinking. The pioneers in the New World had embarked on their winemaking ventures certain that, given warm, sunny climates, and water for irrigation where necessary, they could plant whichever grape varieties suited their own aspirations. Soil was dirt and didn't matter. It was of no concern to them that they lacked the limestone of Burgundy, the chalk of Champagne, the Kimmeridgian marl of Chablis, the gravel of the Médoc and Graves, the granite of the Douro, or any other terrain. They planted Bordeaux's great red grape, cabernet sauvignon, alongside Burgundy's great white grape, chardonnay, and they planted both alongside sauvignon blanc, the grape of Sancerre. And their vines flourished. Unlike so many European vines, growing on soils too poor to sustain most other crops, they didn't have to struggle for water and nutrients; they didn't have to push their roots yards down through layers of subsoil and resistant rock.

But neither did their vines produce wines with complex flavors that reflected the particular places from which they had come. Their wines reflected the grape varieties and the choices the winemaker had made during the fermentation and maturation processes. They tended to be strong on fruit flavors and alcohol (because the grapes ripened to high sugar levels in the warm climates), and equally strong on flavors that come from the winemaker's armory – the buttery taste of white wines in which a malolactic fermentation has taken place (*see page 128*), and the sweetness and flavor of new oak in red and in white wines.

VINEYARD CHARACTER

This didn't mean that they weren't good wines. On the contrary, some were so good they beat the finest French wines in competitions predominantly judged by French tasters. The everyday wines were more consistent in quality than almost anything produced in Europe at the time. But, unlike the great European wines, they didn't express the character of a vineyard. (As if to reinforce this, they were labeled primarily by grape variety and producer or brand, rather than geographically.)

The French call this spirit of place, or "somewhereness" as an American commentator has referred to it, *terroir*. It means the complete package of growing conditions that are specific to a vineyard or site and which, in combination, influence the style and quality of the wine that can be produced there. Terroir encompasses topography (altitude, slope, and orientation), climate (temperature, sunshine, and rainfall), soil, subsoil, and bedrock. For the French, terroir is an article of faith, and their appellation contrôlée system is based on it.

Roses mark the perimeter of Château de Sours' vineyards in the Entre-Deux-Mers region of Bordeaux. The merlot grape dominates the red wines here.

Terroir means the complete **package** of growing **conditions** that are specific to a **vineyard**.

soil

French tradition insists that the chemical composition of the soil, especially its mineral content, can contribute to the taste of a wine. Reluctantly, some New World growers are beginning to agree.

"Look at the flinty, mineral character of Chablis, the earthy-gravelly flavors of Graves, or even the slaty taste of Mosel," say the French. Modernists, predominantly New World producers, don't accept the link between soil and flavor, and it has to be said that scientific inquiry hasn't given a lot of support to the traditional view. But New World producers are coming around to it. You should hear riesling producers in Australia's Clare Valley talking about the differences in the soils and the taste of the wines from Watervale and Polish Hill.

What no thinking winemaker now doubts is that the physical properties of the soil have an enormous influence on wine quality and broad style. To produce wine of quality, vines are generally better served by relatively poor soils that encourage the roots to grow, rather than fertile soils that promote foliage growth, ultimately at the expense of fruit-ripening.

WATER AND HEAT

Vines need soils that are well drained, but which are capable of holding water at depth for the roots to draw on when necessary. Where irrigation is essential (as it is in much of Australia and South America), this water-retaining capacity is likely to be even more crucial. In the northern hemisphere and other cool regions, the soils also need to be able to store heat – something which stony soils do well. It's no empty coincidence that the chalky Champagne soils, the limestone of Burgundy, the Haut-Médoc gravels, and the clay and gravel layers of Pomerol all fulfill these criteria. Europe, of course, has had centuries to get to know its soil types. Growers didn't necessarily know the science behind the successful soils, but they knew which ones, in which climates, suited which grape varieties, and which parts of which small slope produced particularly fine results. Of course, most of that knowledge is now enshrined in individual appellation contrôlée rules.

LOOKING FOR TERROIR

In the now more soil- and geology-conscious New World, growers are making up for lost time, exploring new regions, identifying prime sites, and seeing where one grape variety does better or less well than another. These growers are seeking, in the first instance, cooler, less easy climates; but, as the climate becomes more difficult, so the soil has more bearing on vine-growth and quality potential. New World growers may not be using the word terroir, but they are increasingly beating the same drum.

KIMMERIDGIAN Chardonnay vines grown in the Kimmeridgian chalky marls of Chablis produce famously steely whites.

SLATE The Mosel River flows through beds of slate, and some of Germany's finest riesling comes from steep, slaty slopes in the Mosel-Saar-Ruwer.

CHALK The Côte des Blancs, in the Champagne region of France, has chalky soil. The chardonnay grown here is celebrated for its finesse.

organic & biodynamic

In wine, as in other branches of farming and food production, the Green movement has been gaining momentum, carried along by those who want to pump fewer agrochemicals into their soils and the environment, and by those who don't want to drink wines in which there might be chemical residues. Where once organic growing was the preserve of small, hands-on producers, big companies have now moved in, doubtless with an eye partly on the commercial opportunities.

ORGANIC GROWERS

In the European Union, organic wine means wine made from organically grown grapes. There are no rules covering what happens next: the winemaking. To be recognized as organically grown, by a confusing array of accredited organizations, the grapes must come from vineyards in which, for at least three years, no synthetic pesticides, fungicides, or weedkillers have been used, and no synthetic fertilizers applied. Compost, manure, and insect and animal predators are used instead. Cover crops, and sometimes weeds, are grown to improve the texture of the soil, to attract desirable insects, and, in some cases, to provide competition for over-vigorous vines. This is not taking place too soon. Years of relentless agrochemical applications have left soils – including some of the finest in Burgundy – compacted, lifeless, and heavy with residues. All we need now are standards for the winemaking processes.

ALTERNATIVE SYSTEMS

In addition to fully fledged organic growers, there are many more who practice systems such as sustainable viticulture and integrated pest management. These are similar in intent to organic viticulture, but more flexible in practice, allowing judicious agrochemical treatments to save a crop when necessary.

There is also a much more rigorous system, *biodynamie* or biodynamism, that has spread with surprising rapidity to the highest echelons of French wine, especially in Burgundy. It is surprising because it is apt to sound eccentric. Growers eschew chemicals in favor of local manure buried in cows' horns and infusions of powdered quartz and various plants (dandelion, nettle, valerian). They also organize their vineyard work, day by day, according to the phases of the moon and stars, harmonizing vine growth and development with what they believe are the natural rhythms of the earth

As a biodynamic alternative to pesticides, phacelia has been planted here in the Romanée-Conti vineyard, Burgundy, to eliminate nematode worms from the soil.

and cosmos. It would be easier for detractors to dismiss all this as nonsense were it not for the quality of the wines of adherents such as Domaine Leflaive and Domaine Leroy in Burgundy, Chapoutier in the Rhône, and Huët and Coulée de Serrant in the Loire.

Do all organic, organic-inspired, and biodynamic wines taste better than ordinary ones? Not by any means. These methods require a greater degree of skill, care, and patience. An inexperienced grower is more likely to botch an organic wine than one where he can fall back on chemicals. But, at their best, such wines do seem to have purer, more intense flavors – not least perhaps because they come from vines that, without synthetic chemical input, produce lower yields and therefore more concentrated flavors.

LIMESTONE Pinot noir grown in the limestone soils of Burgundy's famous Côte d'Or appellations attains a complexity seldom achieved elsewhere.

CLAY AND GRAVEL The prices of Château Pétrus and other estates in Pomerol, Bordeaux, testify to the quality of their merlot, grown in clay and gravel.

LARGE PEBBLES Big, round stones sitting on clay and sand in Châteauneuf-du-Pape absorb heat in the day and radiate it at night.

grape growth

Every year the drama of the grape crop begins anew, with every grower praying to be spared the frosts, hail, or lingering rain that can spell disaster.

1 BUD BURST As spring arrives, buds start to open on the vine. Foliage and shoots develop rapidly, turning the dead-looking vine green. Grape varieties that bud early are more at risk from spring frosts.

2 FLOWERING The vine flowers in late spring/early summer, 6–12 weeks after bud burst. Flowering usually lasts for up to 10 days. For successful flowering to occur, the weather must be warm, dry, and not too windy.

3 FRUIT SET Immediately after flowering, grapes start to develop from the fertilized flowers. This is called fruit set. The percentage that sets varies according to variety and the weather, but averages about 30 percent.

Depending on **climate** and **grape variety**, 130–200 days separate the first **buds** in spring and the **harvest**.

(4)

RIPENING During high summer the grapes begin to ripen. The sugar content of the grapes increases and the grapes start to change color and soften. This process is called *véraison*. Good weather conditions are vitally important for the ripening process, which continues into late summer/early autumn. Once the grapes are fully ripe, the harvesting can begin.

climate

As far as climate is concerned, the classic European wine regions are mostly near to the margins of successful vine cultivation – where vines are most at risk from the weather.

The growing season in Europe can be a nail-biting experience from start to finish. Too much rain dilutes the flavor of the grapes; too little sunshine results in unripe grapes. Hazards such as spring frost, poor weather when the vines are flowering (preventing the fruit from setting satisfactorily), hail, mildew, and fall rot are always in the cards. Sometimes even drought can be a problem, especially in those regions where irrigation is frowned on, and largely banned, because of the potential to use it to increase yields and thus dilute quality.

It's not only Europe that suffers: this vineyard, in Mendoza, Argentina, was stripped of its foliage by midsummer hail.

MESOCLIMATES

The Old World grower tends to look for sites where the severity of the climate is moderated in some way – for example, near a body of water that warms the adjoining land, on a slope sheltered from the prevailing wind, or in a frost-free pocket above the valley floor. Sites such as these are described as having a mesoclimate (a climate within a climate). And if previous generations haven't disclosed which vineyard or slope is the most favored, and which the least reliable, experience will soon reveal all, as it does for any other kind of farmer. Yet, however well a site is selected, and however carefully the vines are tended through the seasons, there will always be difficult years in these marginal regions, resulting in disappointing wines.

CLIMATIC EXTREMES

Warm regions are not without their threats. Argentina suffered badly from El Niño in 1998; the Hunter Valley in Australia is prone to harvesttime rain; Western Australia and New Zealand sometimes suffer the effects of passing cyclones; and a variety of abnormal weather conditions made 2000 an unusually difficult vintage for some of South Australia's key regions. But these are the exception, not the rule. Whereas the Old World hopes for good weather, the New World expects it. The latter's problem is more likely to be too much warmth too soon, resulting in grapes that are ripe before they have developed much flavor.

So, the Old World grower looks for an extra degree of sunshine or frost protection, while the quality-oriented grower in the southern hemisphere and California increasingly looks for the cooler site up in the hills, the one that catches chilling sea breezes or morning fogs, or the one where the temperature drops lower at night. The result of all this is that the world's finest wines tend to come from the warmer years in favored northern Europe vineyards and, increasingly, from those vineyards in the New World that are cooler and more European than the average.

vine cultivation

Vines need planting, training, and pruning in the right way – right for the vine and the environmental conditions and, no less important, appropriate to the quality of wine being made.

Just as poor grapes won't make good wine, some places will never make great wine, no matter how much money is lavished on them.

CLONED VINES

In fact, it's not only the grape type but differences between individual clones that the quality-conscious grower will be aware of. Clones can be chosen for their disease resistancy, productivity, aromatic potential, and all kinds of other attributes. Nowadays, it is considered preferable to have a variety of clones in a vineyard rather than a single clone, because the variety results in a greater spectrum of flavors and potential complexity. For the same reason, some growers prefer vines that have been propagated en masse from a vineyard, rather than those which have been clonally selected.

VINE SPACING

Having chosen a grape variety and clone, the grower has to decide how closely the vines should be planted. This may not sound important, but it can have a huge bearing on quality. The very rough rule of thumb is that vines are planted closer together in poorer soils and more marginal climates, so that they have to compete harder for the available nutrients. They put more effort into extending their roots and, ultimately, into ripening a smaller number of bunches of grapes (the smaller number making it more likely that they will ripen). Relatively close planting and narrower rows are therefore more typical of Europe, and wider spacing is more typical of the New World, where soils tend to be more fertile and where vineyards were planted with mechanization in mind.

genetic engineering

At the time of writing, genetically modified (GM) vines are not commercially available, but that could change in the next few years. Certainly, laboratories all over the world have been developing GM vines for some time.

Most of the work has been on developing vines with resistance to viral, fungal, and insect-spread diseases, and vines that will ripen their fruit more readily. But in Australia, where wine has been becoming increasingly alcoholic, one line of research has been in developing vines on which grapes develop their flavors earlier. The grapes can then be picked before their sugar rises to those levels that are converted to high levels of alcohol by fermentation. As for other GM organisms (GMOs), GM yeast may have been used in Champagne since the 1980s – but the Champenois prefer not to talk about it. GMOs are not allowed in any European Union organic products, including wine.

Below left: widely spaced vines allow mechanized harvesting. Below: with closer rows, all work is done by hand.

CONTROLLING YIELDS

Training, trellising, and pruning vines are all ways of controlling how well the grapes will ripen and how many are produced (the yield). A vine that over-burdens itself with bunches of grapes simply won't be able to ripen them properly, however much sunshine there is. Ideally, winter pruning will result in the right number of bunches, but a grower may thin the crop in the summer by removing and discarding some of the bunches (known as green pruning or a green harvest). The question of yield, or crop level, is always a critical one, but there's no simple formula. It depends on the location, the grape varieties, the density of planting, the age of the vines, which treatments and fertilizers have been used, and the intended quality level of the wine (everyday drinking or medal-winner).

BUSH VINES

Precise methods will, similarly, depend on the vineyard environment and type of vines, and very possibly on local custom. In places such as the south of France, southern Italy, and the Barossa Valley in Australia, where there are very old vines, there may be no training and very little pruning because old vines – in this untrained state called "bush vines" – naturally produce lower yields. Old vines, meaning of any age from about 25 years to well over a century,

Top: cabernet sauvignon vines trained on and supported by a "split cordon" trellis system in Napa County, California.
Center: excess shoots are stripped from vines in Puglia, Italy, to expose the grapes.
Left: mechanized training in Alsace – the machine lifts new foliage, clipping it to wires that it runs on either side of support posts.

are prized because of these lower yields, which are associated with higher quality and more complex flavors. Young vines are naturally vigorous, but their fruit tends to be simple in flavor.

In other places, training and pruning methods have been designed to deal with particular conditions. In New Zealand, for example, vines naturally produce extravagant amounts of foliage. This not only diminishes root growth and fruit ripening, but also prevents the grapes from ripening simply by shading them. A "canopy management" system, involving thinning shoots and removing leaves in summer, has been developed to deal with the phenomenon. And it has been very successful.

HARVESTING

Choosing when and how to harvest might seem easy enough, but even without the vagaries of the weather, there is potential for getting it wrong. With few exceptions, the aim is to pick grapes at perfect ripeness; but in warm climates the essential acidity, especially in white wines, can drop suddenly. This leaves the grower with a crop of overripe grapes that will need just the right amount of acid added in the winery – provided that the regulations allow additions of acid, which they usually do in the New World, but may not in the Old.

One way of catching the optimum moment is to pick at night by machine, ensuring that the grapes are gathered swiftly in ideally cool temperatures. It's popular in Australia and it's also cheap. But machine harvesters have their critics and aren't suitable for all grapes, vineyards, and weather conditions, particularly in Europe.

They can't be used, for example, for botrytized grapes, or in vineyards where rot-affected bunches need to be discarded. They can't be used on terraced or steep hillsides, and they can be trouble in muddy, waterlogged vineyards. They're not allowed in Champagne, where the grapes must arrive at the winery intact (not split), and, although they are allowed in Bordeaux and Burgundy, they aren't used by top estates.

TIMING THE HARVEST

In the classic European regions, underripeness, not overripeness, is more likely to be the worry; picking a fraction too early may give tart white wines and thin, tannic red ones. In general, grapes are being picked riper than in the past, but sometimes it is impossible to pick at the ideal moment. The prospect of wet weather or incipient rot (or even, in Australia, marauding cockatoos) may force growers to pick at any time, whether they want to or not.

The exceptions to the "optimum ripeness" rule include champagne grapes, which are picked with deliberately high acidity, and grapes used for sweet wines. These are harvested late in the season or beyond, sometimes shriveled with noble rot and picked gradually over several weeks, sometimes dessicated by sun and wind, and sometimes frozen solid and picked by hand in the dead of night.

Clockwise from top left: quality-conscious harvesting – individual grape bunches are cut, carried away in small hods, and sorted while still in the vineyard.
Right: machine-harvesting at night enables growers to pick rapidly in the cool of the night.

in the
winery

Combine healthy grapes with a natural bloom and the yeast populations that build up over time in wine regions, and the result will be wine. If you're lucky.

But you probably wouldn't be lucky all of the time – perhaps not much of the time, even with nice, clean fermentation containers, and with weather warm enough to get the fermentation started, but not so hot that it happened too quickly. On the other occasions, all too often, the result would be more like vinegar than wine, your precious liquid having succumbed to attack from bacteria or unfriendly yeast. With plenty of both always dying to get ahold in any wine-producing environment, protecting the incipient wine from contact with air, or oxidation, is one of the key roles of the winemaker. But there are other things to do, too, and crucial decisions to make.

New oak barrels give **richer** and more **complex** **flavors**, and a richer **texture**.

CRUSHING THE GRAPES

Once the grapes have been harvested, they need to be delivered to the winery (in the New World) or cellar (Old World) as soon as possible; but they must arrive in good condition, not squashed to a pulp and wide open

Treading grapes is arduous work, but for some red wines and vintage port the resulting quality justifies the time and trouble.

to a blitz of bacteria. Transporting them in small plastic crates is ideal. Piling them up in the back of a large open truck in the heat of the day, for a slow, bumpy journey in the company of a cloud of flies, is about as bad as it gets.

At the winery, white grapes go off to be crushed and pressed. They may be chilled first, but the winemaker's main goal is to get the clear, fresh juice flowing from the grapes. Red grapes go to the crusher to have their skins broken and stems removed, but they don't go to the press until after fermentation. Thus the big difference between making white wine and red is that the juice is fermented without the skins for white wines, whereas for red wine the juice ferments with the skins.

In fact, that's how red wine gets its color: the flesh of almost all red wine grapes is colorless, which is why you can make white wine, and rosé, out of red grapes. Champagne and sparkling-wine producers do it all the time, pressing the clear juice from whole bunches of red grapes and discarding the skins (which come in very useful for the local spirit, marc de Champagne).

MACERATION

Rosé can be made in several ways. The most usual for wine with any aspirations to quality is to crush grapes as if making red wine, leaving the resulting mush of juice and skins for anything from four to 24 hours, depending on the grape variety and the depth of flavor and color desired. You then run the juice off the skins and ferment it as if making white wine. This maceration period is known as skin contact, and is sometimes carried out with white grapes (chilled and protected from air) to extract extra aroma and flavor from the skins. The running-off process is known as a saignée, a "bleeding."

Variations on the theme of crushing red wine include leaving a proportion of bunches whole, complete with stalks, for some low-tannin grape varieties,

The juice of white grapes is separated from the skins before fermentation; the skins of red grapes stay with the juice to color the wine.

Traditional basket presses, such as this one at Krug Champagne, have been brought back into service in some Australian wineries.

notably pinot noir; and a process called carbonic maceration, used for Beaujolais and other wines designed to be drunk young and fruity. Whole bunches are put in the fermentation tank, blanketed with carbon dioxide, and sealed; fermentation then starts without yeast inside the berries, and the resulting wine is juicy in style and has a distinctive perfume of banana, peardrops, or bubblegum.

TREADING BY FOOT

Another variation is treading by foot, which, in select circles, has been making something of a comeback. It's gentle, which is why some New World producers now tread their pinot noir, and it's a very efficient way of extracting color. Top-quality vintage port continues to rely on treading for its color, even to the extent of using robotic "foot" treaders. Just for the record, foot-treading is perfectly hygienic. The average foot is a lot less dusty than many of the grapes you see arriving at wineries.

from grapes
into wine

Fermentation will turn any grape juice into some kind of wine, but winemakers who seek quality will make sure they are in control at every stage.

1
SORTING Good grapes are needed for good wine, so, ideally, any diseased, immature, or rotten grapes are discarded at the outset. The higher the aspirations of the producer, the greater the care that is taken.

2
INTO THE WINERY Because of the risk of bacterial infection, the sooner the processing of the grapes starts the better. Here, the grapes are conveyed directly through the winery roof to the grape-crusher inside.

3
CRUSHING The winemaker chooses a crushing method that suits the grape variety and the intended wine. Varieties with relatively tough skins are usually crushed by faster, more powerful machines.

There is no one **perfect** kind of **winery** for all wines. It depends on the **type** of wine, the **location**, the **climate**, the availability of **labor**, and the intended or likely **marketplace**.

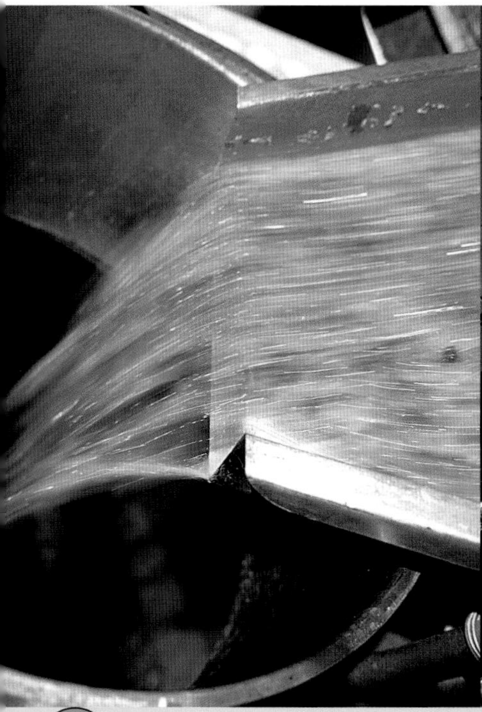

4

INTO FERMENTATION If a white wine is being made, only the separated juice is fermented and the rest is removed. For red wines, the juice and skins are fermented together to give the wines their color.

5

FILTERING After fermentation, the resulting wine is usually cloudy. To make the wine stable – and look more appealing – winemakers use various methods to clarify the wine, including cold stabilization, as shown here.

6

OAK AGING Many wines never come into contact with oak and are bottled immediately after filtering. But others, both white and red, are aged in oak barrels to give them more complex flavors and a richer texture.

FERMENTATION

The type and size of the container used for fermentation has an enormous effect on the wine – and on its price. There are still glass-lined concrete and fiberglass tanks in use, but large, stainless-steel tanks equipped with temperature-control systems are the modern, easy-care choice, particularly for the cool, slow kind of fermentation required to produce crisp, lively whites and rosés. Many reds are also fermented in stainless steel, but traditional, large, open-topped wooden vats are still popular. In fact, some have been introduced into ultra-modern New World wineries by wine-makers impressed by their color-extraction and heat-holding potential. Similar wooden vats, but closed at the top, are also used in some of the classic white wine areas, especially in Germany and Alsace.

THE ROLE OF OAK

Then there are expensive, new oak barrels, which no producer aiming for top-quality full-bodied whites or reds can be without. Many woods have been tried (including chesnut in Italy, rauli in Chile, and eucalyptus in Australia), and some continue to be used, but there is no question that oak produces the most sophisticated results. And not just any old oak. Fine-grained oak from French forests is held to be the best. American oak is regarded as more robustly flavored, but can be subtle when skillfully selected, seasoned, and coopered.

New oak barrels give richer flavors (not just the taste of oak, but a more complex character), and a richer texture. White wines can readily be fermented in these small containers, but with red wines the skins are a problem. They rise to the surface and need constant pushing down – as they do in any container – so that they don't form a crust on top of the wine. For this reason, red wine is usually matured, but not fermented, in barrels; although some producers transfer the wine, minus the skins, to barrels as soon as the maceration (the color and tannin-extraction period) is complete, but before fermentation has finished.

Below: it's not only in traditional cellars that you see large wooden fermentation vats; some New World wineries have introduced them. Below right: stainless-steel tanks offer a fine degree of temperature control. The purity of flavor of varietal wines is often best preserved by fermentation in stainless steel.

making oak barrels

It is no longer common for oak barrels to be made at the château where they will see service, but at Château Haut-Brion in Bordeaux the tradition of in-house cooperage continues.

Before assembly, each stave is tapered at each end. The cooper stands shaped staves in a circle, while an iron "raising-up" hoop attached at their head maintains their position.

Once the circle of staves is complete, the cooper knocks down two temporary hoops tightly over the end of the barrel. The raising-up hoop is replaced during this process.

One end after the other, the barrel is shaped over a firepot. The cooper knocks hoops tightly over the staves, aided by the heat and water liberally applied to the sides.

The barrel is toasted inside to create a buffer for the wine.

The stave-ends form an irregular lip when barrel formation is completed, so they are planed smooth before the barrel is released.

Some winemakers suspend small pieces of oak in their tanks of wine as a quick, cheap way of getting some oak flavor into the wine.

Shortcuts to oak, for winemakers on a tight budget, include suspending bags of oak chips or oak staves in tanks or vats of wine during fermentation and/or aging. This can give a useful short-term blast of oak flavor, but the results are never as subtle or rich as in wine nurtured through the same processes in a carefully prepared barrel. Oak essence also exists, but is mostly illegal. But liquid and powdered tannin products, made from oak and other woods, have a long and legal history in many wine regions. They're used to improve the color, shelf life, and texture of red wines.

ADDITIVES
It's a fact of life that few wines are made without any additives, but it's equally true that most additives are used in tiny amounts and, more importantly, leave no residues in the wine. The most commonly used, although at deliberately lower levels than in the past, is sulfur dioxide, which is usually added as an extremely effective disinfectant and preservative when the grapes go into the crusher.

Once inside the fermentation vessel, the must may start fermenting without any help, but it may not, especially if the weather is cool. In the past, all you could do was heat the must in some way. Nowadays, many winemakers use cultured yeasts, which behave more predictably than wild (or ambient) yeasts. The argument against cultured yeasts is that they can't produce the potential complexity of flavor of wild yeast fermentations. Modern winemakers often also use commercial yeast nutrients to make sure that the fermentation starts quickly.

There are also additives to make up for nature's inadequacies. In northern Europe, the primary one is sugar. The sugar isn't added to make the wine sweeter, but to make it fuller-bodied by providing more "fuel" for the yeasts to convert into alcohol. In the New World, where sunshine usually ensures high sugar levels, the principal adjustment is acidification – the addition of acid. Chaptalization (adding sugar) is rare in the New World.

THE MALOLACTIC
The alcoholic fermentation varies in duration according to the temperature (it can be quite rapid for red wines at temperatures of up to 90° F/32° C), the yeast used, and the amount of sugar in the grapes (fermentation of sweet wines can be very prolonged). There is then, potentially, a second kind of fermentation, the malolactic. This softens the acidity by converting malic acid to lactic, and gives, to white wines especially, a buttery taste.

Red wines invariably go through a malolactic fermentation – and taste harsh if they don't. With white wines,

the winemaker must decide whether to allow one to occur. In warm climates, where white wines often need every scrap of freshening acidity they can get, the malolactic may be prevented. The same applies to wines, such as German riesling, that depend on tingling, racy acidity. But in cooler regions that produce full-bodied wines, such as Burgundy, the malolactic can help to give the wine richness. Often, especially in the New World, winemakers encourage it in only a proportion of tanks or barrels, and then blend those with the rest.

AGING ON THE LEES
Another choice for white winemakers is whether to rack the wine (draw it off into another container) or leave it with its lees – the sediment of dead yeasts and grape fragments that drops to the bottom of the wine after fermentation.

White wines that are aged on their lees (dead yeasts) may be stirred to enhance the creamy flavor and texture the lees give.

The lees give a richer, creamier flavor to wine and also keep it fresher. Wine labeled *sur lie* (on its lees), the best known of which is Muscadet, stays on its lees right to the point of bottling to give it extra zip and freshness.

If the wine is to stay on its lees, the next decision is whether to stir them periodically to enhance the effect, as is traditional in Burgundy. Stirring the lees has the added advantage of aerating the wine at a time when it can easily develop smelly sulfide aromas.

RACKING

A red wine may be left on its lees, but not usually for a prolonged period before pressing and racking (when it is poured off the lees and transferred into a new barrel). And the lees aren't stirred for red wines. Winemakers who want to make their reds fashionably rich and soft, particularly in Old World regions of relatively tannic grape varieties such as Bordeaux and Madiran, may, if they can afford the equipment, use a technique called micro-oxygenation,

which involves sending tiny bubbles of oxygen through the wine. Otherwise, winemakers rack in the time-honored way and then blend in relatively little press-wine – the tannic wine that is eventually pressed from the skins.

BLENDING AND AGING

Sometimes different grape varieties are fermented together. Most blending, however, whether of different grape varieties or of different treatments of the same basic wine, is done after fermentation, and often some months later in the spring. It can be even later. Wine may be matured for almost no time at all – as in many inexpensive white wines and simple, fruity reds – or it may be allowed lengthy and expensive sojourns of two or more years in oak barrels.

FINING AND FILTERING

Contact with oak can contribute to a wine's flavor and complexity, but it also has other advantages. With long oak-aging, complete with periodic

racking, the wine needs less fining and filtering to make it clear and stable, because most of the particles will have settled out naturally. And that's a positive feature, because fining and filtering, however gentle, inevitably remove some of the aroma, flavor, and character from a wine.

The difference between fining and filtering is that, with the former, you add a fining agent to the wine, such as fresh egg whites (favored by leading European wine estates), bentonite, or casein. These fining agents pass through the liquid, attracting any solids, and shouldn't leave any residues. Other processes, more often used for cheaper, commercial wines, are cold stabilization (chilling to precipitate crystals), and adding preservatives such as ascorbic acid and sulfur dioxide. The cheaper wines often also undergo a fairly severe filtration process.

Below left: as part of the racking procedure, a barrel is tilted to pour the wine off its lees. Below: samples of the wine are regularly held up to a candle to assess their clarity.

sparkling wines

From the grandest, most expensive champagne down to the cheapest bottle of non-champagne fizz, all sparkling wine is wine with carbon dioxide bubbles in it. But all are by no means equal.

When you buy a top champagne, you're undoubtedly paying a premium for the product's image. But you're also paying for the painstaking, time-consuming, and money-eating method that transforms not very nice-tasting, high-acid, relatively low-alcohol, still wine into an infinitely more fascinating and flavorsome sparkling wine (a more alcoholic one, too).

Sparkling wine is the one time that you can turn a harvest of apparently unripe grapes into something very special. Indeed, you actually need tart, thin-flavored still wine to make fine sparkling wine. This is why New World countries, with their bigger, riper flavors, find it impossible to achieve the finesse and subtlety of champagne without going to their coolest vineyards, growing chardonnay, pinot noir, and, very occasionally, meunier, the third champagne grape, and producing much smaller crops than usual.

BLENDED WINES

Turning the neutral-tasting, acid wine into fine fizz begins late in the winter, after the tasting and blending of still wines made from the different grape varieties. In the Champagne region itself, the grapes may come from a great many different villages – sometimes 50 or more. The resulting blend is put in bottles with a precise amount of yeast and sugar, and sealed. A second fermentation takes place, but this time the carbon dioxide given off has no escape and remains as bubbles in the wine. You now have fizzy wine, but still not very interesting wine. It's during the next stage, when the dead yeasts gradually break down, that champagne acquires its quintessential creamy, bready, brioche flavors.

REMOVING SEDIMENT

Champagne is left aging on its lees like this for a minimum of 15 months, and more often several years. Before it can be despatched to the public, the yeasty sludge, which would soon make the wine cloudy, has to be removed. This is done by *remuage* or riddling. The bottles are gradually inverted, either by hand over several weeks in special racks or more quickly by machine, so that the sediment slips down into the neck of the bottle. The neck is then frozen, so that when the cap is removed the frozen lump of sediment shoots out. This is known as *dégorgement,* or disgorging. The bottle is then topped up with a *dosage* of wine and sugar, the amount of sugar depending on the style. Even *brut* (dry) champagne has some sugar added. A sparkling wine made in this way outside the Champagne region can describe itself as made by the classic or traditional method (as in *classique, classico, traditionelle*, and so on).

Remuage is costly, so one cheaper way of making sparkling wine is to transfer the wine to another bottle, filtering out the sediment en route. Inevitably, this method – called "bottle fermented" or "transfer method" – results in some loss of flavor. Cheaper and still more inferior is the tank method, or *cuve close*, in which the second fermentation takes place in a huge tank. And at the bottom of the pile is carbonation, or the "bicycle-pump" method, in which carbon dioxide is pumped into wine as if it were a soft drink.

Sediment thrown by a champagne's second fermentation is slowly tilted down the bottle until removed by the *dégorgement* process.

sweet wines

Winemakers use a variety of tricks to achieve sweetness in their cheaper sweet wines, but the world's finest examples rely on nothing more than the sugar in the grapes.

Some cheap sweet wines are made by stopping their fermentation before all the sugar (including any added during chaptalization, *see page 128*) has been turned into alcohol. The wines are then dosed heavily with sulfur dioxide to stop them from refermenting. Others, especially in Germany, are sweetened with grape concentrate. The best sweet wines, however, don't need such intervention from the winemaker.

Grapes may be extra sweet because they have been harvested late – for example, those used for German and Austrian Auslese, Alsace vendange tardive, and New World wines labeled "late harvest." They may have begun to dry out like raisins, as in sweet Jurançon. Or they may be made from grapes deliberately dried after picking: in Italy, Recioto is made in various regions from grapes, red or white, spread out on trays or hung from the roof to dry. France has its vin de paille, made from grapes dried on straw; and Austria, likewise, has its Strohwein.

BOTRYTIZED WINES

Grapes used to make Sauternes and other botrytized wines, such as German and Austrian Beerenauselese and Trockenbeerenauslese, Tokaji, Alsace sélection de grains nobles, and New World botrytis wines, are shriveled and concentrated by a fungus, botrytis cinerea, or noble rot. Botrytis appears in vineyards when the weather conditions are right: misty in the morning, dry and warm in the afternoon. In the New World, the same effect is sometimes achieved by spraying botrytis spores onto grapes in the winery and then subjecting them to alternating humid and dry conditions. In Sauternes, some châteaux help themselves in wet vintages by using a cryoextraction machine to freeze the excess water out of rain-diluted grapes, thus "reconcentrating" them.

To make Eiswein or icewine, grapes are picked when they are frozen, then pressed before thawing to release sweet, concentrated juice.

But cryoextraction is frowned on by producers of Eiswein in Germany and Austria, and icewine in Canada. These wines are made from grapes frozen on the vine and picked after they have been at 16° F (–8° C) or colder for at least eight hours; sometimes in Germany this means a harvest in January of the new year. The frozen grapes are gently pressed and yield a concentrated, syrupy juice, very high in both sugar and acidity because the water remains as ice in the press.

These muscat grapes have been allowed to dry while still on the vine. When finally harvested, they will yield very sweet juice.

The unappetizing-looking noble rot on these chenin blanc grapes will concentrate the sugar, acidity, and other flavors.

fortified wines

Fortifying wines – adding alcohol, usually grape spirit, to them – is another way of making them sweet. The alcohol incapacitates the yeasts, leaving unfermented sugar.

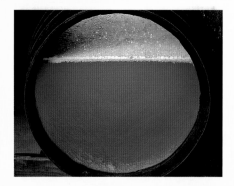

In this glass-ended show barrel, a thick layer of yeast, known as flor, grows on the surface of fino sherry, shielding it from the air.

Occasionally, the alcohol is added before the grape juice even starts to ferment, the best-known example being the Cognac region's Pineau de Charentes. Usually, it's added part way through fermentation. France's vins doux naturels, such as Muscat de Beaumes-de-Venise, Rivesaltes, and Banyuls, are made in this way, as are port, Madeira, Marsala, and Málaga. Sherry and Montilla differ in that fortification takes place after fermentation, which means that they begin as dry wines, although they may be sweetened afterward.

SHERRY

Fortification is only one aspect of the great fortified wines. The other essential and distinguishing element is maturation. Sherry is aged through a "solera" system of fractional, or serial, blending: as it ages, each row of barrels has sherry from the next, younger, row blended into it. This constantly "refreshes" the maturing sherry. As a very rough average, on each occasion a quarter to a third of each barrel is moved to the next stage. Some solera systems date back more than a century.

The other distinctive feature of sherry is *flor*, a yeast that grows in a layer on the surface of the young wine. If the growth is vigorous (looking rather like porridge), the wine will be classified as a fino (or manzanilla) and only lightly fortified. If there is little or no flor, the wine will be fortified more strongly and will be classified as an oloroso. The other sherry styles, such as amontillado and palo cortado, fall between fino/manzanilla and oloroso.

MADEIRA

Madeira has an equally distinctive but entirely different aging process. It is either heated in large tanks for about six months (the estufagem process), or it is aged in warehouses at the ambient temperature. This varies from about 66–76° F (18–25° C) through the year and is considerably warmer than is advisable for other wines. The effect, either way, is to give Madeira its characteristic burnt tang and to make the wine incredibly long-lived, if not virtually indestructible.

PORT

Port is aged more conventionally, but in two different ways. Tawny or wood ports are aged for many years in barrels and are ready to drink when bottled and sold. Vintage, single-quinta (*see page 187*), and vintage-type ports are aged for a much shorter time in barrel and then need to finish their development in bottle. In the case of true vintage port, this may take decades.

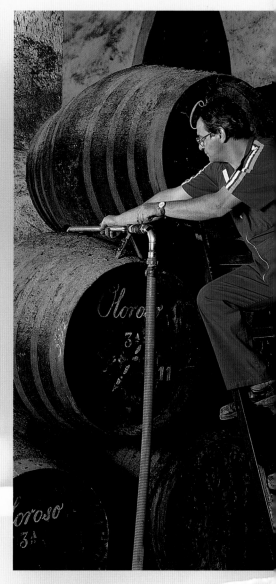

In the solera system of Osborne's La Palma bodega, young oloroso sherry is pumped into a barrel of maturing oloroso to "refresh" it.

Whether you're buying wines
experimentally for everyday
drinking or for laying down,
it pays to know your options.

buying
wine

looking for value

Whether you're in a store, a restaurant, or overseas, price is almost always a consideration, but there is more than that to buying a good bottle.

Buying wine ought to be one of life's pleasures, and yet navigating wine shelves and restaurant wine lists can be a daunting experience. Even a supermarket may have as many as 600 different wines from more than 20 countries – and no one with any wine knowledge on hand to give advice. If you don't want or need help, that's fine, but, if you do, there are probably better alternatives. And it's not just a question of service: different kinds of outlets offer different kinds of wines.

STORES, MERCHANTS, AND MAIL ORDER

In many countries, most wine is sold through supermarkets. In Britain, for example, they generally offer large lines of well-made, ready-for-drinking wines at competitive prices. Increasingly, they have wines made for them to their own specifications – modern, easy-going, fruity styles made by itinerant Australian or Australian-influenced winemakers (so called flying winemakers). Supermarkets also focus on mass-market, heavily promoted wine brands, on which profit margins are generous. What they can't offer to any very useful extent, because of their size and the nature of their business, is wines from small, independent producers, wines that are daringly innovative or idiosyncratic, and wines that need aging – although some offer a few token wines of these kinds in their flagship stores.

Unsupported by sales of laundry detergent and pet food, prices in chain stores and wine warehouses tend to be higher, but the best of these retailers list more of the world's interesting, limited-production wines and are staffed by people with enthusiasm and at least some knowledge.

For the most individual selections of wines, together with personal service and passion for the subject, you need to seek out independent wine stores, some of which are partly or wholly mail-order businesses. They are also the principal retail source of the finite volumes of sought-after, sometimes cult, wines that are allocated around the world and which sell out almost as soon as they are offered (often while the wine is still in the producer's cellars, *see page 138*). Some retailers also put on tasting events – fun, educational, and intended to encourage you to buy more wine.

For the most **individual** selections of wines, you need to **seek** out **independent** wine stores.

Mail-order wine clubs are a variation on the theme, often with more club events, newsletters, and so on. They range from one-man operations to large enterprises. Either way, they should be offering wines that aren't available in the big chains – either because quantities are too small, or, conversely, because the club is big enough to buy up all available stock or has its own winemakers in the regions. Buying wine online is yet another variation on the theme, but one that has yet to catch on significantly, even among the established mail-order wine companies who have added cyberspace as another avenue.

AUCTIONS AND EXCHANGES

Two areas of online business that are developing are wine auctions and wine exchanges (where wine is traded a little like stocks). Both, like traditional terra-firma auctions, are forums for buying rare fine wines, notably mature wines, and lesser (but usually mature) wines. The potential for picking up bargains is real, but neither auctions nor exchanges should be approached casually or in ignorance. You need to know the current (or recent) prices of the kinds of wines you're interested in; you need to be aware of any extra costs involved (buyer's premium and taxes); and you need to be able to understand the catalog well enough to ask questions in advance where necessary – particularly about provenance. It's essential to know the history of wine being sold in this way. If, for example, it has changed hands several times, or has been across the Atlantic and back, its storage conditions have almost certainly been less than ideal.

EN PRIMEUR AND INVESTING IN WINE

Buying wine by the case en primeur (also known as futures) means ordering and paying for it (but not necessarily the taxes and transport costs) when it's still maturing in casks in the producer's cellars. In the past, en primeur sales were largely restricted to red Bordeaux from leading châteaux. Bordeaux is still the mainstay of the market, but it has been joined by other fine wines, including burgundy (red and white), Rhône, Barolo, Californian, and Australian wines.

The reason for buying at this early stage is to secure, at the lowest prices (known as opening prices), sought-after wines that are likely to become very much more expensive and hard, if not impossible, to come by as they approach maturity. But there are risks. Currencies and economies fluctuate; vintages and/or châteaux are sometimes overhyped and overpriced (as 1997 Bordeaux was); and wines sometimes don't turn out as well as expected. It's also imperative to buy from a well-established seller with impeccable credentials and faultless administration systems, because you've got to be certain that, two years or so after you've handed over your money, the company is still going to be around to hand over your wine.

If you know what you're doing, you can make good money out of investing in wine. Not only that but, once you've made your initial outlay, you can drink well, more or less free, for the rest of your life. All you do is buy fine wines by the case en primeur, ensure that they are stored in perfect conditions, and then, several years later when the wines are mature, or nearly so, sell what you don't want.

Whether you buy en primeur or select wine by the case from a retailer, you need good storage conditions to protect your investment.

You then invest some of the profits in more young wine. It all sounds straightfoward enough, and in many ways it is, but it's not for amateurs. Without good advice, it's not even for modestly knowledgeable wine drinkers. Nor is it for anyone bent on making big money overnight. That can be done, but it is more sensible to think in terms of at least five years.

Investing wisely is a matter of choosing the right wines in the right vintages and dealing with the right companies. This last element is crucial. As with buying en primeur, it's a prerequisite to buy from a company with a proven track record in wine. Beware the so-called wine investment companies that try to lure investors by making extravagant claims about potential profits.

As for the wines, reds are the staples, because more of them last for longer, and the two classics are red Bordeaux and vintage port, both notably long-lived. Burgundy has become more important in recent years, as has a small portfolio of wines from the Rhône, Italy, Spain, California, and Australia. But the point is that it is individual producers and vintages, not regions in general, that count. Wines for investment have to be among the very best of their kind.

BUYING IN SITU

For many people, buying wine directly from the grower is easily the most enjoyable way of stocking up, whether in France, California, or Australia. Some regions are more geared up for visitors than others, but with most producers you will usually get some wine to taste and possibly a tour of the cellars.

some top wines

Port: Taylor, Graham, Fonseca, and Quinta do Noval Nacional.

Bordeaux: Médoc first growths, or premier crus classés (such as Lafite and Latour); the "super-seconds" (leading second growths, such as Léoville-Las-Cases and Ducru-Beaucaillou); a few other famous Médoc châteaux, such as Palmer and Lynch-Bages; and St.-Emilions and Pomerols such as Cheval-Blanc and Pétrus (but beware the new high-profile, small-production, very expensive wines with no track record).

Burgundy: Domaine de la Romanée Conti (or DRC) leads, but de Vogüé, Lafon, Leroy, and Rousseau are increasingly sought.

Rhône: wines such as Jaboulet's Hermitage La Chapelle and Guigal's Côte-Rôties.

Italy: Sassicaia, Ornellaia, Gaja, and Conterno.

Spain: Vega Sicilia.

California: Opus One, Dominus, and Ridge now have good track records. California also has its own breed of exceptionally expensive, new cult wines (such as Screaming Eagle).

Australia: the investment wines are led by Penfolds Grange and Henschke's Hill of Grace.

The price of 1982 Le Pin shot up to nearly $50,000 a case in 1997, before slipping back to around $8,250 a year later.

One advantage of tasting wines where they are made is that you often have the opportunity to compare vintages of the same wine.

In the more rural, less ritzy regions of Europe, and at grand estates, it is often best to make an appointment (by phone or in writing), but avoid trying to do so at harvest time. You aren't obliged to buy wine on such occasions, but if you've tasted several wines free, it's generally expected. If you don't think you're going to want to buy, make your excuses and leave sooner rather than later – and buy the minimum amount if you think it's necessary.

It's worth noting that buying wine in supermarkets in continental Europe, particularly France, can be a hit-and-miss affair. It's possible, during special promotions (foires aux vins), to pick up red Bordeaux bargains, but wine quality overall is much lower than in British supermarkets, and the choice is largely restricted to French wines, with only a few token foreigners among them.

TRAVELING AND WINE

In theory, any wine in a bottle with a cork is packaged to travel, but this doesn't mean being shaken around in a hot car for two weeks. In practice, red wines are generally more robust travelers than whites and rosés, and any wine with less than 11.5 percent alcohol is not likely to be a good traveler – and was probably made to be drunk young anyway. The trouble often is that the wine travels, but the vacation ambience doesn't. A wine that tastes eminently refreshing or suitably rustique with a backdrop of sun, cicadas, and local food often isn't remotely appropriate in the real, post-vacation world of suburbia. So, the answer when bringing wine back home is usually to trade up from your vacation staple. It will probably still seem cheap in comparison with domestic prices.

Very cheap wine, including most of the "plonk" in liter bottles, plastic bottles, and giant plastic containers, often at alcohol levels of 11 percent or lower, is not designed to travel more than a few miles or to last more than a few months. You bring back that kind of wine at your peril; it may not even be fit to cook with.

BUYING IN RESTAURANTS

Most restaurants have far fewer wines to choose from than any wine store or supermarket, but that doesn't mean it's easier to make a decision, especially if you're choosing for people eating different things (keep in mind the list of wines that go well, *see page 100*). Even if matching the food isn't a problem, it's easy to be discouraged by horrendous prices and unfamiliar and hard-to-pronounce names (the pronunciation guide should help, *see pages 218–19*). In an ideal world, there is a friendly, well-informed wine waiter at the ready – not to mention a varied range of wines with modest markups, interesting house wines, wines by the glass, and half-bottles. But restaurant life isn't always like that, and along with other shortcomings, the lists themselves can be woefully inadequate – chaotically organized and lacking vital information such as vintages or producers' names. If the waiter doesn't know, ask to see the bottle(s) and check such details yourself.

INTERPRETING PRICES

Even leaving restaurant prices and individual countries' taxes out of the discussion, do you get what you pay for? There are no hard and fast answers, but, very broadly speaking, at under $10 a bottle in the US you get more or less what you pay for, whereas at over $10 you may also be paying for such things as rarity, fashion status, and the producer's unalloyed ambition. At over $20, you are almost certainly paying for some of these things – nowhere more obviously than in the wave of new, tiny volume, "superpremium" wines emerging all over the world. Sometimes these wines are created jointly by two high-profile producers (often one European and one New World) who save their greatest creativity for the pricing. All these wines prove is that, if you make something in small enough quantities and price it highly enough, some people will form a line to buy it.

PRICE AND QUALITY

Ignoring fashion and egos, elements that make one wine more expensive than another include high land prices (in Burgundy and California's Napa Valley, for example); ground that is expensive to work (such as the steep, rocky slopes of Priorato, in Spain); and low crop levels. The latter may occur because the vines are old (but give beautifully-flavored fruit), the soil is infertile, and the climate cool, or because the grower is pruning deliberately to limit the crop. Another factor that affects price is the grape variety: some, such as viognier and pinot noir, are temperamental; others, such as chardonnay, will do anything for anyone anywhere. And those are only the vineyard variables. Winemakers can increase their costs enormously by buying expensive, high-tech equipment and new French oak barrels annually, by maturing the wine in oak for a long time and aging it further in bottle, and by any number of other time-consuming, skill-demanding techniques. At the other end of the scale, especially in the southern hemisphere, there are areas where sunshine is plentiful, land is cheap to buy and cheap to work, vines are grown in such a way that they produce huge crops, and wines are made and sold within a matter of months.

restaurant wine lists

- Household generic names such as Chablis and Sancerre tend to have heavy markups. Cult wines, such as Cloudy Bay, are generally the most overpriced of all.

- Red Bordeaux, burgundy, and California wines also tend to be heavily marked up, but look out for the less famous burgundies, such as Auxey-Duresses, St.-Aubin, and St.-Romain.

- Riesling is the insider's bargain. Dry or medium dry, its acidity is an asset with food. Look to Austria, Germany, Alsace, Australia, and the US.

- Little-known wines are often the least greedily priced. Look for reds from Portugal, Italy, the Loire, Languedoc-Roussillon, and Rhône villages such as Lirac, Valréas, and Séguret.

- Alsace dry whites are seldom bargains, but are rarely extortionately priced either, and they tend to go well with food.

reading
the label

If you can master the art of reading a wine label, you'll know what kind of wine to expect in the bottle and be able to choose wine with more confidence.

what to look for

- **grape variety/varieties** If more than one, they are listed in order of importance in the blend.

- **region of origin** This might be small and specific, such as Brézème-Côtes du Rhône, or a large catchall that doesn't tell you much, like Southeast Australia.

- **property or producer name or brand name** Examples, in order, are Schloss Vollrads, Hunter's, and Jacob's Creek.

- **quality category** This includes any official classification, such as denominazione di origine controllata (DOC) or premier cru classé.

- **term indicating style** Seco or mousseux are examples.

- **alcohol content** This is a clue to how full-bodied the wine is.

Learning to read a wine label isn't quite as simple as it sounds – a bewildering amount of information is often squeezed on that small square of paper pasted on the bottle. If it's any consolation, I was floored recently by a wine called Enantio. Until I had established that enantio was an obscure north Italian red grape, I didn't know whether it was a brand name, the name of an estate, an individual vineyard, the producer's name, or, indeed, a grape variety. I would have enjoyed the wine anyway, but it was all the more interesting for knowing what it was, where it came from, and who, with such evident care, had made it.

PLACES OF ORIGIN AND GRAPES

While certain information has to appear on bottles (sometimes divided between front and back labels), there is no one convention for naming wines. The traditional European approach is to call them after the place from which they come (Chablis or Chianti Classico, for example), sometimes giving precedence to the actual property (Domaine Nom de Plume, or whatever). Producers in the New World broke the mold by naming wines varietally – they gave primacy to grape variety over geography and made words like chardonnay, cabernet, and shiraz common currency (these had the advantage of being easier to pronounce than many of Europe's regional names). Varietal wines were so successful that growers in some traditional European regions began to adopt the idea. The authorities in areas such as Burgundy and Bordeaux frown, not always effectively, on the naming of grape varieties on labels, but regions that reinvented themselves in the 1990s, such as Vins de Pay d'Oc and Puglia, use them to great effect.

Another sign of the success of New World wines is the trend to name Old World wines in a way that disguises their origins and makes them sound like New World wines – ranging from gimmicky puns and slang to names that have an, often spurious, local reference (Ridge-this, Gully-that, and Creek-the-other). While there is nothing wrong with many of the names, hiding the wines' true geographical origins in the smallest legal type-size seems a retrograde step.

bottles and closures

Choosing a wine just by the bottle's shape or color was never very wise. Now that some New and Old World producers are ignoring the traditions, it really is necessary to read the label, too.

When Europe dominated the wine world, the shape of the bottle, and sometimes its color, was a useful indication as to the kind of wine it contained. Bordeaux (red, dry white, or sweet) came in a high-shouldered bottle, with clear glass used for Sauternes; red and white burgundy, Rhône wines, and Sancerre came in a wider, sloping-shouldered shape; German and Alsace wines came in tall, slim bottles, with Germany's Rhine wines in brown glass. The classic wine regions still respect these shapes, by and large, and many New World producers use Bordeaux-style bottles for their cabernets and merlots and burgundy-style bottles for their chardonnays and pinot noirs.

But not necessarily. Shiraz and unoaked chardonnay can be found in Bordeaux-style bottles, and Australian rieslings in Bordeaux, burgundy, and tall, slim bottles. The picture has also been clouded by producers all over the world splurging out on extra-tall bottles to indicate expensive, ambitious wines, and by the appearance of the increasingly popular so-called flanged ("lipped") bottles.

Even the way bottles are sealed has changed. Because of problems with corks (*see* Wine Faults, *page 73*), synthetic corks are making inroads into the mass market for wines not intended to be aged. For the same reason, some quality-oriented producers, notably riesling-makers in Australia's Clare Valley, are using screw caps. Other producers, especially in California and Austria, have dispensed with capsules (foil) on their bottles on environmental grounds, some of them replacing the capsules with wax discs.

Below, from left to right: sloping-shouldered burgundy bottle; high-shouldered Bordeaux bottles – clear glass is used for sweet wines; flanged and tapered bottles from the New World; tall white wine bottles from the Rhine in Germany (brown glass) and Alsace (green).

Varietal wines were so **successful** that growers in some traditional **European** regions began to adopt the **idea**.

label information

Since wines are named in different ways, there is no one formula for reading all labels, but here are some useful models.

GERMANY

vintage (year of harvest)

from the village of Deidesheim

from the Mäushöhle vineyard in Deidesheim

Produce of Germany

L. A.P.Nr. 5 106 044 26 99 — Entwurf Franz v. Stuck 1887

1998er Deidesheimer Mäushöhle
Riesling Spätlese halbtrocken
Qualitätswein mit Prädikat · Gutsabfüllung
PFALZ
750 ml — Weingut Reichsrat von Buhl GmbH · D-67146 Deidesheim — alc. 12.5%vol.

AP number (given to the wine when it is officially approved)

grape variety

late-picked grapes

region

bottled at the estate, a useful indication of quality

quality category (QmP): wines made from grapes of superior ripeness

AUSTRALIA (SPARKLING)

French term for dry, used for sparkling wines

name of producer

vintage (year of harvest)

grape variety

SEAVIEW
BRUT
CHARDONNAY
Vintage Reserve
BLANC DE BLANCS
TRADITIONAL METHOD

1996

recognized term for sparkling wine made in the same way as champagne

white wine made from white grapes only

vintage: the wine of a single harvest, as opposed to a blend of years. Reserve: no legal definition, so it means whatever the producer wants it to mean

FRANCE

name of estate

region of origin

classification (appellation contrôlée, or AC) in the French wine hierarchy

PRODUCE OF FRANCE
DOMAINE J.M. BROCARD
CHABLIS
APPELLATION CHABLIS CONTRÔLÉE
VIEILLES VIGNES
Mis en bouteille au domaine
J.M. BROCARD, Vigneron à Préhy 89800 Chablis France

13% vol. — 750 ml

alcohol content

old vines: in theory an indication of quality, but the term is unregulated

name of grower

bottled at the domaine (not always as clear-cut as here, because some cooperatives can use the term)

contents of bottle

address of grower

half-dry, or medium-dry (due to be replaced by Classic and Selection)

name of wine (or brand name)

vintage (year of harvest)

ITALY

region of origin (Langhe). Rosso simply means it's a red wine

classification (DOC)

made from barbera grapes in vineyards at Austri and San Fereolo, and bottled by the Azienda Agricola San Fereolo in Dogliani

Brumaio
1997
Langhe Rosso
Denominazione di Origine Controllata
Prodotto con uve Barbera provenienti dalle vigne degli Austri e di San Fereolo e imbottigliato dall'Azienda Agricola San Fereolo - Dogliani Italia
75 cl — L 3.99 — 14% vol
www.italywines.com
NON DISPERDERE IL VETRO NELL'AMBIENTE

contents of bottle and European Union's "e" mark

in effect, "Don't dispose of this bottle carelessly"

lot number: the official code that reveals when the wine was bottled. It is obligatory for all wines sold in the European Union

SPAIN

name of wine (or brand name)

wine aged in both oak barrels and bottle in accordance with the Rioja rules

alcohol content and contents of bottle

GLORIOSO
RIOJA
DENOMINACIÓN DE ORIGEN CALIFICADA
RESERVA
1996
PRODUCTO DE ESPAÑA
BODEGAS PALACIO
CASA FUNDADA EN 1894
13% vol. 750 ml

region of origin and its classification (denominación de origen calificada, or DOCa)

name of producer (bodega means winery or cellar) and, underneath, the date it was established

vintage (year of harvest)

CHILE

vintage (year of harvest)

name of producer (in effect, the brand name)

1999
ERRAZURIZ
CASABLANCA VALLEY
Wild Ferment
CHARDONNAY
75cl.
PRODUCED AND BOTTLED BY VIÑA ERRAZURIZ
PRODUCT OF CHILE
14.0% vol.

contents of bottle

region of origin

a wine made using the naturally present yeasts, rather than cultured yeasts

grape variety

AUSTRALIA

vintage (year of harvest)

name of producer

region of origin

legal requirements: producer's name and address, country of origin, contents of bottle, and alcohol content

VINTAGE 1990
EST 1844
Penfolds
BIN 128
COONAWARRA
SHIRAZ
This wine is made from lighter style Shiraz grown at Penfolds Coonawarra Vineyards. It has a distinct bouquet and characteristic soft fruit flavour for which Coonawarra is renowned. This vintage is ready to drink now and will improve with further bottle age.
PRODUCED BY PENFOLDS WINES PTY. LTD, TANUNDA ROAD, NURIOOTPA, AUSTRALIA 5355
PRODUCT OF AUSTRALIA • 750ML • ALCOHOL 13.0% BY VOLUME

name of wine by bin number, a traditional Australian way of distinguishing winery batches, but now usually just a brand name

grape variety

producer's description – more useful than many such descriptions

origin & quality

European wine countries categorize their wines as follows, with the best at the top of each list, going down to basic table wine.

FRANCE
- Appellation Contrôlée (AC or AOC)
- Vin Délimité de Qualité Supérieur (VDQS)
- Vin de Pays
- Vin de Table

ITALY
- Denominazione di Origine Controllata e Garantita (DOCG)
- Denominazione di Origine Controllata (DOC)
- Indicazione Geografica Tipica (IGT)
- Vino da Tavola

SPAIN
- Denominación de Origen Calificada (DOCa)
- Denominación de Origen (DO)
- Vino de la Tierra
- Vino da Mesa

PORTUGAL
- Denominação de Origem Controlada (DOC)
- Indicação de Proveniência Regulamentada (IPR)
- Vinho Regional (VR)
- Vinho de Mesa

GERMANY
- Qualitätswein mit Prädikat (QmP)
- Qualitätswein bestimmter Anbaugebiete (QbA)
- Landwein
- Tafelwein

the language
of labels

Wine labels provide a wealth of useful information about what's in the bottle, but you need to know the precise meaning of the terms that are used.

aged with oak/in contact with oak Could mean aged in barrel, but more likely to be aged much more cheaply in tanks with oak chips or staves.

almacenista Sherry from a small, private producer.

barrel/barrique fermented, or barrel selection If the words barrel or barrique are used, it means that the wine has been fermented or matured in a barrel, rather than given its oak flavor via cheap oak chips or staves.

basket pressed Traditional, circular, wooden basket presses are supposed to be gentler on the grapes.

bin Traditional Australian way of identifying a particular batch of wine (as in "Bin 52"); now often just a brand name.

biologique French word for organic.

blanc de blancs/noirs Champagne or still white wine made entirely from white/black grapes.

botrytis Made from botrytis-affected grapes and therefore lusciously sweet.

bush vines Untrained vines – implies vines of some age and therefore quality.

carbonic maceration Method for making fruity wines to drink young.

cava Sparkling wine made in Spain using the same methods as for champagne.

classic Meaningless term, except in Germany where it is a new term for dry wine.

classico As in "Soave Classico" – the heartland, and traditionally the best part, of an Italian DOC(G).

contains sulphites/contains preservative (220) All labels in the US must carry the former phrase; those in Australia must state additives used, such as 220 (sulfur dioxide).

crianza Spanish wine aged for at least two years (if red), partly in oak.

cru French term literally meaning "growth" and indicating a wine from a superior site or subregion. For example, the best Beaujolais are those from the 10 crus, such as Fleurie.

cru bourgeois A classification of Médoc châteaux below the ranks of cru classé. Cru grand bourgeois exceptionnel is the highest rank of cru bourgeois.

cru classé "Classed growth" – wines ranked as the best in various Bordeaux classifications, but most notably Médoc.

cuvée Often used in conjunction with another word (*see below*), but on its own simply means a particular batch of wine.

cuvée spéciale/personelle/réserve Implies something special (and more expensive), but can mean whatever the producer chooses.

dry grown Unirrigated vines – mostly used to imply old vines and therefore quality.

élevé en futs de chêne Aged in oak barrels.

erstes gewächs "First growth" – a top vineyard in Germany's Rheingau region.

espumante/espumoso Sparkling (Portugal/Spain, respectively).

estate bottled Bottled at the place where the grapes were grown and the wine was made; implies quality.

fûts neufs New barrels (adds to the flavor – and the cost).

garrafeira Portuguese wine from a superior vintage aged at least two years in oak.

grand cru Top individual vineyards of Burgundy, Champagne, and Alsace (superior to premier cru).

grand cru classé St.-Emilion, the second division, below premier grand cru classé.

grande cuvée Implies a top batch of wine, but usage is unregulated.

grand vin Mostly used in Bordeaux for the best wine of a château, the wine that takes the château's name; an unregulated term.

gran reserva Spanish wine from a superior vintage aged five years (if red), at least two of them in oak.

gutsabfüllung Rigorously regulated, estate-bottled German wine (due to replace the less rigorous Erzeugerabfüllung).

late harvest Implies extra-ripe grapes and usually sweet wine.

lees Dead yeast matter that enriches wine flavor and texture, and also keeps the wine fresh (as in "aged on its lees," or "lees stirred regularly").

malolactic A fermentation that has an acid-softening effect.

méthode classique/ traditionnelle/metodo classico Sparkling wine made in the same way as champagne.

mis en bouteille au château/domaine/à la propriété Estate-bottled – implies quality and individuality, but can be a wine made and bottled at a cooperative and named after the estate the grapes came from.

mousseux Sparkling (France).

new oak/barrels Adds to the flavor – and the cost.

oak aged/matured May be aged in barrels, but *see also* "aged with oak."

old vines See "vieilles vignes."

petit chablis Lesser Chablis from the outlying area.

petit château Unofficial name for thousands of unclassified Bordeaux châteaux.

premier cru The top-ranked châteaux of the Médoc, Graves, and Sauternes (although there is a single grand premier cru in Sauternes); but, in Burgundy and Champagne, premier cru vineyards, confusingly, come second after grand cru.

prestige cuvée See "cuvée spéciale."

récoltant manipulant (RM) A grower who makes his own champagne, as opposed to a big champagne house (NM) or a cooperative (CM).

reserva Spanish wine aged for three years (if red), at least one year in oak; in Portugal, implies special quality, but unregulated.

réserve/reserve As in "Réserve Personnelle" or "Private/Family/Winemaker's Reserve" – an almost wholly unregulated term meaning whatever the proprietor/winemaker chooses. Washington State is the only significant region to define the word Reserve, applying it to wines of exceptional quality.

riserva Italian DOC or DOCG wine specially aged in accordance with DOC rules.

sekt Sparkling (Germany).

selection New term for top dry German wine. Otherwise, Selection, as in "Sélection Spéciale," "Private Selection," and so on, is as meaningless as Réserve.

sélection de grains nobles Very sweet Alsace wines made from botrytized grapes.

show reserve Supposedly superior Australian wine, but can mean anything the winemaker chooses.

solera System of gradual blending during the aging of sherry.

spumante Sparkling (Italy).

supérieur Usually means nothing more than slightly higher alcohol than the straight appellation contrôlée wine.

superiore Theoretically, a wine of superior quality (Italy).

sur lie Kept on its lees (dead yeasts) until bottling to give the wine, above all Muscadet, extra zip and freshness.

unfiltered/non-filtré Fashionable term to describe wine that has been minimally treated and processed.

vendange tardive A sweet (not botrytis) wine, especially Alsace and Jurançon.

vieilles vignes Old vines imply quality, but there's no definition of old. It might be 15, 50, or 100 years.

villages Wines from the better part of the region, as in Mâcon-Villages or Beaujolais-Villages.

vintage Year of harvest – can be good or bad, except when referring to vintage champagne or vintage port, which are supposed to be made in good years only.

wild ferment/yeast Wild yeasts can give more complex flavors to wine than cultured yeasts.

dry & sweet

abboccato between medium dry and medium sweet (Italy)

amabile medium sweet (Italy)

brut very dry (champagne)

classic dry (Germany)

demi-sec medium dry (but more like medium sweet in champagne)

doce, dolce, & dulce sweet (Portugal, Italy, and Spain, respectively)

doux medium sweet or sweet (France)

extra dry dry (champagne; not as dry as brut)

halbtrocken medium dry (Germany; being phased out)

liquoureux very sweet (France)

moelleux sweet (France)

sec, secco, & seco dry (France, Italy, and Portugal and Spain, respectively)

selection dry (Germany)

semi-seco medium dry (Spain)

trocken dry (Germany; being phased out)

vin doux naturel very sweet with high alcohol (France)

(For the sweetness/ripeness classification of German and Austrian wines, *see pages 192 and 193*.)

Whether you maintain a wine cellar or not, every glass you drink will benefit from being served as its makers intended.

1911

storing & serving wine

keep the best
& enjoy the rest

One of the great and enduring myths is that wine improves with keeping. A small proportion does, but most is best drunk sooner rather than later.

The vast majority of wines today are made to be drunk within a year or two of the vintage. Not only that but they are perfectly ready the minute they appear for sale. Some may last happily for four or five years, but very few will actually taste better and more interesting for the wait.

It wasn't always like this, of course. In the past, more wine was made with cellars in mind. Wine was also made differently because it had to be. Grapes were picked less ripe, with more astringent acid and tannin, because there wasn't the understanding, and even less the technology, to cope with riper, more sugar-rich fruit. The wines produced from these "greener" grapes needed aging to soften their tannins and more rasping acidity. Nowadays, temperature-controlled fermentation equipment is commonplace, as is a better knowledge of the processes and potential pitfalls. European wines can be made in a softer, riper, fuller style for immediate consumption, while most New World wines, coming from warmer climates, are naturally in that style. And that's how we like our wines: tastes have changed alongside technology.

IDENTIFYING WINES TO KEEP

If most wines are not designed to last more than a few years, that still leaves a high-quality minority that will improve and deserves to be cellared. Sometimes the back labels on wine bottles advise on aging potential, but, in the absence of any such help, the best initial guide to which wines can and can't be kept is price.

Inexpensive wines simply aren't made to be kept: they won't have the concentration of flavor and tannin or acid to last, let alone evolve. The cheapest whites and rosés should be consumed within a year of the vintage, and the cheapest reds within two years. Nonvintage wine (which is undated on the label) should be drunk as soon as possible. The exception is good nonvintage champagne, which can benefit from a year or two's extra aging. Cheap nonvintage champagne and almost all other sparkling wines are at their best within months of purchase.

Overall, more **red wines** than **whites** reward **cellaring**; reds take **longer** to **reach** their **peak** and **stay** there longer.

Mid-priced wines generally last longer, but most don't keep more than five years, and many of the whites will taste better at two or three years. This is particularly true of sauvignon blanc, viognier, New World chardonnay, semillon, and torrontes.

The core of any cellar inevitably ends up being relatively expensive wines, but that's not to suggest that all expensive wines benefit from extended aging: some don't. Dry white wines made from the viognier grape can be superlative and very expensive – Condrieu, for example – but viognier is low in acid and loses its heady perfume and voluptuous fruit within a few years, without developing layers of other flavors to compensate. Similarly, sauvignon blanc, despite its natural high acid, rarely develops more complex flavors with age. Its charm, and sometimes its considerable quality, is in its vibrant acidity and vivid, youthful fruit. Even chardonnay isn't a long keeper, except for the finest white burgundies.

AGING RED WINES

Not all high-priced reds benefit from prolonged aging either. Pinot noir is rarely long-lived. Top-level burgundy is the exception, but even so it doesn't have the longevity of red Bordeaux. And merlot is not as long-lived as cabernet sauvignon. The red wine picture is also increasingly being skewed by new wines with no track record, especially from the New World but also from the Bordeaux garagistes (*see page 167*), being marketed at very ambitious prices. We can make an assessment, from tasting, about how they may mature, especially if we're familiar with the vineyards, grape varieties, the winemaker, and his cellar, but that's not the same as having experience of a succession of vintages.

Overall, more red wines than whites reward cellaring; reds take longer to reach their peak and stay there longer. (In fact, talking about a wine's peak is rather misleading: it's more of an extended plateau of maturity.) Furthermore, there are more Old World wines that improve with age and last well than there are New World wines. But, as New World producers increasingly push out into cooler regions to find naturally higher acid and tannin levels, they are sure to produce more ageworthy wines. It's already more than possible to build up an exciting cellar exclusively of New World wines – and even one devoted entirely to New World white wines. The one color likely to be conspicuous by its absence from any long-term cellar, New or Old World, is pink: almost no rosés benefit from age.

VINTAGE AND BOTTLE SIZE

Another crucial consideration is vintage. If you are laying down wine, you should buy superior vintages, rather than mediocre, unless you know that a producer has outperformed the average. There is guidance on good and bad years in the section on the world's wines (*see pages 162–217*), and there are more detailed charts in wine lists and magazines. It is also worth knowing that the ideal bottle size for maturing wine is a magnum (1.5 l, or equal to two standard bottles): with a smaller proportion of air to wine, the wine ages more slowly. Half-bottles, with their greater percentage of air to wine, are less satisfactory cellar candidates than bottles because the wine ages more quickly.

white wines to keep

austrian grüner veltliner
Can be drunk young, but the top wines, especially from the Wachau, Kremstal, and Kamptal regions, age like riesling and can easily be kept 8–10 years.

chardonnay
From the New World: only the very best from cooler regions and higher altitudes, such as Santa Barbara and Carneros in California; Adelaide Hills, Margaret River, Yarra Valley, and Tasmania in Australia; South Africa; and New Zealand. Think in terms of five years; more is a bonus.

graves & pessac–léognan
Only the best and in top vintages. Drink at between six and 12 years, occasionally more.

hunter valley semillon
Traditional, unoaked Hunter semillon, thin and sharp when young, becomes deliciously toasty and honeyed (yet dry) from about five years of age, and can last up to 20 years.

loire chenin blanc
The very sweet, botrytized wines from the Coteaux du Layon region (including Bonnezeaux and Quarts de Chaume), and from Vouvray and Montlouis, as well as dry and demi-sec Vouvray and Montlouis from top producers; and the rare, dry Savennières. The Loire is very vintage-sensitive, but the top wines, especially the sweet ones, are very long-lived – 10, 20, sometimes more years.

riesling
Dry or sweet, this is one of the longest-lived and most undervalued wines. Germany, Alsace, Austria, the Clare and Eden valleys in Australia, and New Zealand all make rieslings to last eight years or more, but they can also be drunk young. With German wines, choose traditional, lightly sweet to very sweet styles (Kabinett, Spätlese, and so on) or Selection (dry). New-wave German wines, with nontraditional bottles and names, are not for keeping.

sauternes & barsac
Plus the best of outlying regions such as Monbazillac, Ste-Croix du Mont, and Saussignac. In a good vintage, the best should be kept 8–15 years.

tokaji aszú
The sweeter the Tokaji (that is, the higher the puttonyos) the longer the wine will keep. Even a 5 putts wine should keep 10 years.

white burgundy
From both the Côte d'Or and Chablis: don't expect anything below premier cru level to keep more than five years, unless you know otherwise; a grand cru will usually be at its best between five and 10 years. Burgundy is very vintage-sensitive, so keep an eye on vintage charts.

red wines to keep

australian reds
The more expensive shiraz, cabernet sauvignon, and blends are often excellent at 7–8 years and may last much longer.

barolo & barbaresco
These wines are ready to drink earlier than they used to be, but are still long-lived. A good vintage deserves 10 years.

brunello di montalcino & bolgheri
These and other expensive Tuscan reds often need at least five years, and can last many more.

cahors & madiran
Buy from top producers only. Both areas are more vintage-sensitive than sometimes thought. Think in terms of five years minimum.

californian cabernet sauvignon
The best may be good at four years, and better after six, eight, or even 10 years. But remember, we're only talking about a tiny minority of wines.

red bordeaux
Crus bourgeois (see page 167) are usually at their best at 4–7 years; most classed growths start to be ready at about seven years, but the very best should be given 10 or more years. Never keep cheap Bordeaux or modest vintages.

red burgundy
Even in good vintages, most village wines (that is, non-cru) are ready within 3–4 years; most premiers crus can be broached at five years; and most grands crus are perfect to drink from around seven or eight years.

rhône
Hermitage, Côte-Rôtie, and Cornas are very long-lived and usually need a minimum of eight years. Châteauneuf-du-Pape is ready sooner, but the best easily last 10–12 years.

ribera del duero & priorato
Concentrated Spanish reds that age well (unless joven or sin crianza). Think of 6–10 years; the best even longer.

rioja gran reserva
These wines are usually ready when released, five or six years after the vintage, but the best will continue to develop for many more years.

vintage port
A minimum of 10 years' age, preferably more, is needed for vintage port, and it should last decades. Single quinta port is often released ready to drink, at around 13 or 14 years, but will usually keep another six or seven years.

zinfandel
This grape is a long-keeper only from exceptional producers and even then should generally be drunk within eight years of the vintage.

storing wines

It's hard to overestimate the importance of good storage conditions, but don't let that discourage you if you haven't got a traditional subterranean cellar.

Knowing the perfect conditions for wine is simple enough. The hard part is achieving them, sometimes even in underground and custom-built cellars. In the average home, the temperature requirement is usually the most problematic. The ideal is between 45–59° F (7–15° C). At lower temperatures, the wine will come to no harm; as long as it doesn't freeze (expanding, and forcing out its cork) it will merely mature at a slower rate.

The problems come at higher temperatures. Think of 68° F (20° C) as the upper limit, but don't panic about a

degree or two over that, especially for medium and full-bodied red wines. The wines with the most delicate constitution tend to be sparkling wines (including champagne); light-bodied (lowish-alcohol) whites; full-bodied, low-acid whites (made from the viognier grape, for example); rosés; inexpensive wines of all kinds that are intended to be drunk relatively young anyway; and old wines (which, like people and furniture, become more fragile with age). Clearly, it doesn't make sense to subject any valuable wines to the average central-heating temperature of 70° F (21° C)

If you don't have anywhere suitable for long-term wine storage, one option is to rent space in a merchant's cellar.

You should **watch** for any **traces** of **seepage** from the **cork** or **capsule**.

for any length of time; and even less to the heat of the average kitchen (no matter how stylish those wine racks look). The thing to bear in mind when storing wine at higher-than-ideal temperatures is that it will age more quickly than the label, the seller, or vintage charts suggest – the higher the temperature, the faster the rate.

EXTREME TEMPERATURES

The other vital element is constancy. Fluctuating temperatures can be very damaging – and it's all too easy to underestimate them. It doesn't have to be much of a heatwave to push all but the darkest, north-facing rooms up to 86° F (30° C). Even an area under the stairs can warm up considerably, and sheds and garages (especially with large metal doors) can be disastrous, plunging below freezing in winter and soaring in the summer. If you want to keep wine in a shed or an attic, you will need insulation; and the same applies to any basement that also houses a furnace. Perhaps an area under the stairs, an alcove, or an unused fireplace on a north-facing wall would prove more suitable, after all. Wherever you choose, a basic thermometer is well worth the modest outlay. You should also watch for any traces of seepage from the cork or capsule – a sign that the wine has gotten too warm and, just as the cork has let wine out, it is now letting air, the enemy, in.

Humidity is also important, which is why European growers often take such pride in the accumulated layers of mold lining their cellars. In too dry an atmosphere, corks dry out, letting air in. The drying effect of air-conditioning can be a problem, but central heating usually is not, although it's good practice to put the occasional bowl of water near your wine racks. The only problem with excessive humidity is that it destroys labels, leaving you to conduct unanticipated blind tastings.

So far as movement is concerned, vibrations are best avoided – certainly for wine with a sediment. This is one of the reasons it is not advisable to keep wine for long in a refrigerator – another is the lack of humidity. But it has to be said that the often priceless wines kept by generations of famous British wine merchants under London's railroad arches don't seem to be adversely affected by vibrations from trains.

OTHER HAZARDS

Light, especially ultraviolet and sunlight, is bad for wine – aging and oxidizing it prematurely (that's why so many wines come in dark bottles) – but light doesn't usually present a problem at home. You can always use a blind, or cover your wine racks with a blanket.

When it comes to odors, you don't need to worry about everyday cooking smells or the hamster's cage, but you do need to keep wine clear of the kind of strong-smelling chemical products often present in a garage or workshop.

If it's impossible to find somewhere suitable to keep wine, probably the cheapest solution is to rent storage space with a reputable wine merchant. Other options are building a cellar, possibly the cylindrical type that comes as a kit and is sunk 7–10 ft (2–3 m) into the ground, or buying one or more special temperature- and humidity-controlled wine cabinets. Self-storage units may also be rented, but be sure to check temperature variability carefully.

Bizarre though they look, layers of mold in a wine cellar indicate a desirably high level of humidity.

lying down or standing?

- **Lying** You won't go wrong if you follow the long-accepted wisdom that bottles should be stored horizontally so that the corks don't dry out and let in air.

- **Standing** Champagne can be cellared equally well standing (because of the pressure inside the bottles). Wines with synthetic corks don't need to be kept lying down – and possibly shouldn't be until more studies have been done on what happens to them over the long term.

- **Lying at an angle** It has been suggested that, for wines that may be subjected to temperature fluctuations, probably the best position for the bottle is lying with the neck pointing up slightly, so that both the wine and the pocket of air touch the cork. But until wine-rack design changes, this is not very practical.

A foil cutter neatly removes the top of the capsule. Most "waiter's friend" corkscrews (*see below*) have a blade for the same purpose.

The hinged part of a "waiter's friend" corkscrew fits onto the top of the bottle and the cork is levered out. The disadvantage of these is that they pull the cork out at an angle.

serving wines

Efficient equipment, serving wine at the appropriate temperature, and choosing the right wine for the occasion all play their part in enjoyment of wine.

It's possible to spend an alarming amount of time and money on wine paraphernalia, but don't be persuaded that you need to. After all, the only essential for opening a bottle of wine in a civilized way is a corkscrew – and the only essential for drinking it, in an equally civilized way, is a glass. Some corkscrews and glasses are better than others, but that's about as far as it goes.

OPENING THE BOTTLE

Any corkscrew with a screw, or worm, with the sharp edge and solid core of an ordinary hardware screw is liable to grind and break the cork, especially a crumbly, old one. The best corkscrews ease the cork out vertically and have an open, smooth-surfaced spiral. For pulling real corks, teflon-coated spirals are a great boon, but they work less well with the new synthetic ("plastic") corks, which have a habit of getting stuck on them. "Waiter's friend" pocket corkscrews are better for synthetic corks, but they can break real corks because they lever the cork out at an angle. If a cork does break, and you can't get it out, the simple solution is to push it into the bottle before pouring the wine.

A foil cutter for removing the capsule is a useful, if not essential, device. But no matter how you remove the capsule, it's a good idea to wipe any dust or sediment from the top of the bottle before you pour (a dampened paper towel is preferable to a well-used dish towel). Brushes on the end of corkscrews are there to remove cellar dust from the bottle – relics of an age when a butler was there to do it for you.

Champagne corks can be removed with a special star-shaped gripping device: I always use one, but you don't actually require anything to open the bottle – except the utmost care, since corks can fly out with surprising force.

Opening a champagne bottle is made easier by this device, which wedges on to the cork and grips it as you turn it or the bottle.

The best **corkscrews**
ease the cork out
vertically and have
an **open**, smooth-
surfaced **spiral**.

① **FOIL AND WIRE** Remove the foil. Hold the bottle at 45 degrees, pointed in a safe direction. Untwist the wire cage, keeping the cork in with your thumb. As you remove the cage, keep your hand over the top of the bottle.

② **REMOVING THE CORK** Gently twist and ease out the cork (in theory, you're supposed to hold the cork and twist the bottle, so that there's no possibility of breaking the cork, but it's not easy to do).

Once you have removed the cork of your champagne (*see above*), hold the bottle at an angle of 45 degrees until you are sure it's not going to froth over. Similarly, when you pour, the champagne is less likely to froth over if you tilt the glass toward the bottle; a finger placed lightly on the rim of the glass will help stop it overflowing if you are caught off guard.

BUYING GLASSES

Glass shape can make or break a wine. You can even buy glasses designed to show specific wines and grape varieties at their best, but it certainly isn't necessary to do so. You don't even need a different type for white and red wines. A good all-purpose glass has a stem, so that you don't mull the wine with your hands, has a generously sized, tulip-shaped bowl that tapers slightly to the top, and is made of fine, plain, colorless glass, so that you can see what you're drinking. Ideally, glasses should be poured no more than a third full; but, if they're on the small side, you may have to go to half-full.

Champagne deserves taller, slimmer flutes to preserve the bubbles (not a bubble-destroying coupe or saucer shape). Good sherry deserves a traditional copita, a small version of the ideal wine glass, and a copita can also be used for drinking port.

WASHING GLASSES

Like wine, glasses need to be well looked after. Use hot water and the minimum of detergent to wash them, and don't be afraid to use the dishwasher, preferably without any

A cloth wrapped around the handle of a wooden spoon will help to dry the insides of narrow glasses – if not done too forcefully.

rinsing agent and not in the company of greasy plates and pans. As soon as the cycle has finished, open the door so that the glasses don't sit in the steam. Linen cloths, rather than cotton, are best for drying – wound around the handle of a wooden spoon if necessary to reach the bottom of the glass. Store glasses upright in cupboards; otherwise, they'll smell stale when you come to use them. If they haven't been used for a while, they'll need washing anyway.

AERATION

An awful lot of – doubtless very enjoyable – effort has been expended on trying to find out whether wine needs to "breathe" (to aerate it), and whether it should be decanted. As there have been no incontrovertible conclusions, no doubt a lot more selfless effort will go into the study of it in future. I fully intend to do my part. What is unarguable is that opening a bottle to let the wine breathe commits you to drinking it, but makes very little difference to the wine, because far too little is in direct contact with the air.

It's easy to be persuaded to buy more sizes and shapes of glass than you really need. A good basic trio is a generously sized, all-purpose glass for reds and whites (*left*); a large copita for sherry, port, and, at a pinch, white wine (*below*); and a flute for sparkling wine (*right*).

Advocates of decanting believe that the wine exposed to air in this way undergoes an aroma-enhancing, softening, mini-maturation process. The arguments against decanting are that the same aerating process will take place anyway once the wine has been poured into the glass, or, simply that the effect is negligible. My own view is that decanting can help to "open up" high-quality, concentrated, young wines – sometimes even white wines such as burgundy – and it can help to soften rather tannic, young reds, such as Barolo, Ribera del Duero, and Californian cabernet sauvignon.

SEDIMENT

The other reason for decanting is to relieve red wine, or port, of its sediment before it lands in anyone's glass. Cheap wines and mass-market brands are usually filtered so that they won't throw a sediment, but the trend for wines with any pretensions to quality is to filter lightly, if at all. Some grape varieties, such as pinot noir and grenache, throw little sediment, but grapes that produce

dark, full-bodied wines, such as cabernet sauvignon, syrah/shiraz, and brunello, can start to throw a sediment in as little as three years. Sometimes labels warn of the likelihood of sediment, or say "unfiltered" or "non-filtré," but often you're on your own and must make a judgment based on the wine's age, quality, type, and what you can see through the bottle with a light shining behind it. If the wine has been lying down, it's usually quite easy to see the sediment lying on the underside, often near the shoulder, if you hold the bottle up to the light (keeping it horizontal, of course).

A good light – a flashlight, candle, or spotlight – is also essential for the decanting process itself, together with a steady hand and something to decant into. It's not difficult to do, provided you've already maneuvered the sediment to the right place by standing the bottle upright for 36 hours or more in advance. When you pour, take it slowly and steadily, and be prepared to sacrifice some wine at the bottom of the bottle – you may need to sacrifice 1–1½ in (3–4 cm). Young wine can be decanted well in advance, but very old wines should be decanted near to the serving time because their aromas and flavors may start to fade quite quickly.

SERVING RED WINES

There is no single correct temperature at which to serve any wine – among other things, it may well depend on the season. But it's a fact that a lot of wines are served at temperatures that don't do them justice. And I'm talking almost

When decanting, any sediment will gradually slide to the neck of the bottle. Use a strong light to catch the moment, then stop pouring.

exclusively about red wines. Whites and rosés are sometimes numbed into aromaless submission by overzealous chilling; and on other occasions, especially crowded ones, white wines sometimes end up too warm. But red wines are habitually served too warm, by people, including restaurateurs, who take the the traditional diktat of "room temperature" too literally, instead of thinking of the old-fashioned, non-centrally heated room temperatures that were originally meant.

Today's average room temperature of 70° F (21° C) is higher than is good for all but the fullest-bodied, oaky New World red wines – and even most of those would be better at 64° F (18° C). Medium-bodied classic reds, such as Bordeaux, should be slightly cooler, and pinot noirs (including burgundy) a little cooler again. Beaujolais, light-bodied reds, and fuller-bodied reds made in a modern, soft, low-tannin style, can be served cool. Half an hour to an hour in the fridge, depending on the setting of the fridge and the temperature of the bottle when it goes in, will probably cool most such red wines sufficiently, but if you want a quick result, use a bucket of iced water.

SERVING WHITE WINES

Iced water is also the most efficient way of cooling white wine, unless you have one of the functional six-minute chillers that you keep in the freezer and then slip over the bottle when required. Porches and balconies can come in useful in the winter, and you can also chill wine in the freezer, but it's a messy business if you forget it and the wine freezes, expands, and breaks its bottle. (Similarly, you can raise the temperature of a cold red wine in a microwave, but it's absolutely essential to get the timing correct. I tend to rely on the simpler option of immersion in a bucket of tepid or, at a pinch, lukewarm water.)

White wines should be served at between 43–52° F (6–11° C), which is useful to know if you have a wine thermometer. I don't, or at least I don't use one. A more useful guide is to know that cheap and/or light-bodied whites and rosés (including many Italian and German whites and Muscadet) should be served at the cooler end of the range. So should most sparkling whites and rosés, but vintage champagne and Australian sparkling red shouldn't be too heavily chilled.

Fuller-bodied whites (including white burgundy and high-quality New World chardonnays) should be served toward the higher end of the range. Sauvignon, riesling, other aromatic, unoaked whites, and manzanilla and fino sherries should be somewhere in the middle. If anything, start to serve with the temperature lower, rather than higher, because any wine will warm up in the glass (unless you're drinking in the cellar).

WINES AND FOODS
The order in which you serve a succession of wines – or just two – will depend to a large extent on the food, but there is a convention, based on the logic of not allowing any wine to be overwhelmed by the one preceding it. Light-bodied wine is served before heavy (that is, strong or full-bodied), dry wine comes before sweet, and white wine is drunk before red – except that the rules have always been challenged. Classic rule-breakers include unctuous,

A lukewarm white wine is never any pleasure – hence these champagne and wine chillers, used straight from the freezer.

sweet wine such as Sauternes as a partner for foie gras and other rich liver pâtés; sherry served with soup; Sancerre accompanying goats' cheeses; and feather-light Asti or other fizzy moscato with desserts. If you use bread and/or water as palate-clearers, and leave a judicious pause between courses, these wines won't pose any insuperable problems. A German wine with a fish course would probably suffer after Sauternes and foie gras, but a good chardonnay or a Chablis would be full-bodied enough to cope. A delicate, old claret served with lamb might also suffer after Sauternes, so it might be an occasion to serve a Coonawarra cabernet or a younger claret instead.

SUITING THE OCCASION
Food is not the only consideration: season, time of day, and occasion can all point you in particular directions. A 14.5 percent-alcohol zinfandel is not often the best of lunchtime wines, nor the best wine to serve to someone who normally only drinks fairly neutral Italian whites; Vinho Verde can lose its appeal on a cold winter's evening; and the backyard on a summer's day is not a good place to serve a venerable bottle – its precious aromas will waft away in no time. Something like a New Zealand sauvignon would be much more suitable.

LEFTOVER WINE
After years of testing gadgets designed to keep leftover wine in prime condition by protecting it from air, I've come to the conclusion that either they

don't work or they do not justify the effort or financial outlay, which leaves the simple bottle-in-the-fridge method. This involves nothing more taxing than pushing the cork back in the bottle and putting the bottle in the fridge.

If you have less than half a bottle of wine remaining, it's worth decanting the wine into a (scrupulously rinsed) half-bottle to exclude more air – and it's worth buying a half-bottle of wine for the purpose, if necessary. Most wines will keep quite well like this for two or three days, but, with red wine, you will need to remember to bring it back up to a suitable temperature. Some people freeze small quantities of leftover wine in containers such as ice trays, for eventual use in cooking.

The one wine-preserving gadget I do use is a sparkling-wine stopper. Sparkling wine keeps its bubbles quite well in the fridge unstoppered, but it does oxidize and pick up smells. As for silver teaspoons, use them for what they were intended; they do nothing to keep bubbles or freshness in sparkling wine.

In a fiercely competitive market, producers all over the world are vying for your attention with wines of ever higher quality.

the world's
wines

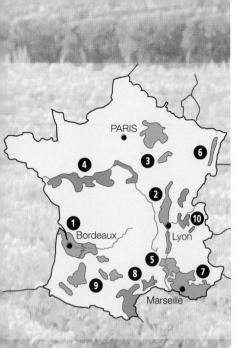

1. BORDEAUX
2. BURGUNDY
3. CHAMPAGNE
4. LOIRE VALLEY
5. RHÔNE VALLEY
6. ALSACE
7. PROVENCE
8. LANGUEDOC-ROUSSILLON
9. THE SOUTHWEST
10. JURA & SAVOIE

Right, clockwise from top:
meticulously maintained Bordeaux
vines; grape harvesting by hand;
Clos de Vougeot, one of Burgundy's
illustrious grand cru vineyards;
St.-Emilion, source of several of
the new "garage" wines.

france

French winegrowers have a unique variety of soils, microclimates, and grapes available to them, plus centuries of expertise in the art of making wine.

No matter what kind of wine you like to drink – Australian, New Zealand, Spanish, Italian – the chances are that in some way, at some time, its flavor has been influenced by the wines of France. The idea of aging wine in small barrels made from new oak originated in France, as did most of the grapes commonly found in wines from the New World – grapes such as chardonnay and cabernet sauvignon, merlot, syrah, and sauvignon blanc.

This is not to say that French wines are the best in the world. It isn't that simple. Wines at the very top level have a subtlety, complexity, and potential to improve with age that make them hard to beat, although they are occasionally, and increasingly, being equaled. Further down the scale, the classic French wine flavors can sometimes seem austere in comparison with their New World equivalents; although now even the most classic – not to say hidebound – of French regions are producing wines that are fresher and fruitier than in the past.

APPELLATIONS AND CLASSIFICATIONS

One of the things, ironically, that has sometimes held France back in recent years is its long-established and much copied, but somewhat inflexible, appellation contrôlée (AC) system. Appellation contrôlée, which you will find on the label of most of the top wines, is the highest category in French wine law. But it's not in itself a guarantee of quality: nearly all top French wines are AC, but not all AC wines are top-quality – in fact, nowhere near all. What appellation contrôlée is intended to guarantee is authenticity, by defining geographical origin, grape varieties, and some aspects of vine cultivation and winemaking.

As you go down the official list of categories, the regulations become progressively less strict. The small VDQS (vin delimité de qualité supérieur) category comes just below AC in its level of regulation. The popular and growing category of vin de pays is lower still, and has rules that are sufficiently relaxed to welcome some ambitious producers who want to experiment with styles outside the AC rules. Vin de table is the most basic category of all.

bordeaux

When English-speaking countries think of French wine, they tend to think first and foremost of Bordeaux, thanks to the region's long history of exporting wines to England.

Wine aging in expensive new oak at Château Ausone, a premier grand cru classé St.-Emilion.

recommended producers

Apart from the classified wines of each region, look out for the following (Ch = Château, Dom = Domaine):

Reds
Ch d'Aiguilhe, Ch d'Archambeau, Ch Canon (Canon-Fronsac), Ch Canon-de-Brem, Ch Carbonnieux, Ch la Dauphine, Ch la Grave (Fronsac), Ch Landiras, Ch Marsau, Ch Meyney, Ch les Ormes-de-Pez, Ch les Ormes-Sorbet, Ch de Pez, Ch Potensac, Ch Poujeaux, Ch Puygueraud, Ch Sociando-Mallet, Ch de Sours, Ch Thieuley, Ch la Tour-de-By, Ch Tour de Mirambeau, Clos Floridène, Calvet, Dourthe, Sirius.

Dry whites
Ch Bonnet, Ch Reynon, Ch de Sours, Ch Thieuley, Ch Tour de Mirambeau, Calvet, Dourthe.

Sweet whites
Ch Cérons, Ch Loubens, Ch Loupiac-Gaudiet, Ch Reynon, Dom du Noble.

VINTAGES

Vintages matter tremendously in the often rainy Bordeaux climate. The great red wine years occur when the fall is long, warm, and dry. 2000 was superb, the finest since 1990; in between, 1998, 1996, and 1995 were good. The worst years of the decade were 1991 and 1992. For sweet wines, 1999, 1997, 1996, and 1990 were the best; 1991, 1992, and 1993 the worst.

This large area in the southwest produces more appellation contrôlée (AC) wine than any other in France, and more fine wine (admittedly an ill-defined term) than any other country. But all Bordeaux is by no means equal. "Bordeaux" itself is an AC, so any wine, red, white, or even pink, that calls itself Bordeaux will be AC. It might be good, occasionally very good, and a good value, but most AC Bordeaux, despite recent concerted efforts to raise standards, is still pretty basic. And don't be fooled by the AC of Bordeaux Supérieur: it means a slightly higher alcohol level, nothing more.

APPELLATIONS

For the wine drinker interested in more elevated quality, the simple guide is that the better wines, those on which the region's reputation stands, aren't labeled Bordeaux. The region as a whole is divided into just over 20 subregions, with their own ACs, and a wine with one of these smaller ACs should be more interesting than one simply labeled AC Bordeaux – but you can't count on it every time.

The Médoc, and its slightly superior neighbor, the Haut-Médoc, are two of the major regional ACs in Bordeaux. Both make red wines only. Another is Graves, and its better-quality enclave, Pessac-Léognan, both of which make good to excellent red and white.

St.-Emilion and tiny Pomerol are red only. The large Entre-Deux-Mers is a source of straightforward dry whites (and AC Bordeaux reds). Up-and-coming Fronsac and Canon-Fronsac are entirely red, as is the tiny but impressive Côtes des Francs. Côtes de Bourg and Premières Côtes de Blaye reds are more rustic (there is also a small amount of white from the latter), while Côtes de Castillon reds, from next to St.-Emilion, are often notably supple and fruity. Sweet white wines come principally from Sauternes, Barsac, Cérons, Ste.-Croix-du-Mont, Loupiac, and Cadillac.

The Haut-Médoc has yet another layer of appellations: six communes (groups of villages), each with its own AC. These are St.-Estèphe, St.-Julien, Margaux, Pauillac, Moulis, and Listrac. Wines bearing these ACs really should be a step up in quality, although Moulis and Listrac have neither the cachet nor the quality of the other four.

CLASSIFICATIONS

Some of these regions go one step further, and have a classification of their best wines. Such classifications are based on quality, though you still get individual properties that either underperform or overperform relative to their category. The most famous classification is that of the Haut-Médoc, which was made in 1855 and divides the top 60 chateaux into five levels:

premier grand cru classé, or first growth, down to cinquième grand cru classé, or fifth growth. Even fifth-growth wines should be of a very high quality, while some seconds and all five firsts (Lafite, Latour, Margaux, Mouton-Rothschild, and Haut-Brion) are blue-chip investment wines. Below the crus classés in the Médoc and Haut-Médoc come the crus bourgeois, and below them are some of the thousands of unclassified Bordeaux wine properties known as petits chateaux.

Sauternes and Barsac classify their fine sweet whites into premier cru supérieur (Château d'Yquem alone), premiers crus, and deuxièmes crus. Graves has a straightforward classification of both reds and whites with no further categories; the only quirk is that Château Haut-Brion also heads the 1855 Médoc classification, as one of the five first growths.

In St.-Emilion, the top wines are the premiers grands crus classés (again, we're in blue-chip country); below them come the grands crus classés, and below them a large number of grands crus, the quality of which can be very mixed and rarely better than that of a Médoc cru bourgeois, despite the fancy title.

Although Pomerol produces some of Bordeaux's finest and most famous reds (notably Château Pétrus and Le Pin), it has no classification. But Pomerol and St.-Emilion have been the source, in recent years, of a different category of wine altogether: the so-called garagistes. From tiny vineyards, garagiste wines, or vins de garage, are made in tiny quantities – perhaps 1,000 cases a year or less. Intensely concentrated wines, they have the best of care lavished on them, including masses of new oak. The best known (Valandraud, La Mondotte, Le Dôme, L'Hermitage) enjoy a cult following and astronomical prices.

GRAPE VARIETIES

The standard red blend in Bordeaux is cabernet sauvignon, merlot, and cabernet franc, with perhaps a dash of petit verdot and occasionally malbec. But while cabernet sauvignon gives the Haut-Médoc and Graves their typically blackcurrant and cedarwood flavors, it is now merlot, long associated with the softer, richer flavors of St.-Emilion and Pomerol, that dominates overall.

Merlot gives wines richness and lushness. This style is now fashionable worldwide, and the proportion of merlot in Bordeaux's vineyards is rising. At the same time, modern winemaking techniques have made even cabernet-dominated wines taste more opulent than they used to. Some critics say that the mania for lushness masks the differences of terroir (*see page 113*) that formerly made Graves taste minerally, St.-Estèphe muscular, and Margaux silky. Others welcome the fact that most red Bordeaux is now drinkable earlier than it used to be.

White Bordeaux is traditionally a blend of semillon and sauvignon blanc, sometimes with a touch of the aromatic muscadelle, although now many dry wines are 100 percent sauvignon for extra crispness. Semillon, adding fatness and weight, is the mainstay of the great sweet wines and is important for dry wines intended for the cellar.

Nearly all relatively inexpensive Bordeaux, both red and white, can be drunk as soon as you buy it, although reds may improve with a year or two's bottle age. Crus bourgeois and their equivalents usually need at least three years' aging; classed growths often deserve at least a decade, although increasingly they are seductively good within five years. Top dry whites from Pessac-Léognan also deserve 10 years, although lesser ones can be broached earlier. Top Sauternes and Barsac can live for decades, but can be so delicious young that few bottles, one suspects, get the chance.

A mecca to wine enthusiasts, the town of St.-Emilion, surrounded by vineyards, is one of the prettiest in all Bordeaux.

The dazzling tiled roof of Château de Corton-André makes it a well-known landmark in the Côte d'Or.

burgundy

Great red burgundy is the most seductive of all wines, with an irresistible silkiness of texture. Everywhere else in the world, producers of pinot noir wines struggle to replicate its quality.

recommended producers

Ghislaine Barthod, J-M Boillot, Champy, Robert Chevillon, J Drouhin, René Engel, J Faiveley, J C Fourrier, Ch de Fuissé, Geantet-Pansiot, Anne Gros, L Jadot, Michel Lafarge, Dom des Comtes Lafon, Laroche, Dominique Laurent, Dom Leflaive, Olivier Leflaive, Bonneau du Martray, Hubert de Montille, François Raveneau, Tollot-Beaut, Verget.

Beaujolais
Duboeuf, Eventail de Vignerons Producteurs, Jacky Janodet, M Lapierre, Loron, Sarrau, Louis Tête.

VINTAGES

The best white burgundy vintages in the last decade are 2000, 1999, 1996, 1995, and 1992; the best red vintages are 2000 (probably), 1999, 1996, 1995, and 1990. No disastrous vintages, but least good for whites were 1991 and 1993; for reds, 1992 and 1994. At a decade old, even the top wines are generally ready; drink simple wines immediately.

Red burgundy can be intensely flavored, but it should never be heavy: those dark, soupy burgundies of the past were invariably beefed up with wine from further south. White burgundy is probably the most famous chardonnay in the world, although the c-word rarely appears on the label.

APPELLATIONS AND CLASSIFICATIONS

Burgundy is not a large region. Its heart is smaller still: the Côte d'Or, a tiny strip of hillside divided into the Côte de Beaune and Côte de Nuits, is the region that built Burgundy's reputation. Along this hillside, every major village has its own appellation. The best individual vineyards have the designation of grand cru, and each grand cru is its own appellation contrôlee (AC). The next best vineyards are the premiers crus; they take the village AC, but add the vineyard name to the label. So, for example, Puligny-Montrachet is a village wine; Montrachet, from the best vineyard in Puligny-Montrachet, is a grand cru; and Puligny-Montrachet les Referts is a premier cru.

Some way to the north of the Côte d'Or is Chablis, home to the world's most steely – and least successfully copied – chardonnays. Here again, the premier cru and grand cru system applies. Wines labeled Petit Chablis come from outlying areas and can be short on true Chablis character. There are also a few light reds from the region, notably the pinot noir-based Irancy, and a sauvignon blanc – Sauvignon de St.-Bris.

To the south of the Côte d'Or is the Côte Chalonnaise. Quality varies, but the best is a good value. The main appellations are Montagny, which produces chardonnay only; Bouzeron, famous for its white aligoté; and Mercurey, Rully, and Givry (red and white). Crémant de Bourgogne, traditional-method sparkling wine, is also produced here and in the Mâconnais to the south. The still Mâconnais wines range from very ordinary unoaked Mâcon Blanc to more serious chardonnays from conscientious producers in the appellations of Pouilly-Fuissé, Viré Clessé, and St.-Véran, and in villages which are allowed to add their names to that of the region (eg Mâcon-Milly). Mâcon Rouge, made from gamay, lacks Beaujolais' charm and is in decline.

Beaujolais itself is a large region to the south, with its better wines concentrated in the northern half. The finest are from 10 villages, known as the crus, which bear their own appellations (such as Fleurie, Brouilly, Morgon) instead of the name Beaujolais. Next in quality comes Beaujolais-Villages, usually well worth trading up to from basic AC

Beaujolais. Beaujolais Nouveau is the young wine of the year, and not to be despised on its own terms.

Buying burgundy is complicated by the fact that each vineyard is divided among umpteen different growers and winemaking styles, which means that you should always pay more attention to the grower's name than to that of the vineyard or appellation. Of course, quality also varies with each vintage but, since chardonnay ripens more reliably than pinot noir in Burgundy, vintage variation for white burgundy is slightly less dramatic.

Right: pinot noir grapes are harvested in the Les Breterins vineyard in Auxey-Duresses, one of the less known Côte d'Or villages. **Below:** vines in Montée de Tonnerre, one of Chablis' premiers crus. The steely character of Chablis chardonnays has proved near impossible to match elsewhere.

Alain Terrier, Chef de Caves of Laurent-Perrier, examines the sediment in a maturing bottle.

recommended producers

Paul Bara, Billecart-Salmon, Bollinger, Charles Heidsieck, Deutz, Fleury, Jacquesson, Krug, Larmandier Bernier, Pol Roger, Louis Roederer, Ruinart, Salon, Veuve Clicquot, Vilmart.

Jean-Pierre Girondin, Chef de Caves of Taittinger, turns jeroboams to shift the sediment.

champagne

For many people, champagne is a synonym for sparkling wine, but that's wrong; while sparkling wine is produced worldwide, champagne comes only from the Champagne region of France.

Buying champagne is complicated by the fact that the champagne appellation covers all qualities. The best villages are ranked as grands crus, the next best as premiers crus, and only wines made from their grapes can be so classified on their labels. But the most expensive wines tend to ignore such details and rely on their names and reputations.

VINTAGE AND NONVINTAGE

The differences between vintage and nonvintage are more significant. The nonvintages are blends of more than one year, made to a consistent house style. They are meant to be mature when sold, although often a further six months of aging can be beneficial.

Vintage wines are made in much smaller quantities, in the best years only, and should reflect the characters of those years. They are richer, deeper, and slower to mature, and can be less easy to get to know: open one too young and you may find a champagne that seems closed and ungenerous. They are often sold well before they are ready to drink, and may need up to five years' further aging. The de luxe or prestige cuvées are the cream of the crop: usually vintage wines made in even smaller volumes, and priced even higher. The best vintage since 1990 is 1996.

There is also a distinction between houses and growers. The former are the big brands: the biggest is Moët & Chandon. The growers are small family businesses that own vineyards and make wine on a much smaller scale. There is no overall difference of quality between the two sides: there are good houses and less good ones, just as there are good and indifferent growers. There are also good to worse-than-indifferent cooperatives.

GRAPES AND STYLES

Champagne is made from three grapes: chardonnay and two black grapes, pinot noir and pinot meunier. Most, including rosé champagne, is a blend of all three: chardonnay for elegance and aging potential, pinot noir for weight, and pinot meunier for early-maturing roundness. But blanc de blancs is an important style made entirely from chardonnay, and blanc de noirs is made from black grapes only.

Relative dryness or sweetness is also important, although the terminology is somewhat confusing. The driest, made only by a few producers, is extra brut; the overwhelmingly popular dry style is brut; extra dry is slightly less dry; sec is less dry again; demi-sec is medium-sweet; and doux is sweet.

The Moulin de la Montagne stands above chenin blanc vines that make fine sweet wines at Bonnezeaux.

loire valley

Following the Loire from central France westward to the Atlantic, this long region is best known for the wines it produces at either end – Sancerre upstream and Muscadet on the Atlantic coast.

recommended producers

Patrick Baudoin, Bossard, Bouvet-Ladubay, Ch de Fesles, Confrérie de Oisly et Thesée, Coulée de Serrant, D Dagueneau, Dom des Aubuisières, Filliatreau, Huët, H Pellé, Jo Pithon, Sauvion, Vacheron.

VINTAGES

Loire wines should be drunk young, except the best reds, sweet whites, and Savennières. 1990, 1995, 1996 (especially), 1997, and 2000 were all good. 1991–1994 were less good.

Joseph Mellot's La Châtellerie vineyard in Sancerre is overlooked by the town of Sancerre itself.

Lying between Sancerre and Muscadet there is a huge variety of whites, reds, and rosés, still and sparkling wines, all with a notably crisp character.

GRAPE VARIETIES

Sancerre and nearby Pouilly-Fumé, Menetou-Salon, and Quincy are sauvignon blanc country, although Sancerre and Menetou-Salon also produce a little light red and rosé pinot noir. Sauvignon continues west, with Sauvignon de Touraine making a decent, cheaper Sancerre substitute. Chenin blanc also becomes important for dry, medium, and sweet whites, both still and sparkling, in Vouvray and Montlouis. The everyday reds of Touraine usually feature gamay more or less heavily and often state gamay on the label, but a host of other varieties play a part; Rosé de Loire is made from whichever of these are on hand. More serious reds made from cabernet franc come from Bourgueil, St.-Nicolas-de-Bourgueil, and Chinon.

Moving west, Savennières produces top-notch dry chenins, while those of Coteaux du Layon are semisweet to sweet, and Quarts de Chaume and Bonnezeaux are outstanding, sweet, long-lived wines. Sparkling Saumur is based on chenin. Sad to say, most of Anjou's rosés are best avoided, but reds (mainly cabernet franc) from Saumur, Anjou, Anjou-Villages, and especially Saumur-Champigny can be very good.

In the Pays Nantais, chenin gives way to melon de bourgogne, otherwise known as the muscadet grape. The best Muscadet comes from the Sèvre-et-Maine area, but the most important words on the label, if you want wine with flavor, are Muscadet Sur Lie.

Château-Grillet, one of the smallest ACs in France, produces extraordinarily expensive viognier.

recommended producers

North
Albert Belle, Chapoutier, Chave, Cave des Clairmonts, A Clape, Colombo, Cuilleron, Ch Curson, Delas, Graillot, Guigal, Jaboulet, Jamet, Jasmin, A Perret, Rostaing, Vernay.

South
Chapoutier, Ch de Beaucastel, Ch de Fonsalette, Ch Fortia, Ch de l'Isolette, Ch Rayas, Clos des Papes, Dom du Cayron, Dom de la Mordorée, Dom Ste.-Anne, Jaboulet, La Vieille Ferme, Vieux Télégraphe.

VINTAGES
Perhaps surprisingly for such a warm region, vintages do vary, and they vary between north and south. The north did very well in 1990, 1991, 1995, 1997, 1998, and 1999, badly in 1992 and 1993; the south did very well in 1990, 1995, 1998, and 1999, poorly in 1991 and 1992. 2000 is promising for both.

rhône valley

The Rhône Valley makes assertive, even forceful wines. They are predominantly full-bodied reds, but there is also a handful of fascinating, rich dry whites.

Major villages in the Rhône Valley have their own appellations, and the only regional appellation is the expansive Côtes du Rhône. While there is no official classification of vineyards, neither is there a shortage of top-quality single-vineyard wines.

THE NORTH
The Rhône divides into two. The steep slopes and granitic soils of the north are dominated by powerful, slow-maturing reds made, often in small quantities, from syrah. The finest and most long-lived wines are from Hermitage, with Côte-Rôtie a close second; Cornas is muscular, if more rustic; St.-Joseph and Crozes-Hermitage slightly lighter. The latter, particularly, can be good value.

The three white grapes make similarly full-bodied wines. The most celebrated, viognier, is either made as a varietal – Condrieu and Château-Grillet are the two (extremely expensive) viognier-only appellations – or blended in tiny quantities into red Côte-Rotie to add perfume. The other two, marsanne and roussanne, together make white Hermitage (the best of which is long-lived), Crozes-Hermitage, St.-Joseph, and the sparkling St.-Péray.

THE SOUTH
The south has 13 grape varieties, although few growers have them all. Grenache, mourvèdre, and the duller carignan are the most important reds, but syrah has been gaining ground to good effect in Côtes du Rhône. Syrah is also important in the leading appellation of the southern Rhône, Châteauneuf-du-Pape, as well as the cheaper alternatives, notably Gigondas, Vacqueyras, and Lirac. Alongside its red, Lirac also produces some rosé, but the village famed for heady, dry rosé is Tavel. Even more of an oddity in this company is the fortified sweet muscat of Beaumes-de-Venise. The other whites of the region tend to be dry, sturdy understudies to the reds, although white Châteauneuf-du-Pape is more aromatic and interesting – and, like the red, expensive.

VILLAGE WINES
Most Côtes du Rhône comes from the south, although there are examples from the north (you can tell by the address of the producer), and these tend to be firmer and more structured. Côtes du Rhône-Villages (from any of 17 better-sited villages in the south) is richer and fruitier, especially when from one of the named villages, such as Cairanne, Rasteau, Sablet, Séguret, Valréas, or Vinsobres, which add their name to the word Villages (as in Côtes du Rhône-Villages Sablet). Côtes du Ventoux, Coteaux du Tricastin, and Côtes du Lubéron are useful and often superior alternatives to Côtes du Rhône.

Gewurztraminer vines in the grand cru Zinnkoepfle vineyard produce highly exotic-tasting Alsace wines.

alsace

Growing both French and German grape varieties, Alsace produces white wines that, although distinctively French, have an aromatic spiciness found nowhere else in France.

Unusually for appellation contrôlée wines, Alsace wines are labeled by grape variety. All take the basic appellation of Alsace except for those from 50 top vineyards, which have the appellation of Alsace grand cru.

Unfortunately, not all grand cru wines are as good as they should be. The biggest hazard when buying Alsace wine, however, is the question of dryness. In theory, the wines are dry unless specified otherwise (vendange tardive wines are sweet; sélection des grains nobles are botrytized and even sweeter). In practice, wines may be off-dry, or even medium-sweet, without any clue on the label.

The best grape varieties, the ones allowed in grand cru sites, are riesling, gewurztraminer, pinot gris, and muscat. The first three age well. Others that appear on labels are sylvaner, pinot blanc, and pinot noir (for lightish reds). Blends of grapes may be labeled Edelzwicker or Gentil (a new term). Crémant d'Alsace is pleasant fizz.

provence

Running east along the Mediterranean coast to the Italian border, Provence has been overshadowed in the last few years by the wine revolution that has taken place in Languedoc-Roussillon.

In comparison with its dynamic neighbor, Provence can look expensive and a bit staid. There hasn't been the same influx of Australian flying wine-makers here, and there's not so much vin de pays action. Nevertheless, there's no shortage of serious producers, and their wines often have more finesse than those made in Languedoc-Roussillon.

The main appellations are Côtes de Provence, Coteaux d'Aix-en-Provence, and Les Baux de Provence, and the slightly more rustic Coteaux Varois.

Bandol is small, but important for its sterling, long-lived, mourvèdre-based red; Cassis (white only), Bellet, and Palette are small but very much in vogue – a status reflected in their high prices. The most famous wines are the rosés, but the best are the reds, based on grenache, cinsaut, mourvèdre, syrah, and cabernet sauvignon. Whites, in the minority but much improved in quality, are made from a variety of grapes, including the characterful local rolle and some chardonnay.

languedoc-roussillon

The huge, sprawling stretch of the Mediterranean coast between Spain and the Rhône has been one of the most dynamic regions of recent decades, yielding some of France's best-value wines.

The winery of Mas de Daumas Gassac, which has been dubbed "the Lafite of Languedoc."

recommended producers

Abbotts, Alquier, Caves de Mont-Tauch, Chais Baumière, Ch de Lastours, Comte Cathare, Dom Capion, Dom Clavel, Dom Gauby, Dom du Mas Blanc, Mas de Daumas Gassac, Mas Jullien, Dom Virginie, Voulte Gasparet.

VINTAGES

Vintages don't vary much, but 1998 was exceptional and 2000 was good. Most wines, except the obviously serious, ageworthy reds, can be drunk on release.

Languedoc-Roussillon has reinvented itself as a source of richly fruited, but still traditionally earthy, southern reds; of modern, international, varietal white and red vins de pays; and of a tiny elite of top-class wines, spearheaded initially by Mas de Daumas Gassac.

Appellations tend to be large, and the same grapes are found pretty well everywhere. In addition, an appellation wine is not necessarily better than a vin de pays – nor is it necessarily more expensive. Fitou and Faugères are appellations with higher-than-average aspirations, as is the Pic St.-Loup commune of Coteaux du Languedoc. Corbières and Minervois are mixed in quality, but at their best are very good. Coteaux du Languedoc, Côtes du Roussillon, and Côtes du Roussillon-Villages are huge catch-all appellations that cover a multitude of qualities. Grenache-based red vins doux naturels (fortified wines) are made in Banyuls and Maury, and muscat fortifieds in Frontignan, Rivesaltes, and others.

Grenache, mourvèdre, syrah, carignan, and cinsaut are the traditional red grapes, but cabernet sauvignon and merlot have crept in. White wines are less important, but chardonnay, viognier, sauvignon blanc, and to a lesser extent marsanne make good New World-influenced vins de pays.

Below left: Aimé Guibert, pioneering proprietor of Mas de Daumas Gassac.
Below: sprawling Languedoc vineyards.

The Château de Monbazillac, one of several properties owned by the local wine cooperative.

southwest

Wines from the southern Atlantic coast, from the regions around Bordeaux to the border with Spain, come in two basic styles: the Bordeaux lookalikes from the north, and the rest.

The Dordogne regions of Bergerac, Monbazillac, Montravel, Pécharmant, Rosette, and Saussignac lie to the east of Bordeaux; Côtes de Duras, Côtes du Marmandais, and Buzet lie a little to the south, closer to Entre-Deux-Mers. The grape varieties in all are predominantly the familiar Bordeaux quartet of merlot and cabernet sauvignon, semillon and sauvignon blanc. The wine styles are equally similar, although the reds are mostly a little softer, and the whites vary from crisp, dry sauvignons in Bergerac and Duras to Sauternes-style sweet wines in Saussignac and Monbazillac.

As you head away from Bordeaux, east to Cahors or deep into Gascony and toward the Pyrenees, the grape varieties change, and with them the styles of wine produced. Bordeaux red grapes give way to malbec (especially in Cahors, where it is sometimes called cot or auxerrois), tannat (especially in Madiran, Béarn, and the Basque Irouléguy), negrette in Côtes du Frontonnais, duras in Gaillac, fer servadou (or braucol), and a clutch of others. If these reds have anything in common, it is a wildness of flavor and a tendency to robust tannins, above all in the wines of Madiran and Cahors.

The white grapes are also distinctive. Gros manseng and petit manseng, the mainstays of Jurançon and the oddly named Pacherenc du Vic-Bihl, give tangy, dry, and intense sweet whites. The appley mauzac is important in white and lightly sparkling Gaillac.

recommended producers

La Chapelle l'Enclos, Ch du Cèdre, Ch de la Jaubertie, Ch Montus, Ch du Plat Faisant, Ch Richard, Ch Tirecule la Gravière, Ch de Tiregand, Clos Triguedina, Clos Uroulat, Clos d'Yvigne, Dom Bru-Baché, Dom Cauhape, Dom du Garinet, Robert Plageoles, Producteurs Plaimont, La Tour des Gendres.

VINTAGES

Vintage variation is roughly as Bordeaux. Dry whites should be drunk young; many reds and the best sweet whites improve in bottle.

vins de pays

Vins de pays are made throughout France, but their origins are not always apparent from their labels. Their names may be derived from one of four huge regions (such as Oc), or from any of 40 départements (such as Aude), or 95 zones (from well-known Côtes de Gascogne to obscure Bigorre). The ones in the news, however, are those of the south, where flying winemakers have been taking advantage of the relaxed vin de pays rules to make international-style wines. But vins de pays can be utterly traditional as well, selling for high prices to a cult following. Or they can be cheap and ordinary. They're supposed to reflect the characteristics of their area, but in the south, especially, a lot seem to make it up as they go along. Not a bad thing.

other regions

The Jura and Savoie make wines that, with the exception of vin jaune, are seldom seen abroad, but which anyone skiing in those areas should try. Vin jaune (which may have the appellation of l'Etoile or Château-Chalon) is the most idiosyncratic: an intensely-flavored, sherry-like yellow wine which seems to live forever. It's made from the savagnin grape, which is also used for Côtes du Jura and Arbois dry whites. Vin de Savoie, Seyssel, Bugey, and Crépy are crisp, fresh styles for drinking young, made from grapes such as jacquère, chasselas, chardonnay, and roussette for the whites, and pinot noir and the heavier mondeuse for reds.

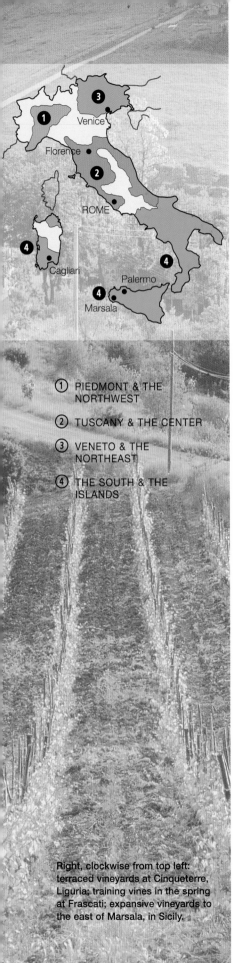

① PIEDMONT & THE
    NORTHWEST

② TUSCANY & THE CENTER

③ VENETO & THE
    NORTHEAST

④ THE SOUTH & THE
    ISLANDS

Right, clockwise from top left:
terraced vineyards at Cinqueterre,
Liguria; training vines in the spring
at Frascati; expansive vineyards to
the east of Marsala, in Sicily.

italy

Traditionally, the wines of Italy have been made only
with indigenous grapes, and most still are, but
international varieties have begun to make their mark.

Italian red wines taste like no others, partly because of the immense range of
indigenous grape varieties and partly because of the way they are handled. Whether
they're light or substantial, there is a unifying bitter-cherry signature that makes
them immensely appetizing. Whites are less easy to categorize. Most are light and
nonaromatic, but the north has some spectacularly aromatic examples, and, dotted
around the country, there are growers trying their hand at rich, oaky chardonnays.
There is also a tradition of making passito wines – sweet wines made from grapes
picked in the normal way and then left to dry before fermentation in order to
concentrate their sweetness. Vin santo and the red and white recioto wines of the
northeast come into this category, although they are not usually labeled passito.

APPELLATIONS AND CLASSIFICATIONS
Denominazione di origine controllata (DOC) and, above that, denominazione di
origine controllata e garantita (DOCG) are the highest legal categories of Italian
wine – the equivalent of French appellation contrôlée. Some consist simply of the
region, with no mention of the grape or grapes – Barolo, for example; others consist
of a grape name and a region – like Nebbiolo delle Langhe. The essential difference
between DOC and DOCG is that DOC, like AC, guarantees only the origin,
grapes, and production methods, while DOCG claims to guarantee quality as well.
Does it succeed? Not beyond a certain point – partly because, although the law was
changed to allow Super Tuscans (high-quality Tuscan "table wines" made with non-
indigenous grapes and new oak barrels) and their cousins from other parts of Italy
into the DOC and DOCG fold, some preferred to remain vini da tavola (VdT). In
between these extremes comes the category of indicazione geografiche tipici (IGT),
which was created to mop up some Super VdTs, but is somewhat underused. The
best guarantee of quality is still the name of the grower.

Some DOCs and DOCGs have a central, and generally better, classico zone, and
the wines are labeled as such, as in Soave Classico. Some have a category of riserva
for wines with extra aging – you can expect these to be higher in quality, too – and
there are also thousands of single-vineyard, or cru, wines. These are generally better
than the regular bottlings from the same growers, and it might be that one day such
vineyards will be officially classified. But don't hold your breath.

piedmont & the northwest

This is where some of Italy's most magnificent reds originate, and some of the country's most delicate, perfumed whites – almost all of them made from idiosyncratic local grapes.

Vines trained on traditional high pergolas, with trees grown specially to support the pergolas.

recommended producers

Altare, Bava, Braida, Ca' del Bosco, Ceretto, Clerico, Aldo Conterno, Giacomo Conterno, Fontanafredda, Angelo Gaja, B Giacosa Prunotto, Sandrone, Scavino, Vajra, Vietti, R Voerzio.

VINTAGES
Vintage variation matters in the north, especially for the late-ripening nebbiolo. Great Barolo and Barbaresco years include 1990, 1996, 1997, 1998, 1999, and 2000; 1991, 1992, and 1994 were duds.

Of the three most important red grapes, nebbiolo is unquestionably the most majestic. Barbera is regarded as the next best, giving everything from simple everyday reds to long-lived wines of great complexity. And dolcetto produces vivid, fruity wines for drinking relatively young, although a dedicated producer in the right place can make something more serious. All are made as varietals for DOC and DOCG wines, but may appear in IGTs and VdTs, which can be blends of anything with anything else – cabernet sauvignon, for example, which pops up here and there. Other red grapes found in lesser quantities include bonarda, brachetto (for sparkling red), freisa, pinot nero, and grignolino.

RED GRAPES
Nebbiolo has its base, and reaches its finest quality, in the DOCG of Barolo, in Piedmont. Prices and quality have both soared here in the last couple of decades, although prices eased off at the turn of the century. These are some of the darkest, tarriest, most complex wines in Italy. They're also among the longest-lived, although most are drinkable younger than in the past. Barbaresco is marginally lighter. Gattinara, Ghemme, Carema, and Spanna (all DOCs) are from outlying

areas: they can be good, but a simple DOC Nebbiolo delle Langhe from a good Barolo or Barbaresco producer is often a better bet.

The best barbera DOCs are the Piedmontese ones of Barbera d'Alba and Barbera d'Asti. The wines are often aged in oak to soften barbera's characteristic acidity and to add perfume and complexity. These are some of Italy's most modern reds, but still with the characteristic Italian bite. Dolcetto is grown in seven zones, including Alba and Dogliani, where it gives denser, firmer wines, and Asti, where it is more delicate.

WHITE GRAPES
The best-known white of the north-west is the light, aromatic, and often fizzy moscato. Among the others are the pear-scented and expensive arneis, cortese (especially for the fashionable Gavi), erbaluce, favorita, vermentino, and the ever-present trebbiano.

The wines of Lombardy, further to the east, are less often seen outside the region than those of Piedmont, but the sparkling wines of Franciacorta and the stylish, rounded white Lugana have been very successful. Sparkling, red, and white wines of Oltrepò Pavese and Alpine Valle d'Aosta, and the whites of coastal Liguria, are all worth a try.

San Gimignano's medieval towers punctuate the skyline above the Monte Oliveto vineyard in Tuscany.

tuscany & the center

Central Italy's best wines are the reds, which are largely based on sangiovese. Whites, heavily dependent on trebbiano, are for the most part light, nonaromatic, everyday wines.

recommended producers

Altesino, Antinori, Argiano, Avignonesi, Banfi, Biondi-Santi, Costanti, Fonterutoli, Fontodi, Frescobaldi, Isole e Olena, Lungarotti, Ornellaia, Le Pupille, Sassicaia, Selvapiana, Tenuta di Capezzana, Tenuta San Guido, Teruzzi & Puthod, Volpaia.

VINTAGES

Good vintages in Tuscany are not necessarily the same as those in other parts of Italy, but vintage variation is more of a factor in selecting serious reds than in choosing whites. For the latter, the most recent year is usually the best. For sangiovese, 1990 was excellent, as were 1997 and 1999. 1995 was very good; 1991 and 1992 were disappointing.

Other red grapes include cabernet sauvignon, merlot, lambrusco (for the eponymous wine), montepulciano, sagrantino, and canaiolo; other whites include vermentino, vernaccia, sauvignon blanc, malvasia, greco, and grechetto. But this is not an area where you need to bone up on grape varieties, as they feature on few labels.

RED GRAPES

The most famous region is, of course, Chianti. The wines of Chianti have improved vastly in the past 20 years, thanks to better vineyard management and winemaking, and are now taken deservedly seriously by the world at large. Tuscan neighbors Brunello di Montalcino and Vino Nobile di Montepulciano (both DOCG) are a little weightier than Chianti, and have always thought themselves a cut above it, even if the reality is now rather different. Vino Nobile di Montepulciano is not to be confused with the robust, fruity montepulciano grape, found as a varietal DOC in Abruzzo, and in the Marches in DOC Rosso Cònero.

Morellino di Scansano is slightly lighter and plummier than Chianti, while Carmignano, which has a good admixture of cabernet sauvignon, is more often complex and elegant. Umbria's Torgiano used to be very fashionable, but has been overtaken in quality by Chianti and others, such as Umbria's new star, Sagrantino di Montefalco, from the sagrantino grape.

Other nonsangiovese reds from this part of Italy include light, slightly fizzy Lambrusco, though this is too often sweetened for export markets, made white as well as red, and entirely lacking the quintessential acid bite of the real thing.

Regular bottlings of Chianti can be drunk with pleasure within a few years of the harvest, but riservas and many single-vineyard wines, and sangiovese-, merlot-, and cabernet-based wines from Bolgheri – and many Super Tuscans – need longer.

WHITE GRAPES

Central Italy's most popular whites are Vernaccia di San Gimignano (nutty, tangy, and made from the vernaccia grape), Galestro (light and leafy), Est! Est!! Est!!!, and Frascati (all made from trebbiano and malvasia), and Orvieto (the same two varieties again, but with some local varieties as well). As a rule of thumb, the more malvasia in the blend, the fuller and nuttier the wine. The same grapes are also widely used for sweet vin santo. Chardonnay usually comes with a VdT classification and a Super Tuscan price tag.

The medieval castle at Soave, near Verona, overlooks the vineyards of this much improved region.

recommended producers

Allegrini, Anselmi, Bolla, Dal Forno, M Felluga, Gini, Gravner, Jermann, Lageder, Maculan, Masi, Pieropan, Pojer & Sandri, Quintarelli, Mario Schiopetto, Tedeschi, Zenato.

VINTAGES

Most of these wines are made for early drinking, so buy the most recent year available. The exceptions are the Reciotos and Amarones of the Veneto, which deserve to be aged for several years before being opened and will often last many more. Best recent vintages for these are 1990, 1993, 1995, 1997, and 2000.

veneto & the northeast

Italy's finest whites come from the northeast: intense, yet never heavy, sometimes very fragrant, sometimes less so, but always pure in flavor. Reds tend to be lightish with a good rasp.

The range of grapes is huge. Whites include chardonnay, gewurztraminer (or traminer), müller-thurgau, pinot grigio, pinot bianco, riesling italico, riesling renano (true riesling), sylvaner, the highly aromatic goldmuskateller, ribolla, garganega, and trebbiano (the latter two being the basis of Soave), tocai friulano, the nutty verduzzo, and prosecco (which is the mainstay of the soft sparkling wine of the same name).

The reds, apart from merlot and the two cabernets, which are found throughout the northeast, are less familiar. They include lagrein, vernatsch or schiava (most reds in Trentino-Alto Adige, including Santa Maddalena and Lago di Caldaro, are based on these), and moscato rosa. There is also Friuli-Venezia Giulia's robust refosco.

Valpolicella is made from corvina, rondinella, and molinara, a trio that, in the hands of a good producer and from a single vineyard, gives a wine of sappy, but rich, cherry fruit – a far cry from mass-produced cheap Valpolicella. Bardolino, from the same blend, is generally lighter.

VENETO BLENDS

In Friuli-Venezia Giulia and Trentino-Alto Adige, most DOC wines are varietals, and labeled as such. This changes with the blends of the Veneto, including the famous dried-grape wines. Valpolicella and Soave reach new heights when made in this way. Recioto di Soave and Recioto di Valpolicella are sweet, concentrated, and complex; Amarone della Valpolicella is made from dried grapes that are fermented out to dryness. The result is a fascinating, bittersweet, rich, and smoky dry wine. Ripasso di Valpolicella is a sort of halfway house: the new wine is "passed over," or refermented on, the lees and skins of Recioto or Amarone to give extra weight and flavor. Prices for all these are higher than for regular versions, but worth it.

Mauro Lunelli of Ferrari among the chardonnay vines used to produce his company's acclaimed sparkling wines in Trentino.

The volcanic soils of Monte Vulture give Basilicata its distinguished red wine, Aglianico del Vulture.

the south & the islands

The quality revolution in southern Italy and Sicily is more recent than that of Tuscany or Piedmont, but judging by what is being achieved, it is probably even more thoroughgoing.

recommended producers

Marco de Bartoli, Calatrasi, Candido (Salice Salentino), Cantina Sociale di Copertino, Donnafugata, Duca di Salaparuta, Fratelli d'Angelo, Librandi, A Mano, Mastroberardino, Planeta, Regaleali, Sella & Mosca, Settesoli, Spadafora, Terre di Ginestra.

The best reds are now lush and rich, and whites are at least clean and fresh, and may be perfumed and complex in the bargain. Inevitably, prices have risen, but they are still very good compared to other regions.

GRAPE VARIETIES

The reds are all the more interesting for not being made from cabernet and merlot, but largely from indigenous southern grapes: aglianico, negroamaro, malvasia nera, primitivo, gaglioppo, monica, nero d'avola, cannonau (grenache), and carignano (carignan), as well as the Italian staples of montepulciano and sangiovese. There is also the red, muscatlike aleatico, which is made into strong, sweet red wines in Puglia. And of the international varieties it may be syrah in Sicily that has the most potential.

The south hasn't escaped incursions from chardonnay (some very successful) and sauvignon, and there are the usual trebbiano and malvasia, but local white varieties, thankfully, are still very widespread, including the fiano, greco, and falanghina in Campania, and catarrato, grillo, and inzolia in Sicily. The moscato grape is turned into sweet wines, notably Moscato di Pantelleria, from the island of Pantelleria, which is closer to Tunisia than to Sicily.

Most wines, unless they have a varietal DOC – such as Aglianico del Vulture (from Basilicata), Primitivo di Manduria (from Puglia), Fiano di Avellino (from Campania), and Moscato di Pantelleria – are made from a cocktail of grapes, although the famous Taurasi from Campania is usually wholly aglianico. Negroamaro is the main grape behind the powerful, spicy, chocolaty flavors of Puglia's Salice Salentino, Copertino, and Brindisi; gaglioppo, which is punchy, if short on finesse, is the mainstay of Cirò from Calabria. But frankly, at this stage of the game, the balance of grape varieties isn't nearly as important for flavor and quality as the attitude of the producer.

FORTIFIED WINE

The other great southern, or rather island, tradition is fortified wine, notably Marsala. This wine has suffered at the hands of fashion – which at one time meant a fashion for sweetened Marsala flavored with eggs, cream, coffee, and so on. Marsala winemakers are now focused on a return to quality, both dry and sweet, but it can't be said that the world's wine drinkers are rushing back. Choose a Superiore Riserva or Vergine style if you intend to judge for yourself. Marsala Fine, despite the name, is a lower grade.

VINTAGES

Vintage variation is not enormous. Most whites should be drunk within two or three years (Fiano di Avellino is an exception). Reds can be drunk on release, but those based on aglianico (such as Taurasi) and negroamaro can age well.

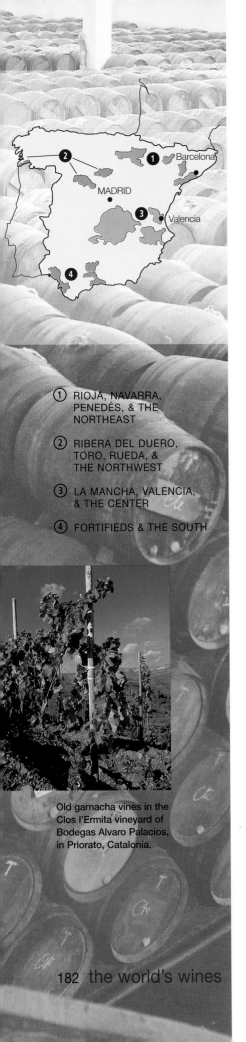

1 RIOJA, NAVARRA, PENEDÉS, & THE NORTHEAST

2 RIBERA DEL DUERO, TORO, RUEDA, & THE NORTHWEST

3 LA MANCHA, VALENCIA, & THE CENTER

4 FORTIFIEDS & THE SOUTH

Old garnacha vines in the Clos l'Ermita vineyard of Bodegas Alvaro Palacios, in Priorato, Catalonia.

spain

Spanish wine is on a roll. Prosperity has increased demand for fine wine, bringing in its wake fresh, new styles and a transformation of traditional wines.

The elegantly faded, vanilla-scented reds that we long associated with Spain still exist, but they are being supplanted by a more vibrant, vigorous style of red, with brighter fruit and fresher oak. This has moved the spotlight from the traditional regions, most notably Rioja, to regions that might have been making wine for centuries but have only recently been discovered by fashion, like Priorato.

White wine has never been Spain's strong point. Once taste moved on from the deep yellow, oxidized wines of the past, most regions struggled to find modern, interesting alternatives to fill the gap. The one shining exception has been the northwest, with its albariños.

APPELLATIONS AND CLASSIFICATIONS

Spain's appellation system is only semi-helpful as a guide to the best wines. There are over 50 denominación de origen, or DO, regions, and they are by no means all of equal quality. Rioja has the higher category of DOCa, or denominación de origen calificada, the equivalent of Italy's DOCG. Below DO and DOCa are vinos comarcales and vinos de la tierra – the rough equivalent of French vins de pays – and, at the bottom, vino de mesa, or table wine. A few prestigious and pricey wines use the last two categories for wines that don't fall geographically into any DO, but the flexibility, in many DOs, of the rules on grape varieties means that there is not the same need, as in France or Italy, to go outside the rules in order to experiment.

What is useful in red wines is the basic classification by age, even though precise details vary by region. Joven (young), or sin crianza (without aging), indicates wine sold with no oak maturation – that is, fresh and fruity. Crianza reds are aged for two years, with one year or six months of that spent in oak. Reservas are generally matured for three years, with a year or two in oak; and gran reservas are aged for longer again – usually two years in cask and three in bottle.

Cypress trees provide a windbreak for the vineyards of Bodegas del Senorio de Sarra, in Navarra.

recommended producers

Agramont, Finca Allende, Artadi, Chivite, Clos l'Ermita, Clos Mogador, Clos de l'Obac, Codorníu, CVNE, Enate, Freixenet, Guelbenzu, Marqués de Murrieta, Marqués de Riscal, Martínez Bujanda, Ochoa, Raimat, Remelluri, La Rioja Alta, Roda, Torres, Viñas del Vero.

VINTAGES

The best Rioja vintage of the 1990s was 1994, closely followed by 1995. Also good were 1996, 1997, 1999, and 2000. 1991 was poor.

rioja, navarra, penedés, & the northeast

If asked to name one Spanish red, most of us would think first of Rioja. Some of Spain's most traditional wines come from the northeastern heartland – and some of its most modern.

The red grape varieties here are those familiar throughout Spain: tempranillo, garnacha, graciano, cariñena, and monastrell, together with the jet set – cabernet sauvignon, merlot, and some pinot noir. Whites include viura, parellada, xarello, chardonnay, sauvignon blanc, and gewurztraminer. Penedés and Somontano are especially hot on international varieties; Rioja has tended to stick to traditional ones, although it's beginning to change.

APPELLATIONS

Rioja, in fact, is changing in all kinds of ways. Its white wines modernized themselves some years ago, becoming fresh and light, but its reds seemed to lose their way for a while, not knowing whether to follow the old path of long oak aging and faded flavors, or to become more fruity. Now the balance is tilting decisively in favor of modernism, with even the most traditional bodegas (wineries or cellars) producing new-style wines. Some are replacing American oak barrels, which have long given Rioja its vanilla flavor, with French oak. Others have chosen to abandon the old categories of reserva and gran reserva in favor of cuvée names.

There is also more stress on regionality. Bodegas traditionally blended their wines from all three sub-regions – Rioja Alavesa, Rioja Alta, and Rioja Baja. Now single-estate wines are appearing – although, to be honest, differences between the terroir of one estate and another can be difficult for outsiders to spot in the glass.

Navarra makes its own Rioja-type wines, together with some impressive cabernet sauvignons and chardonnays, and a lot of attractive rosado. Somontano, in the Pyrenean foothills, is one of Spain's new stars, making exhilarating, modern reds and whites. Costers del Segre, which is dominated by the firm of Raimat and came to fame in the 1980s, continues to be a reliable source of cabernet sauvignon and chardonnay. Penedés produces most of Spain's cava (traditional-method sparkling wine), which has become a huge international success. Penedés still wines are dominated by Torres, a company that pioneered international grape varieties, but which is now taking a fresh look at the indigenous ones.

The red wine region of the moment, however, is Priorato. Its massive, concentrated wines from very old vines fetch high prices, and new vineyards are being planted apace as producers leap onto the bandwagon. It remains to be seen whether quality can be maintained in the face of strong demand.

ribera del duero, toro, rueda, & the northwest

The regions of the northwest, some of which have found fame and fortune only in recent years, include Spain's two best, though very different, white wine areas: Rías Baixas and Rueda.

recommended producers

Alion, Belondrade y Lurton, Felix Callejo, Martín Códax, Condes del Albarei, Marqués de Griñon, Marqués de Riscal, Pazo de Seoane, Pesquera, Pingus, Protos, Senorio de Nava, Teofilo Reyes, Vega Sicilia.

VINTAGES

Of all these regions it is Ribera del Duero that is most subject to vintage variation, but really poor years are rare. 1994 and 1996 were especially successful; 1990, 1991, 1995, 1997, 1998, and 1999 were all good.

The albariños of Rías Baixas have peachy fruit and zesty acidity; Rueda, made from verdejo and sauvignon blanc, has an attractive gentle nuttiness and a grassy, greengagey tang.

It is, nevertheless, the reds that get most of the attention, especially those of Ribera del Duero. This is one of Spain's star regions; but until the 1980s it consisted of little more than one wine, the famous Vega Sicilia, which was in such demand that it was pretty well permanently rationed. The best Ribera del Duero wines combine Rioja-like elegance with greater concentration and power. They age well, but quality can be unexpectedly uneven – no doubt because growth has been so rapid.

The main red grape, the backbone of both Ribera del Duero and nearby Toro, is tempranillo, supported by garnacha, mencía, and small amounts of cabernet sauvignon and merlot. Toro is a more rustic proposition than Ribera del Duero: tempranillo at its most solid. Quality has slipped in recent years, but interest from Vega Sicilia suggests that we may be seeing the start of a recovery.

la mancha, valencia, & the center

These are regions, largely, of simple, young everyday wines. In the vast La Mancha region, to the south of Madrid, the dull white airen is still the main grape, but its days are numbered.

recommended producers

Agapito Rico, Bodegas Castaño, Casa de la Viña, Señorio del Condestable, Félix Solís (Viña Albali), Castilla de Liria, Nuestro Padre Jesús del Perdón coop (Yuntero), Rodriguez y Berger, Los Llanos, Vinícola de Castilla.

VINTAGES

Vintage variations are modest.

La Mancha's airen vineyards are being uprooted and replaced with tempranillo and some cabernet, syrah, petit verdot, and merlot, to produce soft young reds and, occasionally, something more serious. The same red varieties in various combinations, together with bobal, garnacha, and monastrell, are also grown to make robust but increasingly fruity wines in Jumilla, Almansa, and Yecla. The reds of Valencia tend to be juicy and a little lighter, and Valdepeñas has a tradition of American-oak reservas à la Rioja.

White grapes include viura and chardonnay, grown especially in Ribera del Guadiana, and moscatel, which is made into simple, barley sugar-flavored sweet wine, but white wine is no longer the focus of attention.

A tall pergola of vines shades a road dividing González Byass' bodegas in Jerez, Andalucia.

recommended producers

Argüeso (Herederos), Barbadillo, González Byass, Domecq, Bodegas Lopez Hermanos, Vinícola Hidalgo, Lustau, Osborne, Valdespino, Williams & Humbert.

A barrel is rolled through cellars of Osborne's La Palma winery in Puerto de Santa Maria, near Cádiz.

fortifieds & the south

The south of Spain is dominated by sherry. There are some table wines but they're seldom worth drinking, whereas the quality of sherry is very high – a fact that isn't wasted on the Spanish.

In Spain, sherry doesn't have the image problem it has abroad. Spanish drinkers like sherry pungently dry. They don't drink the sherries that are sweetened to make them more commercial on export markets. This is true whether the sherry has been classified as manzanilla, fino, amontillado, or oloroso.

CLASSIFICATIONS

The sherry grape is usually palomino, but it's style, not grape variety, that is important. Manzanilla is the lightest and most delicate. It comes only from the town of Sanlúcar de Barrameda, and has a distinctive, salty, yeasty tang. Like the almost equally light fino, it should be chilled and drunk in one sitting, or within days if kept in the fridge in the meantime. It will start to deteriorate in an unopened bottle about six months after bottling, so only buy from a shop with a quick turnover.

Amontillado is darker in color, more robust, nutty, and, unless sweetened, austere and elegant. Oloroso is darker again, richer, and with flavors of dried fruit and nuts. High-quality, sweet versions of oloroso do exist: they are usually labeled dulce in Spanish (where dry sherries will normally say seco). Anything called, in English, cream will be commercially sweetened. Such Spanish phrases on the label as muy viejo (very old) may seem vague but are generally a sign of a serious wine. Almost all sherry is nonvintage.

OTHER FORTIFIEDS

Although it is true that sherry is made from palomino, there is a very small amount of dark, treacly, dessert sherry made from the pedro ximenéz grape. The same grape is grown in Montilla-Moriles for lighter, less pungent sherry lookalikes (both sweet and dry). Similar wines are made in Condado de Huelva, but are seldom seen outside the region. While southern Spain's other fortified wine region, Málaga, is a shadow of its former self, the remaining bodegas produce good, rich, raisiny, toffee-flavored wines.

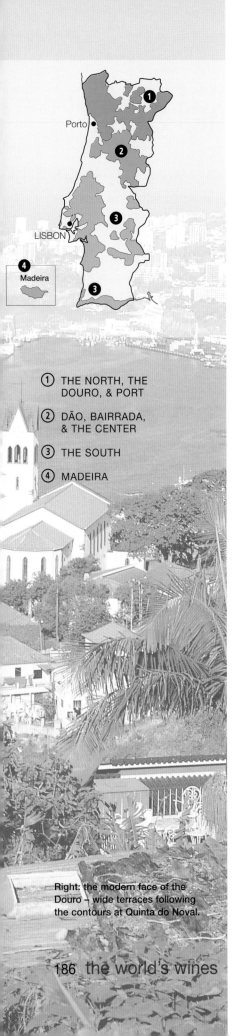

① THE NORTH, THE
DAO, & PORT

② DÃO, BAIRRADA,
& THE CENTER

③ THE SOUTH

④ MADEIRA

Right: the modern face of the
Douro – wide terraces following
the contours at Quinta do Noval.

portugal

A country rapidly reinventing itself as a source of
modern wines, Portugal is doing so with a wealth
of characterful indigenous grape varieties.

Fortunately, the equally characterful names of some of these grapes haven't held
them back. Borrado das moscas (fly droppings) and esgana cão (dog strangler)
spring to mind. With a few exceptions, Portugal's best wines are the rich,
chocolaty reds – a little more elegant in the north, slightly broader-flavored in the
south, but still, in many regions, in the process of finding a distinct style. A few
fashionable estates are putting up their prices beyond all reason, and the best of
luck to them, but the great majority of wines offer excellent value.

APPELLATIONS AND CLASSIFICATIONS

The appellation system is basically the same as that found throughout Europe.
At the top is denominacão de origem controlada, or DOC (with a category of
reserva for better-quality wines with extra aging.) Below that is indicação de
proveninência regulamentada, or IPR; below that is vinho regional, or VR,
and, at the bottom, vinho de mesa, or table wine.

A traditional basket in use during harvesting at Quinta do Bonfim, the Dow's port flagship estate.

recommended producers

Churchill, Cockburn, Dow, Ferreira (Barca Velha), Fonseca Guimaraens, JM da Fonseca, Graham, Niepoort, Quinta do Côtto, Quinta do Crasto, Quinta do Noval, Quinta da Rosa, Quinta de Vesuvio, Ramos Pinto, Smith Woodhouse, Taylor, Warre.

VINTAGES

Vintages in northern Portugal vary a lot, but only really for vintage port. The most important vintages of the 1990s were 1991, 1992, 1994, and 1997. Douro table wine vintages are more even, although 1993 was a disaster for all, while 1994 and 1997 were outstanding. Drink Vinho Verde as young as possible.

the north, the douro, & port

In the far northwest is Vinho Verde, home to Portugal's one significant white wine export – but one that has been losing out in the global race for fuller-bodied, fruitier wines.

Until recently, much Vinho Verde was actually red – red, rasping, acidic, and very much an acquired taste. It is still made in ever-diminishing quantities for the local market. But it was the sharp, light-bodied, dry white that traveled, and it still does, although the label now sometimes mentions a grape variety, especially alvarinho (which becomes albariño when it crosses the nearby border into Spain).

PORT WINES

Port comes from the steep-sided, granite Douro Valley, just to the south of Vinho Verde. Umpteen grape varieties are grown, including a tiny minority of whites, but the most significant are touriga nacional, touriga franca, tinta barocca, tinta roriz, and tinto cão. These are used both for port and for the increasingly fine red table wines. The latter have the DOC of Douro, and better wines may be labeled reserva.

Port, however, which is made by stopping the fermentation of the young wine by the addition of fortifying brandy, leaving the wine sweet (and more alcoholic), has a number of different categories. Vintage is the crème de la crème. This is wine from a single top-quality year, bottled two years after the harvest and designed to age in bottle. It's the most expensive port and bears the name of the shipping house – Dow's, Taylor's, Sandeman, and so on. Single-quinta vintage wines are similar, but they're made in the years when a port shipper (producer) is not declaring (that is, making) a vintage port. They're made from the shipper's best single property (or quinta), rather than being a blend of top vineyards. Single-quinta ports, labeled Quinta de Something-or-Other, are lighter and may be drunk slightly earlier – at perhaps seven or eight years old, instead of the 10 years plus that full-blooded vintage port needs.

Vintage ports throw a heavy sediment, or crust, and need to be decanted. The same applies to crusted port, which is a blend of vintages – a very small category, but a good value. Ports in the much larger late bottled vintage (or LBV) category are mostly released filtered (that is, sediment-free) and ready to drink. Exceptions are usually labeled unfiltered.

Vintage Character is a blend from several years, released when ready to drink. Despite its name, it doesn't have the character of vintage port: it's more like an upmarket ruby. Ruby itself is simple, young, red, and sweet – the bottom rung of the quality ladder, along with the cheapest tawny ports.

Cheap tawny ports are young rubies, their color adjusted by using white port and other winemaking tricks.

True tawny port is something else. Matured in wooden casks for many years, its color fades to a pale brick, or tawny, and it develops an increasingly nutty, raisiny character. The best carry an age statement – 10, 20, 30, or 40 years old – indicating the average age of the blend. Colheita port is similar, but is from a single year. Serve both of these kinds of tawny lightly chilled.

White port should be served well-chilled as an aperitif – if at all. The best white ports are golden, dry, and nutty, and few and far between; the worst of them are heavy and coarse.

Leading Bairrada producer Luis Pato in the barrel room of his Quinta da Cha winery.

recommended producers

Casa da Saima, Casa de Santar, Caves Aliança, Caves São João, Luis Pato, Quinta dos Roques, Sogrape.

VINTAGES

Traditionally, the reds were often kept a long time, but modern examples need little further aging when they are released. Vintage variation is not great, but 1993 was poor, and 1997 excellent.

A woman harvesting corn passes unpruned vines near Mangualde in windswept hills of the Dão region.

dão, bairrada, & the center

For many years, Dão and Bairrada were Portugal's best table wines, but they began to be overtaken by developments in the north and the south, and are only now beginning to catch up.

The grapes in red Dão are a cocktail, with an obligatory one-fifth touriga nacional, accompanied by bastardo, jaen, tinta roriz, tinta pinheira, alfrocheiro preto, and others. The wetter Bairrada region relies primarily on one variety, the tannic baga. That should mean a big difference in style between the two regions. In practice, it doesn't necessarily, and it doesn't in the way one would expect. Bairrada tends to have more insistent fruit – a ripe blackberry and raspberry character; while Dão, with its climatic advantages, is often tougher: it's simply a question of winemaking. Dão still has a way to go, despite recent progress, and the same goes for its tiny proportion of white wines. Bairrada makes a limited amount of modern, crisp, herby white.

the south

Things are on the move throughout Portugal, but it's in some of the southern regions – the Alentejo, Ribatejo, and Estremadura – that Portugal's most far-reaching wine revolution is taking place.

At present, there's no automatic quality difference between DOC, IPR, and VR, and frankly little need to take note of one DOC name over another. The name of the producer and any grape variety on the label are better guides to quality and style. The grapes include almost everything grown in Portugal – touriga nacional, joão santarem (alias trincadeira, castelão, periquita, and others), and alfrocheiro preto among the reds; arinto, esgana cão, and fernão pires among the whites. There are also international varieties, especially cabernet sauvignon and chardonnay in the Terras do Sado region.

Long-aged and long-lived – Madeira maturing at Adegas de São Francisco.

madeira

The fortified wines from the subtropical island of Madeira have been exported around the world for several hundred years. But tradition is no safeguard: these days they fight for a market.

Quality is not a problem; it is more that fortified wines of all kinds are drunk much less than they were.

CLASSIFICATIONS

The grape varieties used are, in theory, the ones that define the four styles of Madeira: sercial for the driest and most austere wines; verdelho for slightly less dry wines; bual for medium-sweet; and malmsey, or malvasia, for very sweet. Any Madeira claiming to be one of these must contain 85 percent of the named grape. If, instead, a Madeira merely calls itself dry, medium, or whatever, then it has been made from the ubiquitous tinta negra mole grape. There is no question that this is not as potentially fine as the other grapes, but it can still make characterful wines. The flavor of Madeira comes, in any case, from the aging process rather than from the grape variety. The degree of sweetness is determined in the winery, but the fascinating, almost sour tang comes from long years of aging in old wooden casks and the unique process of prolonged heating that the wines undergo, known as estufagem. This can either take place naturally in warm warehouses or, as is more usual, with the aid of a heating mechanism.

Madeira is famous for its ability to live for a century or even longer, and examples of this age, and old vintage-dated wines, can still be bought.

germany

If ever there was a country ripe for rediscovery, it's Germany. The days of Liebfraumilch are not past, but the country is returning to its fine heritage.

VINTAGES

German rieslings age extremely well in bottle, and in fact usually need several years to show at their best: young riesling can taste closed and lean. Other grape varieties are usually drinkable earlier. Germany has had an exceptional run of vintages recently: none in the last decade has been disastrous, and 1990, 1993, 1995, and 1997 were especially successful.

Right, clockwise from top left: slopes too steep for any machine in the Mittelrhein; the Bassgeige vineyard above Oberbergen in Baden; St. Hildegardis Abbey and the Klosterberg vineyard, Rudesheim, in the Rheingau.

Of course, it's still very easy to find cheap, dull German wine, if that's what you want, but the pendulum is swinging back in favor of the fine, racy, elegant whites that built Germany's reputation. Producers have also succeeded in developing a new style of drier, more contemporary-looking wines for the export market.

APPELLATIONS AND CLASSIFICATIONS

The German system of classifying wine is more precise than that of any other European country, if also more complicated. Most European countries tell you where the wine came from and which grapes it was made from: German wines, in addition, tell you how ripe the grapes were when they were harvested.

For QbA wine (Qualitätswein bestimmter Anbaugebiete, the equivalent of French appellation contrôlée), Germany is divided into 13 different regions: Ahr, Baden, Franken, Hessische Bergstrasse, Mittelrhein, Mosel-Saar-Ruwer, Nahe, Pfalz, Rheingau, Rheinhessen, Saale-Unstrut, Sachsen, and Württemberg. For Landwein, the German equivalent of vin de pays, the regions are different, but this is not a category that is much exported. The most basic category is Tafelwein (table wine), a classification that producers of an experimental bent occasionally use for wines that do not conform to the rules.

Each of the 13 QbA regions is subdivided into Bereiche, or districts; Bereiche are subdivided into Grosslagen, or groups of vineyards, and Grosslagen are subdivided into Einzellagen, or single vineyards. Always choose an Einzellagen wine over a Bereich or Grosslage one. Bereich wines are easy to avoid: they have the word Bereich on the label, as in Bereich Bernkastel; Grosslage wines, however, do not identify themselves as such. Separating your Grosslagen from your Einzellagen is the biggest problem in buying German wine. Most top producers have voted with their feet, and do not use Grosslage names. There is a proposal to replace Grosslagen with more tightly regulated Ursprungslagen, or sites of origin, with much clearer labeling. The Rheingau is also establishing Germany's first system of premier cru vineyards, or Erstes Gewächs, beginning with the 1999 vintage.

Single-vineyard wines bear first the name of their village, and then the name of the vineyard. Bernkasteler Doktor thus comes from the Doktor vineyard in the village of Bernkastel. (Beware of Bernkastel Badstube, which is a Grosslage.)

Riesling vines in the precipitous Brauneberger Juffer vineyard, one of the Mosel's finest.

Next, ripeness and sweetness. There is an additional category above QbA for wines of higher quality. This is QmP, or Qualitätswein mit Prädikat. There are six classes of QmP: in ascending order of grape ripeness they are Kabinett (ripe grapes), Spätlese (late-picked), Auslese (selected super-ripe bunches), Beerenauslese (individually selected botrytized berries), Trockenbeerenauslese (individually selected berries so affected by noble rot that they have shriveled), and Eiswein (bunches frozen solid by winter cold). The higher you go up these classes, the sweeter the wines become. Kabinett wines are usually medium-dry; Spätlese medium-sweet; Auslese medium-sweet to sweet; and all the others very sweet.

But not invariably, because many producers now opt to make drier wines, particularly in the more southerly parts – the Pfalz, Franken, and Baden. The terms that have been used for these are Trocken (dry) and Halbtrocken (half-dry), and you can still see them on Kabinett, Spätlese, and even Auslese labels; but, as from the 2000 vintage, they are being phased out. A new system divides dry (and half-dry) wines into two categories according to their quality, rather than degree of dryness: Classic wines come from a particular region; Selection wines are top-quality dry wines from an individual vineyard in a specified region. Neither term can be used with any other style (so no Trocken, Spätlese, and so on).

If all the above has made you think that the complexities of German wine are beyond understanding, don't despair. Just look for the name of a grape; wines of the poorest quality simply won't give a grape name.

GRAPE VARIETIES

The finest grape is riesling – the best by far in the Rheingau, Mosel-Saar-Ruwer, and many other regions. The exceptions are the Pfalz and Baden, where the pinot family – pinots blanc, gris, and noir – claim equal star billing, and Franken, where silvaner is usually the best. Pinot blanc is often called weissburgunder; pinot gris may appear as rulander or (in a dry wine) grauburgunder; and pinot noir is known as spätburgunder. Other quality grapes are rieslaner, gewurztraminer (often called traminer), scheurebe, and, to a lesser extent, kerner. Avoid müller-thurgau. Red wines have come a long way in recent years, with spätburgunder making the most authoritative, and dornfelder and lemberger also producing some convincing wines.

Not all the 13 regions are equal in quality or prestige, though most have at least some star producers. The Mosel-Saar-Ruwer and the Rheingau are the most famous, with high concentrations of top estates. The former makes some of the lightest, most delicate, and yet concentrated and long-lived rieslings in Germany; Rheingau rieslings are bigger, as are those of the Nahe. Rheinhessen wines are softer; look out particularly for silvaners labeled RS for Rheinhessen Silvaner. Mittelrhein rieslings are leaner. Baden and Pfalz wines can be relatively weighty, including the reds, and Pfalz whites are often notably spicy. Franken's distinctive silvaners are dry and slightly earthy; the wines of Sachsen are seldom seen elsewhere, but the dry whites are worth trying. Ahr is a traditional red wine region, now moving away from the traditional sweet style. Württemberg also produces a lot of reds that at their best are excellent, but are mostly rather anemic.

austria

Austria's classification system has a lot in common with Germany's, but it's by no means identical, and the wine styles produced are even less so.

As in Germany, the classification system is based on the level of ripeness of the grapes and the grape varieties themselves. But Austria's more southerly latitude gives fuller, more alcoholic wines and a greater emphasis on dry wines.

APPELLATIONS AND CLASSIFICATIONS

Qualitätswein, Austria's basic-quality wine category, is superior to simple QbA in Germany; and Kabinett in Austria is a higher-quality subcategory of Qualitätswein. The following Prädikat categories are for wines of ascending levels of ripeness and sweetness: Spätlese; Auslese; Beerenauslese; Strohwein (wines made from grapes picked and left to shrivel on straw, to concentrate their sweetness), together with Eiswein; Ausbruch (sweet wines from botrytized grapes); and Trockenbeerenauslese.

Austrian wines, at Qualitätswein, Kabinett, and often Spätlese levels, are generally dry. Red Auslese, too, may be dry – look for the word Trocken. At Strohwein levels and above, the wines are sweet to very sweet. The Wachau, one of Austria's finest wine regions, has some quality categories of its own for dry white wines. In ascending order of ripeness and body, these are Steinfeder (light and crisp), Federspiel, and Smaragd.

The most planted vine by far is the white grüner veltliner. It provides the base for many light, dry blends, but also gives some of Austria's finest aromatic, steely, peppery whites, particularly in Wachau, Kremstal, and Kamptal, in Niederösterreich. Welschriesling is popular for making good sweet and dry wines, while müller-thurgau is still significant, but declining fast. Among other white varieties are chardonnay (still sometimes called either morillon or feinburgunder), riesling, neuburger, muskat ottonel, traminer, pinot gris, pinot blanc, and sauvignon blanc.

Weissenkirchen in the beautiful Wachau region, source of fine riesling and grüner veltliner.

recommended producers

W Brundlmayer, Feiler-Artinger, Freie Weingärtner Wachau, F Hirtzberger, E Knoll, A Kracher, H Lang, Malat, Lenz Moser, Nikolaihof, W Opitz, Pfaffl, F X Pichler, F Prager, Prieler, Salomon-Undhof, Schloss Gobelsburg, H Schröck, E Triebaumer, J Umathum.

VINTAGES

Vintages vary considerably, although sweet wines can be made every year. 1990 and 1995 were excellent; 1993, 1994, 1997, 1998, 1999, and 2000 were all very good. Top grüner veltliners and rieslings can be long-lived.

Two oddities are grown only in Thermenregion – zierfandler (or spätrot) and rotgipfler. The most common red is the indigenous, cherry-scented zweigelt, followed closely by blaufränkisch and blauer portugieser. More interesting is the pinot noir-like st. laurent and blauer burgunder (pinot noir itself). Cabernet sauvignon is a new and fashionable import.

Steadily, Austria's reds have been getting fuller-bodied and more substantial over recent years, to the point where they can be overextracted and overoaked. Prices are high, too, since the domestic market laps them up. Most of the best come from the warmer south, in particular Burgenland. Burgenland is also the source of Austria's luscious sweet wines, which are often more Sauterneslike than German. The broad, shallow lake of Neusiedlersee provides the humidity that noble rot loves, but good dry whites are produced too. Neusiedlersee-Hügelland, on the other side of the lake, also makes all three styles. Other important regions are Donauland, Weinviertel (the largest region and producer of much everyday dry white), Carnuntum and Traisental; Styria; and Wien, or Vienna itself.

switzerland

High prices see to it that Swiss wines are little exported, much to the regret of many producers in Valais and Vaud, the two largest regions.

The French-speaking cantons of Switzerland have an appellation contrôlée system for their best wines, and this is gradually being applied to the German- and Italian-speaking cantons. In addition, the best merlots produced in Italian-speaking Ticino bear the VITI seal.

The main grape in the French-speaking parts is chasselas (or fendant in Valais), a soft, relatively neutral variety that, if not overcropped, is adept at reflecting differences in terroir. Sylvaner (alias johannisberg in the Valais), pinot gris, pinot blanc, and ermitage (marsanne) are among the other familar grapes grown alongside such indigenous, characterful, and often aromatic varieties as amigne, petite arvine, and humagne blanche. Red wines are made from pinot noir and gamay, sometimes blended to make simple, fruity Dôle; there is also a little promising syrah. German-speaking Switzerland focuses on blauburgunder (pinot noir) and riesling-sylvaner (müller-thurgau). Ticino concentrates on its long-established merlot, which varies from lightweight to serious Bordeaux-style.

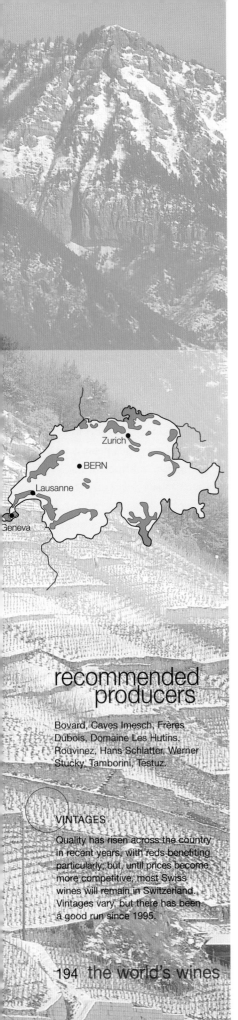

recommended producers

Bovard, Caves Imesch, Frères Dubois, Domaine Les Hutins, Rouvinez, Hans Schlatter, Werner Stucky, Tamborini, Testuz.

VINTAGES

Quality has risen across the country in recent years, with reds benefiting particularly; but, until prices become more competitive, most Swiss wines will remain in Switzerland. Vintages vary, but there has been a good run since 1995.

recommended producers

Breaky Bottom, Chapel Down, Chiddingstone, Davenport, Denbies, Nyetimber, Ridge View, Sharpham, Three Choirs, Valley Vineyards, Warden Abbey.

Pinot noir and meunier grown for sparkling wine at Nyetimber in Sussex.

england & wales

There are about 400 vineyards in England and Wales, and yet it can be hard to find any English or Welsh wine without going all the way to the farm gate.

The British, patriotic to a fault on some points and avid wine consumers, can be remarkably churlish when it comes to their own country's wines. Perhaps they are put off by memories of insipid medium-sweet whites, in Germanic-looking bottles bearing pictures of Kent oasthouses, encountered in the early 1980s. The good news is that English wine isn't like that any more. Many who established vineyards in the 1960s and 1970s (there was a boom after the hot summer of '76) knew nothing about grape-growing or winemaking. Only when people began to approach wine as a business rather than a hobby did things start to change.

GRAPE VARIETIES

England's damp climate means that finding the warmest, driest sites with the best-draining soil is essential. Most of these, inevitably, are in the south and east, but there are vineyards as far north as Durham and as far west as Cornwall. Early plantings were of grapes such as müller-thurgau, bacchus, and schönburger, as well as the hybrid seyval blanc, and they still dominate; but varieties such as riesling, chardonnay, pinot noir, and pinot gris have begun to appear.

The climate largely dictates the styles of wines produced. A few people persist with red wines, and a couple of vineyards even boast some cabernet sauvignon, but whites are far more common. The styles have evolved from the Germanic medium-dry and floral toward a drier, more herbaceous style that is more reminiscent of wines from the Loire. Malolactic fermentation and oak aging are now often used to round out the ever-sharp acidity. The rare sweet whites can be very good, but probably England's most promising style is sparkling wine. The best are those that unashamedly copy champagne, being made in the same way from the same grapes grown on broadly similar soils.

Chapel Down is based in Tenterden, Kent, but also buys grapes from several other counties.

eastern mediterranean

Declining markets for their traditional wines have forced many eastern Mediterranean winemakers to change – sometimes with remarkable results.

greece

If your opinion of wines from Greece is based on Retsina, it's time to take another look. Until recently, the Greeks were on the periphery of the revolution sweeping through southern Europe, but now they're doing their best to catch up. As in Portugal, southern France, and southern Italy, the story is of a quaintly flaccid industry, based on quantity rather than quality, receiving a shake-up. Faced with falling domestic consumption of Retsina, producers have realized that they either have to opt out, a common choice since on average grape-growers are over 60 years of age, or follow the quality path.

The best red grapes are the spicy, red-berry and cherrylike xynomavro, which turns gamey with age in the wines of Naoussa and Goumenissa; the deep, plummy agiorgitiko (or st. george) of Nemea; mavrodaphne, often used for fortified wines, particularly in Patras; and the herby limnio.

White grapes outnumber reds by more than three to one. The most notable are the aromatic moscophilero, responsible for the dry, muscatlike

Winemaker Evanghelos Gerovassiliou; harvest in Sithonia in Greece (right).

wines of Mantinia; Cephalonia's tangy, lemony robola; and assyrtiko, an appetizingly zesty specialty of Santorini with, sometimes, a whiff of the local volcanic soils. Among familiar grapes, muscat is used for some sweet wines, including the admired Samos, and chardonnay, cabernet sauvignon, merlot, and syrah are gaining ground – sometimes blended, to good effect, with varieties such as agiorgitiko.

Large companies such as Kourtakis, Boutari, Tsantalis, and Achaia Clauss are generally reliable, but the best wines are those from small estates. Excessive use of new oak gets in the way of some wines, but the best are excellent and improving with each vintage. Producers to look out for include Antonopoulos (for chardonnay), Domaine Carras, Gaia, Gentilini, Gerovassiliou, Ktima, Kyr-Yanni, Kosta Lazaridi, Domaine Mercouri, Strofilia, and Tselepos.

lebanon

Contrary to popular opinion, there's more to Lebanon than the famous Chateau Musar. The country's other main wineries, Ksara and Kefraya, both make wines that can hold their own on an international stage, with Comte de M, Kefraya's cabernet/syrah/mourvèdre blend, being especially good. But Musar remains Lebanon's most distinctive wine. Serge Hochar's idiosyncratic blend of cabernet sauvignon with cinsaut and carignan comes from the Bekaa Valley, where the altitude tempers the heat. The result is a wine that, depending on the vintage, has more or less of the cedary elegance of Bordeaux combined with

more or less of the warmth, power, and spice of the southern Rhône. Released at seven years old, the wines continue to evolve for many years. Hochar himself says the ideal age to drink them is at 15 years. There is also an attractive, younger wine called Hochar Père et Fils for those who can't wait.

israel

If the thought of Israeli wine conjures up images of old-fashioned, cloying, kosher reds, think again. Much of the country is too hot for vines, but in elevated parts, such as the Golan Heights, Galilee, and the hills around Jerusalem, viticulture is more than possible. Most wines are made from cabernet sauvignon, chardonnay, and the usual globetrotters, and the best have much in common with wines from California, where several of the winemakers have trained. The two leading producers are the Golan Heights Winery (under the Yarden and Gamla labels) and Domaine du Castel, near Jerusalem, whose wines could be mistaken for claret. Other estates to keep an eye out for include Baron Wine Cellars, Dalton, Margalit, and Tishbi.

Cabernet sauvignon, cinsaut, and grenache on Serge Hochar's estate high in the hills of the Bekaa Valley, Lebanon.

turkey

Turkey is the world's fourth largest grape-grower, but as it is a Moslem country, most of the harvest is used for table grapes. Less than 3 percent ends up as wine each year. Producers such as Kavaklidere and Doluca make reasonable wines occasionally, but don't hold your breath.

cyprus

The best-known wine on Cyprus is Commandaria, made from sun-dried mavrodaphne and xynisteri grapes. It's rich, brown, and molasses-sweet, and a little like Australia's liqueur muscats, but without the complexity of flavor. Table-wine production is dominated by four cooperatives, of which KEO and ETKO are the best known. There's little that's exciting, although the reds and whites under the Ancient Isle, Island Vines, and Mountain Vines labels are presentable.

eastern europe

Inadequate investment has prevented most Eastern European wine regions from realizing their full potential – and the exceptions prove the rule.

bulgaria

Oaky Bulgarian cabernet sauvignon was one of the success stories of the 1980s. But that was before Australia and all the other New World countries arrived on the scene, with their fruitier, more modern, oaked wines, and before the lengthy post-Communist restructuring of land ownership and cooperative wineries. Today, several wineries are privately owned and well equipped, and benefit from the involvement of foreign winemaking consultants; but until more producers own more of their own vineyards, it's unrealistic to expect definitive improvements to the wines.

The occasional mature cabernet still emerges, but in general, the wines are released when fairly young, and often it's the less ambitious reds, bottled younger and fresher, that work best.

More is not necessarily better where oak-aging of wine is concerned. Among the most consistent wines are Oriachovitza cabernet and merlot (from the Stara Zagora winery); Haskovo merlot (Haskovo); Suhindol cabernet (Lovico Suhindol); Iambol cabernet (Iambol); and Yantra Valley cabernet (Rousse). Boyar Estates' lavish new Blueridge winery in Sliven is one to watch for the future.

With whites, the improved wine-making has meant that old-style, flat, dull wines are now thin on the ground, and fresh, young chardonnays from the Rousse, Black Sea Pomorie, and Slaviantzi wineries can be a good value.

Bulgaria does have an appellation system, placing Controliran and oak-aged reserve wines at the top, but you're better off looking for the name of the producer and the grape variety.

Right: hand-picking grapes in the Bulgarian Suhindol region.

hungary

The legendary mold-encrusted cellars of Tokaj – Gyula Borsos fills a tasting glass with golden, sweet Aszú.

Hungary is the one Eastern European country that has investors lining up to take a stake in the vineyards. Interest is centered mostly on the Tokaj region in the northeast, source of the fabled sweet Tokaji Aszú, made from botrytis-affected local grapes (of which furmint is the most important). The wines are categorized by sweetness, measured in puttonyos, from 3 putts to 7 putts, the sweetest. There is also a vineyard classification, first drawn up in 1700, with first-, second-, and third-class sites. The best producers are Disznókö, Megyer, Oremus, Pajzos, Royal Tokaji Wine Company, and István Szepsy.

Elsewhere, one of Hungary's most talked-about producers is the Hilltop Neszmély winery, where Akos Kamocsay and his team make an excellent range of modern wines, including Eastern Europe's best sauvignon blancs. In Eger, home of Bull's Blood, leading red wine producers include Tibor G'al and Vilmos Thummerer. In the Villány region, near the Croatian border, Austrian grower Franz Weninger is making wine in conjunction with a celebrated local producer, Attila Gere. He also has an estate in Sopron, close to the Austrian border. Near Lake Balaton, Australian winemaker Kym Milne overseas the reliable, good value Chapel Hill range, in between other international winemaking assignments.

romania

Romania is a classic case of vast potential unrealized because of lack of investment. Even so, the very occasional plummy pinot noir (usually from the Dealul Mare region), and the odd juicy cabernet and fresh, spicy gewurztraminer, show what can be achieved. A winery to watch out for in the future is Prahova Winecellars, which recently benefited from a $3 million refit. For the moment, arguably Romania's best wines, and certainly the most striking, are the inexpensive sweet wines from Cotnari and Murfatlar (sometimes labeled with the grape variety tamiîosa).

Vineyards by the canal at Cernavoda, east of Constantia in the Murfatlar region of Romania, a source of good-value sweet wines.

others

Within the former states of Yugoslavia, Ljutomer in Slovenia is famous for laski rizling but can produce better whites. For reds, Croatia has plavac mali, reputedly related to zinfandel, as well as several other interesting varieties. Californian Croat Mike Grgich makes decent if rather expensive wines here.

In both Slovakia and the Czech Republic, frankovka (blaufränkisch) and st. laurent are the favored varieties for reds, and welschriesling, pinot blanc, pinot gris, and the light, spicy irsay oliver are popular whites. On the Czech side, highlights include the Moravenka whites from the producer Znovin Znojmo, and the sparkling Bohemia Sekt. On the Slovak side, the wines of the Vino Nitra coop and the sweet wines of Tokaj (adjacent to the famous Hungarian region) stand out.

Moldova boasts extensive vineyards full of well-known grape varieties. But little of note is exported, apart from a few flying winemaker wines from the Hincesti winery, the odd cabernet from Cricova, and some older vintages of a rather claretlike red called Negru de Purkar. In the Ukraine, the most important region is the Crimea, source of some remarkable sweet wines from the Massandra winery.

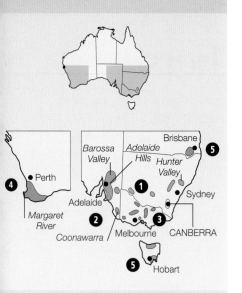

1. NEW SOUTH WALES
2. SOUTH AUSTRALIA
3. VICTORIA
4. WESTERN AUSTRALIA
5. QUEENSLAND/TASMANIA

VINTAGES

While it's seldom a struggle to ripen grapes in Australia, vintage variation does exist, and its effect will become more apparent as vineyards are established in cooler areas. Given the size of the country, blanket assessments are impossible, but broadly speaking, 1998 was a countrywide success for red wines; 2000 was also a success for most (with Barossa and McLaren Vale notable exceptions). 1995 is a year that most growers would prefer to forget.

Almost all Australian wines are ready to drink on release and, while many change with time in bottle, only a few improve. Of the whites, the better rieslings and semillons can be kept for at least five years from the vintage. Most reds above $12 per bottle (except pinot noir) benefit from keeping for at least two years, and the best shirazes and cabernets much longer.

australia

Reliability, flavor, and simple, friendly labeling have enabled Australian wines to elbow other countries off wine-store shelves all over the world.

After spending the past 15 years showing the world how to make and market wines, Australia's producers, among the most technically competent in the world, have now turned their attention from the wineries to the vineyards. Many established regions have proved to be too warm for grapes such as sauvignon blanc and pinot noir, so cooler areas, such as the Adelaide Hills, have been sought out and developed. Elsewhere, gnarled old vines – some planted more than a century ago in the Barossa Valley – are being resurrected after years of neglect. The small quantities of deeply colored, richly flavored wines they yield command high prices across the globe. At the opposite end of the spectrum, an extensive planting program in the 1990s has meant that cheaper wines no longer have to rely on inferior grapes such as sultana and trebbiano, but can now be made from chardonnay, cabernet sauvignon, and merlot.

Not that Australia is perfect. Wines that are undeniably correct technically can lack the soul (which the French would attribute to terroir) that differentiates the great from the good. Equally, if you're seeking subtlety, you will have to sift through a lot of fairly boisterous wines to find it. But if these are the only criticisms that can be leveled at the Australians, they don't have too much to worry about.

APPELLATIONS AND CLASSIFICATIONS

Most Australian wines are labeled by grape variety, the grape variety (or varieties) and the producer's name or brand name being the main keys to style and quality. This is not going to change overnight, especially as many wines will continue to be blends of, say, chardonnay from several regions and/or states. Nevertheless, the appellation system currently being introduced will lead to a greater emphasis on regions and regional differences. The three-tiered system, known as geographical indications, or GIs, will specify where at least 85 percent of the grapes come from. The three levels are states/zones, regions, and subregions. Each state has its own GI, while the zones are divisions within each state (the only exception is South Eastern Australia, which takes in every major wine district except those in Western Australia). Regions are districts within the zones; subregions are further divisions. For example, Lenswood is a subregion of the Adelaide Hills, which is a region within the Mount Lofty Ranges zone.

WHITE GRAPES

Chardonnay takes up as much vineyard space as all other quality white varieties combined. In general, it makes ripe, generously fruity wines, many with obvious oak, but unoaked versions are gaining ground. The lemony semillon also appears in oaked and unoaked guises: the richest and oakiest come from the Barossa, and the longest-lived (without any oak, despite a toasty flavor) from the Hunter Valley. The sumptuous, sweet, botrytized semillons are also well worth trying. Riesling is another grape used for sweet wines, but it's mostly made into dry or off-dry wines with a distinct lime-juice character. The best sauvignon blanc, of which there isn't much, is like a plumper version of New Zealand sauvignon. Other whites to seek out are the rich, tropical fruit-flavored marsanne, and the ripe but tangy verdelho.

RED GRAPES

Shiraz, the most widely planted grape, makes full-bodied red wines with berry fruit flavors and often the sweet, spicy, vanilla character of American oak. Those from warmer climes have chocolate and licorice hints, while cooler areas give more pepper or eucalyptus. The same nuances can often be found overlaying the blackcurrant fruit in Australian cabernet sauvignon. While shiraz/cabernet is a popular, traditional blend, merlot is on the increase, especially as a single varietal. Fans of full-blooded shiraz should try grenache and mourvèdre (sometimes labeled mataro) and any blends of these three. Those who want something lighter can turn to Australia's pinot noirs. Most offer easy-drinking strawberry fruit in an oaky overcoat, but a few have some of the exotic aromas and silky texture of burgundy.

Pinot noir is also used for sparkling wine, as is chardonnay. Simpler wines are exuberantly frothy, while the more ambitious have less overt fruit flavor and more finesse and yeasty complexity. The Australians also make sparkling reds, mostly from shiraz. Love 'em or hate 'em, you can't ignore them, and they are de rigueur for an Australian Christmas dinner. So too are the fortified muscats and tokays (or muscadelles) of Rutherglen – liquid dessert.

Right: Henschke's famous Hill of Grace vineyard high up in the Eden Valley, South Australia.
Below: chardonnay vines stretch to the horizon in Cowra, New South Wales.

new south wales

While the humid conditions in the Hunter Valley hamper viticulture, especially at harvest time, the unique style of unoaked semillon made there remains a national treasure.

recommended producers

de Bortoli, Brokenwood, Evans Family, Lake's Folly, McWilliams, Rosemount, Rothbury, Tyrrells.

Hunter Valley shiraz, still sometimes with an old-fashioned overtone of "sweaty saddle," is also one of Australia's distinct regional styles. Mudgee is beginning to fulfill its potential for both reds and whites, and may eventually become more important than the Hunter. Nearby Orange and Cowra are becoming known for chardonnay, while, further south, some delicious shiraz is being made near Canberra. The Murrumbidgee Irrigation Area (MIA), otherwise known as Riverina, produces vast quantities of simple, everyday wine, plus heady botrytized semillons near Griffith.

south australia

The vast, irrigated vineyards of the Riverland provide wine in quantity, but South Australia is also home to several of the country's finest and most famous regions.

recommended producers

Tim Adams, d'Arenberg, Ashton Hills, Wolf Blass, Grant Burge, Chapel Hill, Grosset, Hardy's, Henschke, Katnook, Leasingham, Peter Lehmann, Lindemans, Charles Melton, Mount Horrocks, Nepenthe, Orlando, Penfolds, Penley Estate, Petaluma, Primo Estate, St. Hallett, Seaview, Shaw & Smith, Tatachilla, Torbreck, Veritas, Wirra Wirra, Wynns, Yalumba.

Top: Darren de Bortoli with a glass of his botrytized semillon, the Riverina's first in the 1980s. Above: spring in South Australia's Clare Valley, a region famous for its rieslings.

South Australia's great advantage is that it has enough variations in altitude, latitude, and proximity to the coast for almost any grape variety to find a good home, somewhere in which to produce quality – or quantity if that is what is required.

Chardonnay, sauvignon blanc, and pinot noir thrive in the hills to the northeast of Adelaide, while the Clare and Eden valleys are renowned for their intense, dry, lime-scented rieslings. Padthaway in the south is admired for its whites, especially chardonnay. Cabernet sauvignon hits its peak in historic Coonawarra, although other, newer districts along the Limestone Coast, such as Robe, Mount Benson, and Wrattonbully, might dispute this in the future. McLaren Vale, to the south of Adelaide, makes a richer style of cabernet, and most regions make shiraz, but none are as famous as the rich, ripe, old-vine shirazes of the Barossa.

Top right: Château Tahbilk was established in 1860, making it the oldest winery in Victoria.

Right: close to the Indian Ocean, the Leeuwin Estate in Margaret River makes superb chardonnay.

recommended producers

Bests, Brown Brothers, Coldstream Hills, Dalwhinnie, Domaine Chandon, Mitchelton, Morris, Mount Langi Ghiran, Mount Mary, Yarra Yering.

recommended producers

Cape Mentelle, Cullens, Evans & Tate, Frankland Estate, Howard Park, Leeuwin Estate, Moss Wood, Pierro, Plantagenet, Vasse Felix.

victoria

Victoria's bulk region is along the Murray River in the northwest, while the state's quirkiest wines are the fortified, so-called liqueur muscats and tokays from Rutherglen, in the northeast.

Central Victoria is peppered with small wineries. The best cabernets and shirazes are produced in Bendigo, Heathcote, the Grampians, the Pyrenees, and the Goulburn Valley (also a source of lovely marsanne), and combine intensity with finesse. Further to the south, the Yarra Valley, Geelong, and the Mornington Peninsula all make fine pinot noir and chardonnay.

western australia

Some pleasant chenin blancs and verdelhos still come from the hot Swan Valley near Perth, but the focus of the WA wine industry has shifted to cooler, more southerly regions.

Margaret River is the source of rich, powerful, but elegant cabernet and chardonnay, and underrated shiraz, semillon, and sauvignon blanc. Great Southern is a vast, varied region along the south coast that produces some of Australia's best riesling (rivaling those of the Clare and Eden valleys in South Australia), as well as good shiraz and cabernet. Pemberton, a newer region between the two, initially made its name with chardonnay and pinot noir, but neither has quite lived up to expectation. It may be that shiraz and merlot would be better bets for the climate.

other regions

Most of Queensland is too hot for the cultivation of wine grapes, but some vineyards can be found at high altitudes in the Granite Belt, where the semillon and shiraz can be surprisingly good. Tasmania has the kind of cool climate in which white varieties such as chardonnay, riesling, pinot gris, sauvignon blanc, and gewurztraminer perform best. There are several wineries, often supplying grapes to mainland wineries for sparkling wines, but only Pipers Brook has made a splash on the international stage.

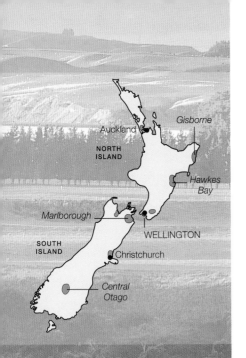

new zealand

Far from the equator, this is the coolest of the southern-hemisphere wine countries – and it shows in the clarity of flavor and freshness of every wine.

By southern-hemisphere standards, the climate of New Zealand was long judged unlikely for serious winegrowing. So unlikely that, right up to the 1970s, the country was dismissed as fit only for inferior Germanic grapes such as müller-thurgau. Then, in the 1980s, the phenomenal international success of Marlborough sauvignon blanc (first planted in 1973) forced a rethink, but many people still concluded that New Zealand would always be a one-wine country, at least in terms of quality. When highly promising chardonnays and sparkling wines began to appear, it was clear that New Zealand didn't have all its eggs in one basket, after all. But, surely, the reds would never amount to anything? Faced with convincingly ripe pinot noirs, the pessimists had to concede a point, but they knew that cabernet and merlot could never amount to anything. Then came the wonderful 1998 vintage...

Today, the doubters question the wisdom of planting nebbiolo, tempranillo, touriga nacional, and viognier, but, thankfully, passionate, pioneering individuals ignore them. It took the Europeans centuries to discover which grapes grew best where (not to mention how best to cultivate them); in comparison, the progress that New Zealand has made in 25 years is remarkable.

WHITE GRAPES

Sauvignon blanc is the grape most readily associated with New Zealand, largely thanks to the sometimes startling wines of Marlborough. A vivid cocktail of gooseberries, grass, currant leaves, and vibrant acidity may not suit everyone, but it's hard to ignore. If you find the Marlborough style too intense, Hawkes Bay sauvignons tend to be a little fuller-bodied, with more tropical fruit.

Although sauvignon grabs more of the headlines, the most widely planted variety is chardonnay, producing styles ranging from simple and peachy to quasi-burgundian. Grown in most regions, from Central Otago in the south of the South Island to Gisborne and Northland way up on the North Island, the best chardonnays are excellent, but pinpointing regional character is difficult because it's still early days and the winemaker's thumbprint tends to make the deepest impression. Oak, decidedly buttery flavors, and a bite of acidity are general hallmarks. Chardonnay, usually from Marlborough, is also used (with or without

recommended producers

Auckland and environs: Babich, Collards, Corbans, Kim Crawford, Delegat's, Goldwater, Kumeu River, Matua Valley, Montana, Nobilo/ Selaks, Stonyridge, Villa Maria.

Canterbury: Giesen, Waipara West.

Central Otago: Felton Road, Rippon.

Gisborne: Millton.

Hawkes Bay: Craggy Range, Esk Valley, Morton Estate, Ngatarawa, Sileni, Stonecroft, Te Mata, Trinity Hill, Unison.

Marlborough: Cloudy Bay, Fromm, Huia, Hunters, Isabel Estate, Jackson Estate, Lawson's Dry Hills, Nautilus, Seresin, Vavasour, Wairau River.

Martinborough: Ata Rangi, Dry River, Martinborough Vineyards, Palliser.

Nelson: Neudorf.

VINTAGES

Vintage matters more in New Zealand than in other New World countries. Since the sodden 1995 vintage, the weather has been mostly favorable, with 1999 and 2000 producing good whites, and the best reds ever in 1998. Most wines are ready to drink on release, but the top Bordeaux-style blends can be kept for five years.

pinot noir) for sparkling wines: the cheaper ones compare favorably with similarly priced wines from anywhere in the world, while the most expensive can match champagne for quality and style. Other successful white grapes are the aromatic trio of gewurztraminer, pinot gris, and riesling. The latter, grown throughout the South Island, is more Alsace than German in style, with powerful citrus and apple flavors, and often quite heady alcohol. New Zealand riesling also produces some excellent sweet wines, but these, like Canada's icewines until recently, are currently banned from the EU (for no good reason, I might add).

Cloudy Bay in Marlborough, the winery that put New Zealand sauvignon blanc on the world map.

RED GRAPES

Among the red grapes, New Zealand pinot noir is a rapidly rising star, with the best wines allying rich, cherry-ish fruit to a velvety texture. Impressive results are coming from Central Otago, Marlborough, the Waipara district of Canterbury, and Nelson, all on the South Island, and Martinborough at the south of the North Island. Cabernet sauvignon and merlot perform best in Hawkes Bay and in small areas close to Auckland, such as Northland and Waiheke Island; but it is merlot in Hawkes Bay that is increasingly dominant in the Bordeaux-style blends, which may also include malbec and cabernet franc. Expect wines with well-defined flavors, often with a leafy (but no longer hard or green) edge. The best come close to fine red Bordeaux – and sometimes in price, too. Hawkes Bay is also starting to produce some promising, dark, peppery syrahs.

Vines planted in wide rows to allow machine harvesters in the Brancott Valley, Marlborough.

united states

California wines are probably the best known outside the US, and for good reason, but California is by no means the end of the American trail.

The US has no vineyard classification system, but it does have Approved Viticultural Areas (AVAs). If one of these is listed on a label, then at least 85 percent of the grapes must have come from the specified regions, although the producer can choose the variety. Some AVAs are vast; some are small and contain just one winery. They are a guarantee of origin, not of quality or style; so, as in most of the New World, the grape variety or varieties and the name or brand name of the producer are the real keys.

california

Although California is the world's fourth largest wine producer, domestic demand keeps prices high and exports low, so it can be difficult for foreign fans to keep track of its exciting progress.

American thirst also explains the dearth of decent wines at the cheaper end of the market, and why, at a slightly higher level, only a handful of producers offer wines that are genuinely a good value. To discover what California is capable of, you need to fork out quite serious money, although serious money isn't itself a guarantee of excellence. Sometimes winemakers try too hard to be the best, and the result is wines that are too ripe, too oaky, and too alcoholic. But at other times, when the power is matched with finesse, the wines compare with and sometimes outclass their European counterparts. It's just a shame that they can cost you an arm, a leg, and half a torso.

WHITE GRAPES

The sunny climate comes through in the generous nature of the wines. Chardonnay is the most important white variety, and veers from simple and actively sweet to opulent and buttery, usually with oak making its presence felt. Sauvignon blanc is often oaked (as in Fumé Blanc), and in general is fuller and less herbaceous than in France or New Zealand.

WASHINGTON

OREGON

New York

San Francisco

WASHINGTON DC

Los Angeles

① CALIFORNIA

② OREGON & WASHINGTON STATE

③ NEW YORK STATE

recommended producers

Au Bon Climat, Beaulieu Vineyard, Beringer, Bonny Doon, Cain, Calera, Caymus, Chalone, Cline Cellars, Clos du Val, Diamond Creek, Dominus, Duckhorn, Fetzer, Frog's Leap, Gallo (the Sonoma range only), Jade Mountain, Kendall-Jackson, Kistler, Robert Mondavi, Mumm Cuvée Napa, Joseph Phelps, Ravenswood, Ridge, Roederer Estate, Saintsbury, Schramsberg, Shafer, Sonoma Cutrer, Stag's Leap Wine Cellars.

VINTAGES & WHEN TO DRINK

Most wines, red and white, are ready on release, although some chardonnays may benefit from an extra year in bottle for the oak to become better integrated. The better zinfandels, merlots, and pinot noirs tend to change rather than improve. The most serious cabernet-based wines need at least five years in bottle, and will last well for several more years. Except for 1998, the vintages of the 1990s and 2000 were good. 1994 and 1997 were the best for reds.

The current popularity of grapes from the Rhône means that many wineries now make viognier, with the best of them matching Condrieu for power, perfume, and price.

RED GRAPES

Cabernet sauvignon, either by itself or in combination with merlot and cabernet franc (a blend sometimes labeled Meritage), regularly makes the greatest wines in California. More money buys more intensity and longevity, but even the less expensive cabernets can pack in plenty of sweet, ripe fruit tinged with aromas of olives, herbs, and mint. Merlot, on the other hand, became something of a fashion victim in the 1990s; the best have a wonderfully lush, sweet, smoky berry flavor, but too many are simply bland and overoaked.

As with viognier, syrah has benefited from Rhône fever and the attentions of a group of dedicated producers – the self-styled Rhône Rangers. Compared to the Rhône originals, California syrahs often have an extra aromatic dimension, but they are less exuberantly ripe and spicy than most Australian shirazes.

California's greatest contribution to the world of big, spicy reds is the brambly, high-alcohol zinfandel, the essence of honest, hearty red wine, but also, in its white zinfandel or blush form, the epitome of vapid, mass-market pink wine. Petite sirah, another long-established specialty, makes even chunkier, chewier reds than zinfandel. The equally well entrenched barbera is used mostly for simple, everyday reds, but sangiovese, another Italian grape, is being nurtured by more ambitious producers. Pinot noir is about as subtle as California gets. Where the sweet cherry and red berry fruit is allowed to shine through the oak, the wines can be superb – and are priced accordingly.

REGIONS

The most famous region is Napa Valley, source of California's best cabernets and merlots. Howell Mountain, Stag's Leap, Oakville, and Rutherford are just a few of the AVAs within Napa. At the cooler, southern end of the region is Carneros, which is the favored spot for pinot noir and chardonnay (for both still and sparkling wine). Carneros runs into Sonoma Valley, which boasts fewer

Young chardonnay vines, near Forestville in the Russian River Valley, Sonoma County.

wineries than Napa, and more diverse conditions, so there's a place here for everything from pinot noir (in the Russian River Valley AVA) to zinfandel (Dry Creek Valley). Further to the north are Lake and Mendocino counties, sources of good-value wines and some fine sparkling wines.

The Central Coast AVA stretches south and east of San Francisco Bay and, thanks to variations in coastal influence and altitude, has a wide variety of growing conditions. In Monterey, Santa Maria Valley, and Santa Ynez Valley, it's cool enough for pinot noir, while in Paso Robles and Santa Cruz, the warmth of the climate comes through in the full-bodied cabernets and zinfandels. The Central Valley covers much of central California, and in general produces large quantities of dreary wine. The Sierra Foothills area is an exception; it has excellent zinfandels and ancient plantings of grapes such as barbera, petite sirah, and grenache, which are sought by producers around the state.

Oregon's Argyle winery in the Willamette Valley – renowned for its sparkling wine.

recommended producers

Oregon
Amity, Argyle, Beaux Frères, Broadley, Domaine Drouhin, Elk Cove, Erath, Eyrie, King Estate, Ponzi, Ken Wright.

Washington State
Andrew Will, Canoe Ridge, Château Ste. Michelle, Columbia Crest, Columbia Winery, Covey Run, l'Ecole No. 41, Hedges, Hogue Cellars, Leonetti.

Vineyards near Benton City, in Red Mountain, part of the Yakima Valley region in Washington State.

oregon & washington state

While California dominates the American Pacific coast, the two very different regions of Oregon and Washington State are both producing wines in their own distinctive styles.

In Oregon's Willamette Valley, south of the state capital of Portland, the climate is similar to that in Burgundy. It's no surprise, then, that pinot noir is already enjoying considerable success (at the hands of the notable Burgundian wine-maker Véronique Drouhin, for one) and, like burgundy, it is experiencing considerable vintage variation. What is surprising is that, although there is some impressive chardonnay, many producers prefer to grow pinot gris. Others reserve their chardonnay for champagne-style sparkling wines.

In theory, Washington State should be cooler and wetter than Oregon, but the main wine region, the Columbia Valley, lies to the east of the Cascade Mountains and is a semidesert in which grapes can be grown only with irrigation. Winters can be extremely cold, and every so often there is a freeze severe enough to kill vines in large numbers. However, quality wine-growing is made possible by long hours of sunshine. Chardonnay, semillon, and riesling can all thrive, but the stars of the Columbia Valley are the full-bodied reds, made from cabernet, merlot, and, increasingly, syrah, which is being planted at the expense of lemberger (Austria's blaufränkisch).

other regions

Most states produce wine, but only for very local consumption. Exceptions include chardonnay and riesling in New York State around the Finger Lakes (look for Lamoreaux Landing, Fox Run, and Wagner), and merlot and chardonnay on the North Fork of Long Island (look for Bridgehampton, Hargrave, Palmer, Peconic Bay, and Pindar). Texas, Virginia, and Maryland all boast burgeoning wine industries, and there are pockets of excellence (such as Callaghan in Arizona) in several other states.

Vancouver

Montréal
OTTAWA
Toronto

NORTH AMERICA

recommended producers

Château des Charmes, Henry of Pelham, Inniskillin, Marynissen, Mission Hill, Quail's Gate, Southbrook.

Right: Quail's Gate vineyard benefits from the moderating effects of Okanagan Lake in British Columbia.

canada

In terms of quantity, Canada's fledgling wine industry will never threaten its southern neighbor, but there are wines that indicate a promising future.

In Ontario, the wineries on and around the Niagara Peninsula produce impressive riesling and chardonnay. When it comes to pinot noir, it isn't just the locals who recognize the potential – the Boisset group of Burgundy is involved in a joint venture with the Inniskillin winery. Much further west in British Columbia (BC), the Okanagan Valley is an extension of Washington State's Columbia Valley (*see opposite page*), and is similarly arid. Temperature varies along the valley and, in theory, there should be a place suitable for almost any grape variety. So far, merlot, chardonnay, and pinot noir have enjoyed the greatest success.

Good as the dry wines can be, it is Canada's icewines that attract the most attention. Nearly every vintage provides the freezing weather conditions needed to make these essence-like dessert wines, usually from riesling or the hybrid grape vidal. Some are cloying, but the best have a streak of acidity to balance the heady sweetness – and the good news is that the European Union's illogical ban on these wines was finally lifted in 2001.

chile

Chile first made a name for itself with its cabernet sauvignons and merlots, which offered soft, juicy flavors at low prices. Now there's much more.

Chile's staple fare of fruity cabernets, merlots, and carmenères is as reliable as ever, but the country is now more focused on premium wines for which grape varieties have been carefully matched to site. Casablanca is a case in point.

APPELLATIONS AND CLASSIFICATIONS

Chile's appellation system splits the vineyard area into Aconcagua in the north (which contains Casablanca), the Central Valley in the middle, and Bío-Bío (containing Nuble and Chillán) in the south. The Central Valley is by far the biggest and most important region, and is subdivided into Maipo, Rapel, and Maule. These in turn are subdivided again: Maipo is subdivided into Santiago, Talagante, Pirque, Llano del Maipo, and Buin; Rapel into Cachapoal, Colchagua, Santa Cruz, and Peralillo; and Maule into Curicó (which includes Lontué), Talca, Cauquenes, Linares, and Parral. Those are the official regions. But Chilean winemakers are discovering the value of terroir – as a marketing tool, if nothing else – and are constantly identifying new valleys within valleys, new subregions within subregions. These don't have appellation status, so won't be named on the front label of a wine, but they may well get a mention on the back label.

Whether the wine of a subregion is necessarily better than one simply labeled Central Valley is another matter. Regional differences do exist in Chile, but at the moment, to you and me, the differences between one producer and another may be more apparent than those between two subregions – not least because even Chilean subregions are large and far from homogeneous. The exception is the cool Casablanca Valley, which is excellent for whites; the crispest, most aromatic sauvignon blanc comes from Casablanca. Other regions grow a full range of grapes, not all of which are necessarily planted in the ideal places.

GRAPE VARIETIES

Much depends, too, on the blend of grapes. Chilean wines may be varietals or they may be blends – but even those labeled as varietals may in fact (and quite legally) be blends. The reason is that, until the early 1990s, carmenère was incorrectly identified in Chile: it was assumed to be merlot. The difference was only officially recognized in 1996, and it is estimated that some 60–90 percent

recommended producers

Almaviva, Caliterra, Carmen, Casa Lapostolle, Concha y Toro, Cono Sur, Cousiño Macul, Dallas Conte, Domaine Paul Bruno, Errazuriz, Gracia, Mont Gras, Montes, San Pedro, Santa Carolina, Santa Rita, Terramater, Torres, Valdivieso, Veramonte, Villard, Viña Casablanca, Viña La Rosa.

VINTAGES

With the exception of 1998, when El Niño caused some problems (although fewer than in Argentina), the Chilean climate is ideal and predictable. All except the most expensive wines are made for drinking young, and even the expensive ones have yet to prove that they age well.

of "merlot" in Chilean vineyards is in fact carmenère, a variety imported from Bordeaux at the end of the 19th century, but now almost extinct there. Since 1998, it has been legal to label wine as carmenère, but the two are often mixed in the vineyards, and so a lot of blends will go on being labeled as merlot.

This also happened with sauvignon blanc and sauvignonasse (or sauvignon vert), with the difference that nobody wants to label their wine as sauvignonasse because it is so much less prestigious. Nobody is planting sauvignonasse now, whereas carmenère is being planted for its own sake – apart from its dark, intense, velvety charms, it gives Chile a point of difference, something it appeared to lack before.

As well as cabernet, merlot, carmenère, and sauvignon, there is pinot noir, malbec, syrah, chardonnay, and some semillon and gewurztraminer. Reds tend to be made in a supple, overtly fruity style – very seductive even if, at the least expensive end, a little repetitive. If you want genuine character, you have to pay a little more. Chardonnays have tropical, pineappley fruit flavors and rely on new oak for structure: look for wines from Casablanca if you want more complexity and elegance. Gewurztraminer is promisingly well balanced and aromatic.

Above: the "tank farm" at Caliterra's La Arboledas vineyard in the Colchagua Valley.

Below: vines – and cactus – at Errazuriz's Don Maximiano estate in the Aconcagua Valley.

recommended producers

La Agricola, Alta Vista, Altos Los Hormigas, Balbi, Catena, Colomé, Etchart, Fabre Montmayou, Finca El Retiro, Finca Flichman, Humberto Canale, J&F Lurton, Nieto & Senetiner, Norton, Ricardo Santos, Valentin Bianchi, Viña Amalia, Weinert.

BODEGAS ETCHART

VINTAGES & WHEN TO DRINK

Vintages are reliably similar unless El Niño strikes, as it did in 1998. Wines are ready to drink when released, although the best reds will keep five years.

argentina

In Argentina, production of the kind of wine likely to appeal to foreign palates is still relatively young, but the industry is making fast progress.

Argentina's international success so far has been helped by the high altitude of its best vineyards. Located in the foothills of the Andes, they are some of the highest vineyards in the world, taking advantage of temperate climates that the country otherwise lacks. But a system of controlled appellations in Argentina is still in its infancy, and most wines simply bear the name of a province.

GRAPE VARIETIES

The most important piece of information on the label, apart from the name of the producer, is the grape variety. Argentina is best known for its concentrated, ripe, spicy malbec, which seems to make far better wine here than it ever did in Bordeaux. Better, too, than many a Cahors, the other main source of the grape.

There is also merlot, cabernet sauvignon, and some impressive syrah, together with the Italian varieties barbera, bonarda, and sangiovese. These generally lack the characteristic bite and intensity of the Italian originals, but perhaps because they are being made to a price. Tempranillo, similarly, tends to be made as a relatively cheap wine. Red wines are Argentina's strength, but there are some good oaked chardonnays, small amounts of viognier, riesling, and semillon, and, possibly the trump card, the distinctive white torrontes. This muscatlike grape produces headily perfumed and often high-alcohol wines. Salta, in particular, with vineyards at up to 5,000 ft (1,500 m) above sea level, suits torrontes.

The biggest wine-producing province is Mendoza, which contains the controlled appellation of Luján de Cuyo. After that, in terms of quantity produced, comes the province of San Juan. La Rioja, Salta, Catamarca, and Patagonia's Río Negro and Neuquen also make wine.

The Andes provide the backdrop for Bodega La Rosa (Michel Torino), in Salta Province.

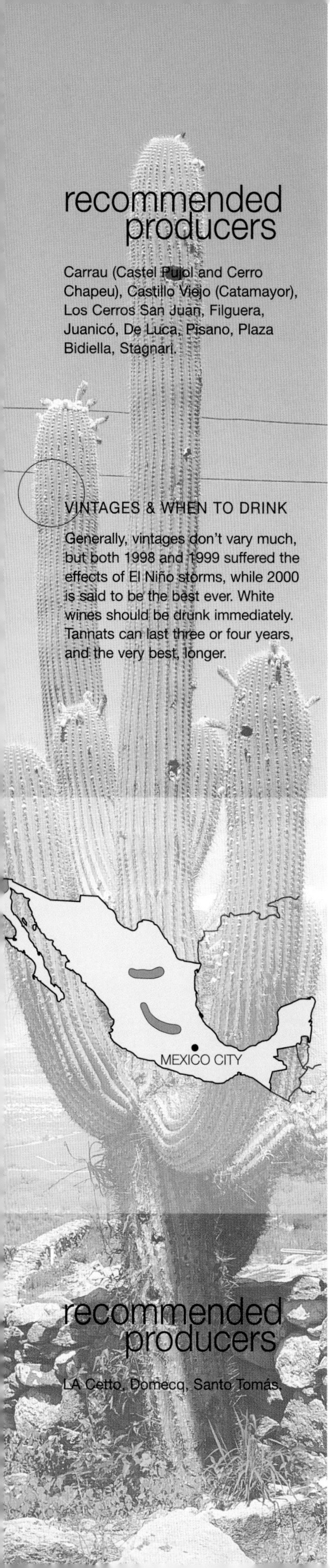

VINTAGES & WHEN TO DRINK

Generally, vintages don't vary much, but both 1998 and 1999 suffered the effects of El Niño storms, while 2000 is said to be the best ever. White wines should be drunk immediately. Tannats can last three or four years, and the very best, longer.

uruguay

Most of Uruguay's output, which compares in size to New Zealand's, sells well on the home market, but the government is eager to build up exports.

The country's specialty is red wine made from tannat, which is also the principal grape behind the muscular Madiran of southwest France. Just as malbec is more supple and succulent in Argentina than in its native Cahors, so tannat is riper, softer, and more approachable in Uruguay than in Madiran. The other red grapes being planted include cabernet sauvignon, merlot, and cabernet franc, some of which are blended with tannat. There is also some promising syrah. White wines are much less important, but include sauvignon blanc, riesling, gewurztraminer, viognier, and various blends of those grapes with the otherwise dreary ugni blanc.

Most of the wine regions are in the south, where the largest, just to the north of Montevideo, is Canelones. Other important regions are San José and Colonia to the west, and Rivera and Salto in the north of the country. For the moment, though, the name of the producer is a far more important guide to wine style than is region.

mexico

Mexico had vines planted before any other American country, north or south, and its modern wines are certainly showing some promise.

Yet Mexico fights to keep up with Chile and Argentina. Baja California, the main growing region, has a wide range of grapes, not all of them especially well suited to the hot, dry climate. Reds such as cabernet sauvignon, petite sirah, merlot, malbec, grenache, zinfandel, and grenache generally do best. There is also some nebbiolo (a difficult variety with which there has been some success) and carignan. Whites, including chenin blanc, trebbiano, colombard, and palomino, are grown for brandy.

MEXICO CITY

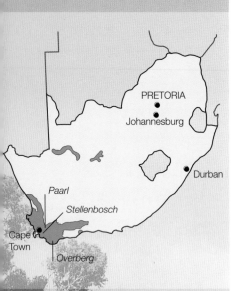

south africa

Winemaking in South Africa has a long history, yet South African wine is struggling to catch up with its principal New World competitors.

One potent reason for South Africa's underachievement is historical: the isolation of the apartheid era. These were formative years for the international wine industry, but South Africa's winemakers were largely cut off from the developments in both technology and consumer taste. By the time apartheid ended in the early 1990s, the gulf between Cape wines and those from other countries was wide.

Farsighted wine producers had realized this long before and had looked abroad for inspiration. Expensive though they were, new French oak barrels began to appear in several cellars during the 1980s, and the improvements in wine quality were often dramatic. But there were other problems. Winemakers were held back by the lack of decent plant material – vines, in other words. Even today, chardonnay, sauvignon blanc, cabernet sauvignon, and merlot together account for only a fifth of the vineyard area and a smaller proportion of the output. There is no lack of people eager to plant, but demand for new vines far exceeds supply – there simply aren't enough commercial nurseries.

Another problem, and not one exclusive to the Cape, is that the vineyards have long been riddled with viral diseases that impede full ripening of the grapes. Many vineyards still need to be replanted with virus-free stock – but, of course, there is a shortage of new vines.

GRAPE VARIETIES

The good news is that, where talented producers have access to good, healthy vines, the wines can be thrilling, with the best combining the ripe fruit flavors of a sunny climate with a firmer, more elegant, European-style structure. Significant progress has been made with cabernet sauvignon, merlot, and chardonnay: also, most recently, with shiraz, which used to exhibit all the worst characteristics of Cape wines – at once green and unripe, overbaked and edgy. Sauvignon, too, is starting to find its feet, in a style that is slightly more herby and tangier than New Zealand's.

In addition, South Africa has two potential trump cards – pinotage and chenin blanc. The red pinotage grape is the Cape's own crossing of pinot noir and cinsaut. Once famously condemned as tasting of "rusty nails," today's bottlings are more likely to show plum, cherry, and banana flavors, in styles ranging from simple, soft, and juicy to robust, full-bodied, oaky, and capable of aging.

recommended producers

Constantia: Buitenverwachting, Klein Constantia, Steenberg.

Stellenbosch: Beyerskloof, Neil Ellis, Grangehurst, Jordan, Kanonkop, Longridge, Meerlust, Mulderbosch, Rust-en-Vrede, Rustenberg, Saxenberg, Simonsig, Stellenzicht, Thelema, Vergelegen, Vriesenhof, Warwick.

Paarl: Bellingham, Boschendal, Cabrière, Cathedral Cellars (part of KWV), Fairview, Glen Carlou, La Motte, Plaisir de Merle, Savanha, Spice Route, Veenwouden, Villiera.

Walker Bay: Beaumont, Bartho Eksteen, Bouchard Finlayson, Hamilton Russell.

Robertson: Graham Beck, Springfield, de Wetshof.

VINTAGES

Apart from a few sweet wines, virtually all whites are at their best on release. So too are most reds, although the better shiraz, pinotage, and any wines based on cabernet sauvignon and merlot benefit from two or three years' bottle age. They can last for several years beyond that, especially in years like 1998 and 2000. 1996 was not good.

Chenin (sometimes called steen), although gradually losing out to more fashionable varieties, is still by far the most widely planted grape. Traditionally, it has been treated as the country's workhorse, but limited yields from old vines, combined with careful winemaking, can produce some characterful wines – both full-bodied, oak-fermented dry whites and sweet, botrytis-affected ones. Even the cheaper dry wines, sometimes with a splash of colombard, can be pleasingly fresh and zippy.

If the availability of plant material improves rapidly, then South Africa could very soon prove as much of a force in wine terms as it has in the field of sports. But racial tension remains an issue; for every nonwhite person making good in the industry, there are still hundreds of others who are working for a pittance in the vineyards. Changing that situation will be a slow and difficult process.

REGIONS AND CLASSIFICATIONS

Nearly 60 appellations of varying size have been recognized by South Africa's wine of origin (WO) program since it began in the early 1970s. The smallest, the wards, such as Constantia and Durbanville, are supposed to have distinctive soil and climatic conditions, but WO status isn't intended to be an indication of style or quality in any region; it is merely a guarantee that origin, grape variety, and vintage are as stated on the label.

Right: bringing in the chardonnay harvest.
Below: Paarl and its outlying vineyards.

Barrels line up outside the cellar of the celebrated Hamilton Russell Estate at Hermanus, in the Walker Bay area of Overberg.

The Boschendal estate in the Groot Drakenstein Valley, Franschhoek, Cape Province.

South Africa's most famous wine regions are clustered around Cape Town. Constantia was famous for its sweet wines in the 18th century, but today it's better known for sauvignon blanc, chardonnay, cabernet cauvignon, and merlot. To the east, Stellenbosch is home to most of South Africa's finest producers. It has more than 45 different soils, and there's a noticeable difference in temperature between vineyards close to the sea (notably those of Helderberg) and those further inland. Stellenbosch, home to a large number of producers, is a remarkable melting pot for ideas. Almost all of the wine industry's administration is found there.

The one exception is found in Paarl, to the north of Stellenbosch. This is where the KWV (Cooperative Winegrowers Association) has its headquarters. The KWV was for many years both the governing body of South African wine, regulating production levels and prices, and a producer of considerable amounts of wine, "sherry," and brandy from grapes grown by its 4,600 members. It no longer has its regulatory role, but remains an important producer. Paarl itself is generally warmer than Stellenbosch, although there are several cooler districts, such as the Franschhoek Valley to the east.

Further inland are Worcester, which is hot and fertile and produces fine fortified wines, and Robertson. Chardonnay thrives in Robertson's limestone soils and is made into both still and sparkling wines. Those made in the same way as champagne are labeled méthode cap classique, but it can't be said that many of them could be mistaken for champagne in a blind tasting. Eastward along the coast from Stellenbosch are Elgin and Walker Bay, part of the larger Overberg region, where the altitude and sea breezes suit sauvignon, chardonnay, and pinot noir. Walker Bay, in particular, produces some outstanding chardonnays and pinot noirs. Swartland is the best known of the regions spreading north up the west coast, although many wines from here appear under the vast Coastal Region or Western Cape appellations. Nevertheless, Swartland is a region to watch in the future.

Above: vines are tended in a vineyard owned by Suntory in Japan.

india &
the far east

East Asian consumers are showing a growing interest in Western wines, and the winemakers are planting more and more international varieties.

india

India's best known wine is the champagne-styled Omar Khayyam from Château Indage in Maharashtra, launched on an unsuspecting and astonished world in the 1980s. It seemed remarkably good at the time, but it hasn't kept up with progress since made in other countries. As a result, it now looks tired when compared with sparkling wines from places such as Australia and New Zealand. Some still wine is also made, from grapes such as chardonnay, cabernet sauvignon, and the irresistibly named bangalore purple. The only other producer of note, making still wines, is Grover Vineyards. The French winemaking consultant Michel Rolland is claimed to advise Grover, but it isn't evident in the wines.

china

China has more vineyards than Chile, but much of the fruit is eaten. A lot of the grape varieties are also peculiarly Chinese, including dragon's eye and cow's nipple, but Western-style wine, both home-produced and imported, is becoming increasingly popular. With a thirsty home market, little of the domestic product is exported. Wines that do emerge tend to come from joint ventures with Western companies, including Dynasty, the Pernod Ricard-owned Dragon Seal, and Huadong, which makes Tsingtao wines. Vineyards, mostly along the northeast coast, have tended to be on rich, alluvial soils, but, with a move toward better-drained slopes, the wines should improve.

japan

Although the Japanese taste has always been for sweet wines, 10 percent of the vineyard area now grows European varieties intended for drier wines. Some winemakers are also starting to make vaguely Alsace-style whites out of the native koshu grape. Large firms such as Château Mercian, Suntory, and Sapporo dominate production, but a few smaller wineries exist. One of the best is Château Lumière.

pronunciation guide

Pronunciations in this guide are given using the "sounding out" phonetic system. Where present, accented syllables are indicated by an <u>underline</u>. The basic sounds used are:

a as in **can**, **ah** as in **father**,
ay as in **play**, **ch** as in **chair**,
e as in **get**, **eh** as in **laid**,
ee as in **cheese**, **eu** as in **fur**,
g as in **go**, **i** as in **hi**, **k** as in **cat**,
oh as in **boat**, **oo** as in **look**,
ow as in **cow**, **u** as in **us**,
y as in **yes**

foreign sounds
h is a guttoral h as in loch;
n is a silent "n" but the preceding vowel should be nasal, similar to the change from "don" to "dong"

countries of origin
If a word relates specifically to a particular country, this is indicated by the following abbreviations:

AU Austria, **AUS** Australia,
CH Chile, **FR** France, **GE** Germany,
GR Greece, **HU** Hungary, **IT** Italy,
MA Madeira, **PO** Portugal,
SA South Africa, **SP** Spain

abboccato a-boh-<u>caht</u>-oh (IT)
Abruzzi a-<u>broot</u>-zee (IT)
adega a-<u>deg</u>-a (PO)
agiorghitiko/agiorgitiko ayor-<u>yeet</u>-ee-koh (GR)
Aglianico del Vulture a-lee-<u>an</u>-eek-o del-vool-<u>too</u>-ray (IT)
albariño al-bah-<u>reen</u>-yo (SP)
Alentejo a-lehn-<u>tay</u>-djo (PO)
aligoté a-lee-go-tay (FR)
Aloxe-Corton al-oss-cort-o*n* (FR)
Alsace al-sass (FR)
Alto Adige al-toh <u>ah</u>-dee-djay (IT)
Amarone a-mar-<u>oh</u>-nay (IT)
amontillado a-mont-ee-<u>yah</u>-doh (SP)
Andalucía and-a-luth-<u>ee</u>-ya (SP)
Anjou o*n*-djoo (FR)
appellation contrôlée a-pell-a-syo*n* con-trol-ay (FR)
Ardèche ahr-desh (FR)
assyrtiko a-<u>seer</u>-tee-koh (GR)

Aszú ah-soo (HU)
Aude ode (FR)
Ausbruch owse-brook (AU)
Auslese ows-lay-zeu (GE)
Ausone oh-zone (FR)
Auxey-Duresses ock-zeh doo-ress (FR)
Baden bah-den (GE)
baga bah-ga (PO)
Bairrada bi-<u>rah</u>-da (PO)
Bandol bo*n*-dole (FR)
Banyuls bo*n*-yool (FR)
barbera bar-<u>beh</u>-ra
Bardolino bar-doh-lee-no (IT)
Barolo bah-<u>ro</u>-lo (IT)
Beaujolais-Villages bo-djaw-lay veel-adj (FR)
Beaumes-de-Venise bome de veu-nees (FR)
Beaune bone (FR)
Beerenauslese bee-rin-ows-lay-zeu (GE)
Bereich beu-rikh (GE)
Bergerac bair-djur-ak (FR)
Bernkasteler Doktor bairn-cass-teller doc-tohr (GE)
blanc de blancs blonk de blonk (FR)
blanc de noirs blonk de nwah (FR)
bodega bo-<u>day</u>-ga (SP)
Bolgheri <u>bol</u>-ger-ee (IT)
Bonnezeaux bon-zoh (FR)
Bordeaux bohr-doh (FR)
botrytis cinerea bot-rite-us sin-er-ee-a
Bourgogne bor-<u>gon</u>-yeu (FR)
Bourgueil bor-guy (FR)
Brouilly broo-yee (FR)
Brunello di Montalcino broon-<u>ell</u>-o dee mon-tal-<u>chee</u>-no (IT)
brut broot (FR)
bual bwahl (MA)
Buzet boo-zay (FR)
Cabardès cab-ar-des (FR)
cabernet franc cab-er-nay fronk
cabernet sauvignon cab-er-nay so-vee-nyo*n*
Cahors ca-ohr (FR)
Cairanne kay-ran (FR)

Calatayud cal-a-ti-<u>yoodth</u> (SP)
Campo de Borja camp-o de bor-*h*ah (SP)
carignan cah-ree-nyo*n*
Carignano del Sulcis cah-ree nyan-oh del sool-chees (IT)
Cariñena cah-ree-<u>nyay</u>-na (SP)
carmenère car-min-air
cave coopérative cahv co-op-eh-rah-teev (FR)
chardonnay shahr-daw-nay
chenin blanc sheu-nin blonk
Chinon shee-no*n* (FR)
cinsaut/cinsault san-soh
climat clee-mah (FR)
Clos de Vougeot clo de voo-joh (FR)
colheita col-yeh-tah (PO)
Collioure col-yoor (FR)
Conca de Barberà con-ca day bahr-bay-rah (SP)
Condrieu con-dree-yeu (FR)
Consejo Regulador con-<u>say</u>-*h*oh ray-goo-la-dor (SP)
Consorzio con-<u>sor</u>-zee-oh (IT)
Corbières corb-<u>yehr</u> (FR)
Cornas cor-nass (FR)
Costers del Segre cost-airs del say-gray (SP)
Côte Rôtie coht roh-tee (FR)
Coteaux Champenois coh-toh shom-peu-nwah (FR)
Coteaux du Languedoc coh-toh doo long-dok (FR)
Côtes de Gascogne coht de gas-con-yeu (FR)
Côtes du Rhône coht doo rohn (FR)
Côtes du Ventoux coht doo von-too (FR)
crémant cray-mo*n* (FR)
crème de cassis craym de cass-eess (FR)
crianza cree-<u>ahn</u>-thah (SP)
Crozes-Hermitage crohz ehr-mee-tadj (FR)
Curicó coo-ree-coh (CH)
cuvée coo-vay (FR)
Dão dow*n* (PO)
dégustation day-goo-stah-see-o*n* (FR)

dolce dohl-chay (IT)
dolcetto dohl-chay-toh (IT)
Douro doo-roh (PO)
doux doo (FR)
dulce dool-thay (SP)
Eiswein ice-vine (GE)
élevé ay-leh-vay (FR)
Entre-Deux-Mers on-treu deu mehr (FR)
Estremadura es-tray-mah-doo-rah (PO)
Faugères foh-djehr (FR)
fernão pires fehr-now pee-resh (PO)
Fitou fee-too (FR)
Fixin fee-sa*n* (FR)
Freixenet fresh-net (SP)
furmint foor-mint (HU)
fût foo (FR)
Gaillac gah-yak (FR)
gamay gah-may
garganega gar-<u>gah</u>-neg-a (IT)
garnacha gar-<u>na</u>-cha (SP)
garrafeira gah-rah-fair-ah (PO)
Gevrey-Chambertin djiv-ray shom-behr-ta*n* (FR)
gewurztraminer geu-voort-stram-ee-nehr
Gigondas djee-gon-dass (FR)
Gironde djee-rond (FR)
Givry djee-vree (FR)
Goya Kgeisje *h*oy-ya kay-see (SA)
grand cru gro*n* croo (FR)
Graves grahv (FR)
grenache grin-<u>ash</u>
grüner veltliner groo-ner velt-lin-er (AU)
Halbtrocken halp-trock-en (GE)
Haut-Brion oh bree-o*n* (FR)
Haut-Poitou oh pwah-too (FR)
Hérault eh-roh (FR)
Hermitage ehr-mee-tadj (FR)
Irouléguy ee-roo-lay-gee (FR)
irsai oliver eer-shy oliver (HU/SL)
jaen jay-en (PO)
Jerez *h*ehr-eth (SP)
Jumilla *h*oo-mee-ya (SP)
Jurançon djoo-ro*n*-son (FR)
kékfrankos kake-fran-kosh (HU)
Klein Constantia klayn con-stan-sha (SA)

Lafite-Rothschild la-feet roth-chihld (FR)
Languedoc lond-dok (FR)
Latour lah-toor (FR)
Léoville-Las-Cases lay-oh-veel lass-cass (FR)
Limoux lee-mooh (FR)
Loire lwahr (FR)
Lynch-Bages lansh badj (FR)
macération carbonique mass-ehr-a-syon car-bon-eek (FR)
Mâcon mah-con (FR)
Mâconnais mah-con-nay (FR)
Maipo mih-poh (CH)
malbec mal-beck
malvasia mal-va-see-ah
La Mancha lah man-cha (SP)
manseng man-seng
manzanilla man-tha-nee-ya (SP)
Marches mahr-kay (IT)
Margaux mar-goh (FR)
Mas de Daumas Gassac mah de doh-mass gass-ak (FR)
mataro mat-ahr-o
Médoc meh-dok (FR)
Menetou-Salon min-it-oo sah-lon (FR)
Mercurey mehr-koo-ray (FR)
merlot mehr-loh
meunier meu-nee-yay
Meursault meur-soh (FR)
Minervois mee-nehr-vwah (FR)
Minho mee-nyo (PO)
mis en bouteille meez on boo-tay (FR)
mis en cave meez on cahv (FR)
moelleux mwahl-eu (FR)
Moët & Chandon moh-wet ay shon-don (FR)
Monbazillac mon-bah-zee-yak (FR)
Montagny mon-tan-yee (FR)
Montalcino mon-tal-chee-noh (IT)
Montepulciano mon-tay-pool-chee-yahn-oh (IT)
Monthelie mon-tay-lee (FR)
Montilla mon-tee-yah (SP)
Montrachet mon-rash-ay (FR)
moscatel moss-cah-tel
Mosel moh-zil (GE)
Moulis moo-lee (FR)
mourvèdre moh-vay-dr
mousseux moo-seu (FR)
Mouton-Rothschild moo-ton roth-chihld (FR)
müller-thurgau moo-lehr toor-gow
Muscadet Sur Lie moo-sca-day soor lee (FR)

muscat moo-scat
Nagyrede nar-grey-der (HU)
Nahe nah-huh (GE)
Navarra nah-vah-rah (SP)
nebbiolo nay-bee-yo-loh
Nederburg nay-dur-burg (SA)
négociant neh-go-see-on (FR)
nero d'avola nay-ro dav-ohl-ah (IT)
Niersteiner Spiegelberg/ Domherr neer-shtiner spee-gil-burg/dawm-hehr (GE)
Nuits-St.-Georges nwee-san-djordj (FR)
Orvieto ohr-vee-et-oh (IT)
Paarl pahl (SA)
Pacherenc de Vic-Bilh pash-er-onk de vik-beel (FR)
palo cortado pahl-oh cor-tah-doh (SP)
passito pass-ee-toh (IT)
Pauillac poh-yak (FR)
pedro ximénez pay-droh heem-ehn-eth (SP)
Penedés pen-eh-dehs (SP)
periquita pay-ree-kee-tah (PO)
Pessac-Léognan pay-sak lay-oh-nyon (FR)
pétillant pay-tee-yon (FR)
petit verdot peu-tee vehr-doh
petite sirah peu-teet see-rah
Pétrus pay-trooss (FR)
Pfalz fahlss (GE)
Pic St.-Loup peek-sah-loo (FR)
Piedmont/Piemonte pee-yed-mont/pee-yeh-mont-ay (IT)
Piesporter Goldtröpfchen pees-port-er gold-trop-fyen (GE)
Le Pin leu pan (FR)
pinot grigio pee-noh gree-djee-oh
pinot gris pee-noh gree
pinot meunier pee-noh meu-nee-yay
pinot noir pee-noh nwah
pinotage pee-noh-tadj
Pomerol paw-may-rohl (FR)
Pommard paw-mahr (FR)
Pouilly-Fuissé poo-yee fwee-say (FR)
Pouilly-Fumé poo-yee foo-may (FR)
Premières Côtes de Blaye prim-yer coht de blah-ee (FR)
primitivo prim-it-eev-oh (IT)
Priorato pree-ohr-ah-toh (SP)
Puglia poo-lee-ah (IT)
Puligny poo-lee-nyee (FR)
puttonyos poo-toh-nyos (HU)

Qualitätswein kvah-lee-tayts-vine (GE)
Quarts de Chaume kahr de shohm (FR)
Quincy kan-see (FR)
quinta kin-tah (PO)
Rapel rah-pel (CH)
Recioto ray-chee-yoh-toh (IT)
Reguengos ru-gehn-gohsh (PO)
Reuilly reu-yee (FR)
Rheingau rine-gow (GE)
Rías Baixas ree-ass bi-shass (SP)
Ribatejo ree-bah-tay-djoh (PO)
Ribera del Duero ree-bay-rah del dway-roh (SP)
riesling reez-ling
Rioja ree-aw-hah (SP)
ripasso ree-pah-soh (IT)
riserva ree-zehr-vah (IT)
Rivesaltes reev-sahlt (FR)
rosado roh-zah-doh (SP)
Roussillon roo-see-yon (FR)
Rueda roo-way-dah (SP)
Rufina roo-fee-nah (IT)
Rully roo-yee (FR)
Ruwer roo-ver (GE)
Saar zahr (GE)
St.-Emilion sant ay-meel-yon (FR)
St.-Estèphe sant ay-stef (FR)
St.-Joseph san djoh-sef (FR)
St.-Julien san djoo-lee-yen (FR)
st. laurent sant law-rent (AU)
St.-Véran san vay-ron (FR)
Ste.-Croix-du-Mont sant kwah-doo-mon (FR)
Salice Salentino sah-lee-chay sahl-en-tee-noh (IT)
Sancerre son-sehr (FR)
sangiovese san-dj-oh-vay-zay
Santenay son-tin-ay (FR)
Sassicaia sass-ee-ki-yah (IT)
Saumur sow-moor (FR)
Saumur-Champigny sow-moor shom-pee-nyee (FR)
Sauternes sow-tehrn (FR)
sauvignon blanc sow-vee-nyon blonk
Savennières sav-en-yehr (FR)
Savigny sav-ee-nyee (FR)
scheurebe shoy-ray-beu
semillon sem-ee-yon
sercial ser-thee-ahl (MA)
Setúbal shtoo-bal (PO)
shiraz shee-raz
Soave swah-vay (IT)
Spätlese shpayt-lay-zeu (GE)
sur lie soor lee (FR)
sylvaner sil-van-er
syrah see-rah

tempranillo temp-ran-ee-yoh
Teroldego Rotaliano tay-rol-day-go rot-al-yah-noh (IT)
terroir ter-wahr (FR)
Tignanello teen-ya-nay-loh (IT)
Tokay/Tokaji toh-ki (HU)
torrontes tor-ont-tehs
Touraine too-rayn (FR)
touriga franca too-ree-gah fran-ka (PO)
touriga nacional too-ree-gah nah-see-yon-al (PO)
trebbiano tray-bee-ahn-oh (IT)
trincadeira preta trinc-ah-deh-rah pray-tah (PO)
Trockenbeerenauslese trock-in-beer-in-ows-lay-zeu (GE)
Utiel-Requena oo-tee-yel ray-kay-nah (SP)
Vacqueyras va-kay-rass (FR)
Valdepeñas val-de-pay-nyas (SP)
Valpolicella val-po-lee-cheh-lah (IT)
vecchio veh-kee-oh (IT)
Vega Sicilia beg-ah see-see-lya (SP)
vendange tardive von-donj tar-deev (FR)
verdejo vehr-deh-ho (SP)
verdelho vur-del-oh
Verdicchio ver-dee-kee-oh (IT)
Vernaccia di San Gimignano vur-nah-chah dee sahn jim-een-yan-oh (IT)
viejo vee-eh-oh (SP)
vigneron vee-nyeh-ron (FR)
vin de paille van de piy (FR)
vin de pays van de pay (FR)
vin de table van de tah-bl (FR)
vin doux naturel van doo nat-oor-el (FR)
Vinho Verde vee-noh vehr-day (PO)
Vin Santo vin sahn-toh (IT)
viognier vee-on-yay
Viré-Clessé vee-ray cless-ay (FR)
Volnay vol-nay (FR)
Vosne-Romanée vohn roh-man-ay (FR)
Vouvray voo-vray (FR)
Wachau vak-ow (AU)
Wehlener Sonnenuhr vay-lin-er zon-en-oor (GE)
Weinviertel vine-feer-til (AU)
weissburgunder vice-bur-goon-dur
Yquem ee-kem (FR)
zinfandel zin-fahn-del
zweigelt tsvi-gelt (AU)

index

acknowledgments

Author's Acknowledgments
Huge numbers of people have, often unwittingly, provided information for this book. I cannot thank them all by name, but I thank them all the same. Among those who have answered more than the usual number or more than averagely time-consuming questions are: John Boodle, Sarah Chadwick, Nicky Forrest, Peter Forrestal, Sue Glasgow, David Gleave MW, Anthony Hanson MW, Catherine Manac'h, Victoria Morrall, Hazel Murphy (and her team), Michael Paul, Phil Reedman MW, Craig Smith, Paul Symington, Katharine Walker, and Karen Wise (together with Natashia Bartlett).

Lucas Hollweg and Robert Johnston at *The Sunday Times* deserve special thanks.

Without Sharon Lucas, Carole Ash, Derek Coombes, Nicki Lampon, Frank Ritter, and Toni Kay, my words would never have made it from computer to book. Without Felicity Bryan and Christopher Davis, there would have been no book. I am grateful to them all.

My name appears as author, but Margaret Rand and Simon Woods contributed substantially and invaluably to the regional section. Jane Boyce MW wrote the expert pronunciation guide.

Finally, thanks to my long-suffering family, which means, essentially, Robin and Poppy.

Publisher's Acknowledgments
Dorling Kindersley would like to thank the following:
Tracy Miles for design assistance; Ludo De'Brito for assisting Ian O'Leary with photography; Eliza Baird for food styling; Amanda Clarke for make-up; Margaret McCormack for the index; Anne Marbot of the Bordeaux Wine Trade Council; the staff at Château Ausone; the staff at Château Haut-Brion; Dickon Johnstone and the staff at Château de Sours; Aimé Guibert, Howard Kaman, and the staff at Mas de Daumas Gassac; François des Ligneris of the restaurant Encour; Fortnum and Mason for the loan of wines; and Oddbins for providing wine labels and wines for photography.

Picture Acknowledgments
The publisher would like to thank the following for their kind permission to reproduce their photographs:
a=above; b=below; c=center; l=left; r=right; t=top
Anthony Blake Photo Library: 30cla, 38cla, 40tl, 46tl, 123tr, 131br, 198br, 198l; J.M.R. Topps 116c, 198clb.
Cephas Picture Library: Jerry Alexander 120tl; Kevin Argue 132tr; Nigel Blythe 191tl, 217cl, 217clb, 217l; Fernando Briones 28b, 42tl; Andy Christodolo 118, 140t, 173, 178tl, 194l, 195cr, 196l, 201tr, 202cl, 210l, 211tr, 211b, 212br, 212l, 213l; David Copeman 186br, 189cl; John Davies 32tl; Juan Espi 214l; Bruce Fleming 140cl; Kevin Judd 28tl, 35br, 39br, 41br, 45bl, 46cl, 54bl , 56bl, 88tl, 116cl, 128tl, 162b, 204l, 205b, 209br; Herbert Lehmann 44tl, 56tl; Diana Mewes 38tl, 51cl, 55tl, 91tl; Alain Proust 215tr, 216tr, 216b; Mick Rock 14br, 15tl, 31br, 33br, 48tl, 48cla, 48clb, 48bl, 51tl, 52cl, 53tl, 54br, 57br, 81tr, 83tr, 84tl, 87br, 89tr, 114bl, 114bc, 114br, 115tr, 115bl, 115bc, 115br, 116cr, 120cl, 120bl, 123cl, 125c, 125cr, 128br, 132cl, 133tr, 133br, 134tl, 139b, 151, 155tr, 163b, 165br, 168tl, 169b, 169t, 170tl, 170bl, 171tl, 171b, 172tl, 173tl, 175tl, 176l, 177tl, 177tr, 177b, 179tl, 180tl, 180bl, 181tl, 181, 182clb, 182l, 183tl, 184, 185tl, 185bl, 186l, 187tl; 188cl, 188br, 189fp, 190l, 191tr, 191b, 192tl, 193br, 193l, 195clb, 195l, 196br, 196bla, 199tl, 199br, 202tl, 202b, 203tl, 203bl, 206l, 207t, 208tl, 208bl, 209l; Ted Stefanski 43tl; TOP/Hervé Amiard 154br; TOP/Tripelon/Jarry 38bl.
Bruce Coleman Ltd: Jens Rydell 36cla.
Corbis Stock Market: Paul Barton 141tr; Rob Lewine 94.
Patrick Eagar Photography: 121br, 124cr, 197tr, 200l, 201b, 205tr, 215b.
Garden Picture Library: Michael Howes 32clb.
Getty Images: Peter Correz 78br; Nick Dolding 92b; Paul Kenward 117cl; Anthony Marsland 24tl, 26cl, 74b, 80; Stefan May 13tr, 87; Bob Thomas 18tl, 89.
Image Bank: Don Klump 8b, 22tl, 76br; O. Pinchart 74tl.
Photonica: Aoi Tsutsumi 148tl.
Superstock Ltd.: 82, 84br, 92tl.
All other images © Dorling Kindersley
For further information see: www.dkimages.com